English Language Teaching

A Creative Approach

By
BHAWNA MISRA

AKANSHA PUBLISHING HOUSE
NEW DELHI - 110 002 (INDIA)

AKANSHA PUBLISHING HOUSE
R-37B, Vani Vihar, Uttam Nagar
New Delhi - 110 059
E-mail: ektabooks@yahoo.com

Showroom
4649/21B, Ansari Road
Daryaganj, New Delhi - 110 002
PHones: 23263193, 9811582579

English Language Teaching

First Published, 2004
Reprint- 2005
Reprint–2006
Reprint : 2012

PRINTED IN INDIA

Published by M.P. Misra for Akansha Publishing House, New Delhi - 110 059 and Printed at Tarun Offset Press, Delhi.

Contents

Preface

English language has been spoken in the Great Britain for some fourteen centuries. During this time, it has undergone such fundamental changes (affecting grammar, vocabulary, and pronunciation) that the speech of an inhabitant of the London region of the 7th century would be totally unintelligible to the modern Londoner. The earliest form of English, brought by Germanic invaders from the 5th century onwards, is known as *Old English* and extends up to about the 11th century. This general term itself embraces a number of separate dialects deriving from the different geographical origins of the invaders.

Over the last five hundred years, the English language has expanded to become the everyday speech of over three hundred million. The expansion has for all practical purposes been a feature of the most recent of the three major phases of development into which linguistic scholarship customarily divides the record history of the language.

Elements of regional differences of pronunciation are evident today, to such an extent that a Cockney and a Glaswegian may still have serious difficulties of communication in speech. Englishmen are still readily able to identify the part of the country from which a person comes simply by listening to his speech, despite the fears of those who predict that dialect forms will soon disappear completely. Indeed, these regional forms of speech are often related to gross statements of regional prejudice—the Southerner who regards the speech of the Northerners as overburnt, and the Northern who characterizes the speaker with a Southern accent as affected. Dialect differences of pronunciation are therefore still important both for reasons of intelligibility and also in social terms. It is worth remarking too that, of all the various accents of British English, that of the

London region has developed most rapidly, the speech of the other regions remaining closer to the historical origins of the language.

The English of India itself shares a number of features with the versions in use in the neighbouring states, all of which resulted ultimately from the influence of the British Raj. Its special vocabulary includes on the one hand words from Indian languages commonly used in English-language books, journals, and newspapers published in India and on the other words that relate particularly to Indian context or that have acquired a special form of meaning in India.

English is in fact now used as a lingua franca of business, science, and sport almost everywhere in the world, whether or not it is spoken as a native language. Its status as a world language has been developing for several centuries, and in the process many exotic varieties, widely different from the native tongue of England, have grown up in places where the influence of the source country has been slight. The increasing use of English in more scholarly contexts after 1500 AD resulted in misgivings about its ability to survive. Historical factors have conditioned the lexicon and grammar of the modified forms of Standard English as well as their sounds.

Now teaching English language. This requires a strategy, time plan, and overall a creative approach. We have gathered here thirteen chapters emphasing the creativity in English language teaching. Though not strictly a conventional handbook, it is unique in its features, which every thoughtful English teacher will like to go through. This will equip the teacher with necessary background information.

The information is drawn from diverse sources. As such we express our gratefulness to the authors of great eminence. Lastly, we owe a deep sense of gratitude to our publishers for bringing out this book.

—**BM**

1

Teaching Creative Writing Techniques

Children's writing cannot really be free or creative until the children themselves feel they have something to say and until they are at least partly satisfied with the way in which they are saying it. One function of the teacher is to provide stimulus which will release ideas, feelings and sensory awareness so that even the most imaginatively impoverished children will feel that they have something worth giving expression to. But it is not enough simply to provide the initial impetus to write the teacher must also help to provide the techniques; only the gifted few can be expected to develop these naturally. The skills of handwriting, spelling, capitalisation, can be fostered naturally and incidentally through the children's own work, and teachers will feel — quite rightly — that they have accomplished a good deal if by the time they have left the junior school most children have mastered these skills. There is another area of expression that the teacher can help to open up.

Anyone who reads a good deal and who is interested in reading becomes aware that writers employ devices, tricks if you like, which may help to convey the sense of what they are saying more succinctly or more dramatically, or perhaps in a way which might simply be called more appealing then the direct statement of fact (although, of course, this itself is a kind of device and can be extremely effective, as it is in the work of writers like Heming-way or Greene). Even a cursory glance through an anthology of poetry for children will reveal a multitude of fairly common devices. For instance, just flicking through the pages of *The Merry go-round,* we have noticed the use of rhyme, repetition, alliteration, sustained metaphor, onomatopoeia, and we expect we could find a good many more if we were to look more closely. Such devices are probably perfected by writers over a long period of experimentation in their own writing, and we have no intention of suggesting that children should be made to learn them, but we do suggest that some of these devices are employed by children quite naturally and that their use can be extended. Children are amused by verbal oddities, by the sound and shape of words; in fact, children like to play with words, and play is an important aspect of mental development as well as a crucial factor in the acquisition of linguistic skills. As W.J.J. Gordon says: 'Play with words invigorates language and by implication reinvigorates perception as well as the way conceptions are used... Play with language not only enlivens metaphor, it also involves an oscillation between particulars and universals.'

We do not envisage what follows as anything like a systematic course but as an occasional lesson, an opportunity for the children to play around with words, devices and forms and it is under these heads that we will make suggestions.

Words

The teacher might introduce a lesson by making some quite simple and arbitrary distinctions, such as words for short fat things and words for long thin things, e.g. examples such as the following might be written on the board:

squat	wafer
stubby	pencil
tub	thread
club	sliver
thumb	stick
blob	spear

Or warm words and cold words:

comfortable	chill
soft	numb

lazy	crisp
sleep	knife
wool	crystal
furry	steel
hay	thin

Or rough words and smooth words:

gnarled	velvet
knobbled	silk
buckled	sleek
coarse	glass
stubble	slither

The idea is to find words which may mean 'rough' or 'smooth but which also have some evocative aspect which suggests in sound or through association the quality in question. The search ought not to be confined to adjectives but should include any parts of speech. What we are doing is indirectly making children aware of the metaphorical extension of words, without necessarily using this terminology. In fact there is no need for generalised or descriptive comment at all, unless the teacher feels that the class would welcome and understand such comment. The function should be evident in the exercise.

It is a good idea to get children to make a collection of words and phrases from the books and poetry they read. There is no need to impose any restrictions on this activity: the teacher might ask the class to 'collect' any words they like for whatever reason. Just to illustrate, here are a few examples from a collection made by 9-year-olds:

> bats flit | sluice | assumption | Jabberwocky
> Clasps the crag with crooked hands | silver pears
> Goldenhair | tournament | gilded | umbrageous
> bangalory | Their five eyes smouldering green
> and bright | porcupine | trigonometry |
> threadbare.

The words appealed to the children, we suppose, because they were odd and pleasant to say, or quite new and perhaps a bit mysterious, and for any number of reasons one can't know. What is valuable about this activity is that the children are considering words as interesting things in themselves, worth collecting, and perhaps worth being concerned about, and an interest in language itself however rudimentary is some way towards assisting in the flexible use of it.

Later on if it seems appropriate to the needs of the class the teacher might encourage the children to collect words under certain heads, perhaps relevant to any of the other work in creative writing, e.g. words suggestive of fire, water, animals, etc., if this is not already being done for such lessons.

We have already mentioned some simple and arbitrary distinctions, made without reference to the function of words as parts of speech, and we see no reason why the linguistic functions should not be introduced as another kind of distinction, so long as the teacher keeps in mind that the purpose of the exercise is not to clutter up their minds with useless terminology but to encourage a more skilful use of language. The class might be asked to think of verbs or words which have verbal force in two quite arbitrary classes, say words which have a turbulent connotation and words which evoke a sense of the opposite:

blunder	creep
Crash	slide
charge	sidle
plunge	steal
clump	glide

One might reasonably hope for some direct carry-over here into their own writing, since it is fairly easy to point out that it is more interesting to read stories which seem to come to life than those which do not, and there is more life or vividness in 'He crept/blundered/clumped/sidled down the empty street...' than 'He went down the empty street....' (we realise of course, that a skilful writer, in the proper context could make this collocation effective.) A sensitive teacher would, we hope, see the possibilities of this as a 'creative' exercise; handled ineptly it can, of course, lead right back to the drudgery and unreality of the old-fashioned kind of exercise with which we are all too familiar. The whole point of the approach it is that it can be a pleasurable way of sharpening the children's awareness of language as well as extending their vocabulary, and in our experience, the more technical restriction imposed, the less proportionally s the gain in genuine interest and verbal dexterity.

Further Suggestions

Words for animals (see section on Animals, page 122), e.g. prowl, stalk, sleek, fierce, vicious, etc.

Words for precious things, e.g. topaz, silver, star, treasure, etc.

Made-up and portmanteau words, e.g. brillig, mimsy, vorpal, slithy (Carroll, naturally, is the obvious source here).

Telescoped words, e.g. Infirtaris, Mollis Abuti, Mairsey Totes.

At this point we must draw attention to Alastair Reid's excellent book *Ounce, Dice, Trice* (Dent) which is full of delightful material and endless amusement for any class. (See also *Junior Voices*).

Once the children have got the idea that different kinds of words have, as it were, different personalities they can be encouraged to write on 'Words' as a theme. Here are some examples:

Elephant, alligator, crocodile,
These are words that make our smile.
Kangaroo, koala bear and giraffe,
These are better, they make our laugh.
Bang, crash, clatter, cling, clout,
These are words that make our shout.
Ring-a-ling, tong, tingle and ting,
These are words that make our sing.

(Kimberly, aged 10 UC)

Some words we like are from Shakespeare's MacBeth. Names like this: Donalbain, Banquo, Macduff, Fleance, 'foul murder.' We like words that we can make up on the spot, sort of. There are some words that we hear sometimes and we think this: 'Dull interesting, stupid, daft, and pointless.' Not until we started reading Shakespeare did we realise that words had very good uses and were quite the opposite of what we had thought. If we said to you, 'Foul murder has been done,' you'd think we were rude. But Shakespeare used it in many plays. He liked murderous (if we may say so) foul words. We like that kind of word too. They're jolly good. (Though we don't use them!).

(A boy, aged 9 UC)

Words! There are millions, uncountable.
Here are some with o's and k's:
Hook, cook, took, look, book.
Here are some with ig's:
Wig, pig, fig, twig, big, dig.
Here are some with ing's:
Thing, sing, ping, ring, wing sting.
It's are common:
Bit, nit, hit, pit, spit, sit, twit, lit.

(Child, aged 9 UC)

Many poems and stories have a language which is appealing to children even though the sense may not be immediately accessible to them. The following extract from Holiday Memory by Dylan Thomas *(Quite Early One Morning,*Dent) is a good example:

August Bank Holiday. A tune on an ice-cream cornet. A slap of sea and a tackle of sand. A fanfare of sunshades opening. A wince and whinny of bathers dancing into deceptive water. A tuck of dresses. A rolling of trousers. A compromise of paddlers. A sunburn of girls and a lark of boys. A silent hullaballoo of balloons.

Probably only 'a compromise of paddlers' would cause any difficulty. Teachers might explain that the paddlers don't want to go into the water completely and aren't content just to lie on the beach away from the sea, so they go halfway.

Other Poems

Jargon *James Reeves* H; WS
The Hen and the Carp *Ian Serraillier* PQ
Uriconium *James Reeves* PQ
Precious Stones; The Bee's Song *Walter de la Mare* PdM
The Straight Night (octave) *Gerard Manley Hopkins* TWD
Jabberwocky; Infirtaris *Lewis Carroll* MGR
English *Eleanor Farjeon* RR, Green
The Land of the Bumbly Boo *Spike Milligan* RR, Green
The End of the Road *Hailaire Belloc* RR, Green; WS
We had a Hippopotamus *Patrick Barrington* RR, Yellow
Blum *Dorothy Aldis* FBNV
Eletelephony *Laura Richards* PL, III
Through Winter *Geoffrey Summerfield* WS
Mean Song *Eve Merriam* JV, I
Jive talk, Rabbit and Pork, Rhyming talk *trad.* JV, IV
Muddy Boots *Philip Paddon* MW
Cargoes *John Masefield* ILTP
Father says *Michael Rosen* YSH

Devices

It used to be the case, and may be still is in some places, that children were taught systematically to recognise a selection of figures of speech ranging from simile to synecdoche, without ever doing anything with this information other than pick out these devices in an examination. We cannot see that this knowledge is of much use unless one needs either to refer to such devices or to use them. As we have already suggested we think that junior children can understand some of the simpler types and be encouraged to use them effectively in their own writing, provided again that the intention is liberative rather than simply descriptive. In other words it is useful it it can be offered as a tool and not simply a terminology. Perhaps the easiest device to encourage children to try out is sustained metaphor, the fundamental principle of which is to find a basic comparison which will allow for as many similarities as possible. Consider a forest fire for instance. There are numerous ways in which one might think of it but suppose we settle on the 'conceit' of fire as a ravenous animal. It is fierce, destructive, violent, releventless, savage; it has a tongue: it might be considered cruel, unfeeling, blundering, etc. A class might be asked to write as many points of likeness as they can and to write a piece, poem or prose, which is a continuous elaboration of the basic comparison. At first this will probably be a bit mechanical if they are an average class and the idea is new to them. Here are some examples from such a class:

Fire is like a tigers claw
And it kills things like animals kill
It goes round things and destroys things
Like an aniconda.

(Charles, aged 11 UC)

Fire is an animal
It spreads as fast as a leopard....
As hungry as an elephant
As mischievous as a monkey.
And if it gets out of hand ... like a lion
It will become king of all things.

(Stuart, aged 11 UC)

Fire is an animal.
It kills, it leaps and it makes noises.
Fire spreads and eats things
It destroys.

Its colour.
Fire dies like an animal.

(David, aged 11 UC)

This was done in the last ten minutes of an English lesson on something else, as were the following pieces on Time. The children in this class, however, had become used to creative writing and were prepared to write freely without much stimulus. The idea of a fundamental comparison was explained and they were asked to write down 'Time is....' and to follow it with as many ideas as they could think up in the remainder of the lesson.

Time is golden
Time is good
Like the clocks you see
Like the sun and moon and stars.
Time is months
Time is a day
Time is seasons
Time is years
Time is everything to you.

(Sue, aged 10 UC)

Time is something that is never still,
When once gone can never come back,
People grow older but never younger.
Time is an old man in the street.
Time is the sea and tide
Time is never enough, enough,
Time is the sound of a bell ringing.
Time is everything

(Susan, aged 10 UC)

In his article on writing poetry for children in *Young Writers Young Readers* James Reeves describes how he worked out his poem 'The Sea' as a sustained metaphor with the hungry dog as the basic comparison. This is a poem children enjoy because they can easily follow the comparison and they take pleasure in recognising the various points of likeness. It also offers the teacher a very simple but direct way of introducing the device. Here is the poem:

The sea is a hungry dog,
Giant and grey.
He rolls on the beach all day.
With his clashing teeth and shaggy jaws
Hour upon hour he gnaws
The rumbling, tumbling stones,
And 'Bones, bones, bones, bones!'
The giant sea-dog moans,
Licking his greasy paws.
And when the night wind roars
And the moon rocks in the stormy cloud,
He bounds to his feet and snuffs and sniffs,
Shaking his wet sides over the cliffs,
And howls and hollos long and loud.

But on quiet days in May or June,
When even the grasses on the dune
Play no more their reedy tune,
With his head between his paws
He lies on the sandy shores.
So quiet, so quiet, he scarcely snores.

Here are two children's attempts at using the device:

The sea is a wild animal,
Leaping, mauling and clawing at the sandy shore.
It lives in anger most of the time

Breaking down rocks, smashing the little boats
With his guilty jaws.
He had no friend to take care of him
But when the wind stops blowing
And the rain stops pelting down
The wild animal can be calm and still

(Carol, aged 10 C)

The Train

The train is like an animal of iron and steel.
It has bones of iron and ribs of steel
And its blood is the steam that pounds
In the cylinders—its heart—is forever beating
When it tears along the track in great haste.
It is like a hungry animal leaping for its supper
Along the iron rails it thunders and screams
Like a vicious animal.

(Kegin, aged 10 C)

The same principle may be used with themes like The River, Storm, Aeroplane, Joy, Old Age, Fear, depending upon the ages of the children.

It may be noticed that there are at least two ways of approaching this idea. One is to present the children with a word, such as 'time,' 'silver,' 'darkness,' 'quickly,' (see Reeves' poems 'Grey' and 'Slowly' and de la Mare's 'Silver') and ask them to think of its application. Here is an example:

Quickly the time passes by when you are on holiday.
Quickly the ice cream melts at the seaside.
Quickly the boys and girls on the breach run about and play on the sand.
Quickly the wheels go round on the coach when it takes you back home.

(John, aged 11 C)

The other way is to suggest a basic comparison (Train like an animal, etc.) and let the children work from there. In some cases where the ability of the class is very mixed only a proportion of the children will be able to worry at the idea until they have written what could reasonably be called a poem; other children will produce lists, but they should receive encouragement nonetheless. It is perhaps wiser to use these ideas as something to be tackled incidentally, possibly at the end of lessons on something else, or to use them as the basis of a group poem in which the whole class participates. With a class of roughly the same ability and especially with older children more time will be necessary.

Other devices which we have found may be isolated and treated successfully are alliteration, onomatopoeia, rhythmical forms, non-finite verbs. All of these may , of course, be used for serious or for humorous writing (although we personally have found it wiser to indicate beforehand what kind of writing we were hoping for, since writing which is a mixture of the serious and the non-serious is usually neither). The main thing is to find a clear example of the use of the appropriate device in a poem or bit of prose, or to make one up which will clearly illustrate what you want the children to do, and then to emphasise the device by reading it in a forcible way. For instance, in 'The Cataract of Lodore' (see page 71) Southey uses strings of non-finite verbs to give the impression of the waterfall pouring, almost wasting itself down the mountainside. When we had read this to a class of 8-9-year-olds we asked them what else might come tumbling down in this way. They made the following suggestions which we wrote up on the blackboard: landslide; snow falling; rain falling; volcano; a river; an aeroplane; iceberg crumbling; building being demolished. We then read them another poem, this time by a child.

Tree Felling

The lumberjack called:
'Tim . . . . .ber!'
And the tree began to fall.
It creaked and groaned

And moaned and sighted;
Cracking and bending,
Its pains were not ending;
Falling and falling,
And staggering and learning,
And tearing and smashing and crashing,
Bettering and shattering and lashing,
Tumbling and falling right down to the ground.

(Derek, aged 10 C)

This, we think, showed them clearly what the possibilities were, as well as providing a little incentive in the fact that another child had written on this theme. Here are some example of their work:

The Snow

Whirling and hurling
Twirling and gurling
The snow came down at such a rate
When we went out it was oh! so cold.
Our friends and we were built a snow man.
Then we were told
The sun will soon come out
And the snow will melt away.

But he will go
To the splashing and restless sea
Where he will have a new life
Once again.

(Lorraine, aged 9 UC)

Train into Station

The train is coming roaring and hissing

Spitting and rocking,
Faster and faster,
It's whistling and clattering,
It's whizzing and shouting,
Faster and faster,
Rattling and battling,
Past the fields and past the trees,
Past the hedges and past the houses,
Racing and spacing through the woods,
It's slowing and slowing,
As it reaches the station.

(Carl, aged 9 UC)

Reading this afterwards to the class we thought it worth emphasising the rhythmic quality of the piece and it was very easy here to demonstrate the way in which this suggested the movement of the train (see Forms, pages 160 ff.) as it does in W.H. Auden's poem 'Night Mail.'

The Sea

The sea comes crashing and booming,
Out of the hollow caves
Bringing all the little rocks and stones with it,
Clashing and banging and spraying,
And playing as it comes out of the caves,
Bringing all the little sea creatures with it,
As it twinkles and wrinkles coming out of the caves.
As it comes it swishes by all of the seaweed.
Banging on to the big rocks

(Karen, aged 9 UC)

We feel that these poems suggest that, for this particular class at least, the exploitation of one device proved a liberating experience. The children used the technique without being tied to it and without it restricting their own ideas. Incidentally, Southey's poem as well as drawing attention to the power of verbs offers a feast for children of limited vocabulary, and is worth keeping in the classroom as a kind of thesaurus.

Further Suggestion

Kites flying; football match; swimming; fishermen hauling in nets; fireworks;storm wind; herds of cattle/horses racing across plain; war dance; plague of insects; bicycle race; crowd at seaside, etc.

It will be noticed that any themes which suggest action will probably offer the necessary scope and, of course, many of the poems in the following list may indicate suitable to topics for children's writing. The list of poems is arranged according to the presence of some particular device in the individual items. This does not mean that this device is necessarily predominant; it simply means that it is easy to demonstrate to children.

Poems

Alliteration, Onomatopoeia and Tongue Twisters (these can,of course, be treated separately)

Jargon *James Reeves* H; WS

Brand the Blacksmith *James Reeves* HJ

Sink Song *J.A. Lindon* RR, Green; WS; JV, III

The Bee's Song *Walter de la Mare* PdM

From'Goulies and Ghosties' *Anon* PL, III

The Donkey *G.K. Chesterton* RR, Yellow

Circus *Margaret Stanley Wrench* RR, Yellow

Engineers *Jimmy Garthwaite* FBNV

A canner *trad.* JV, IV

One Old Ox *Anon* WS

Betty Botter *Anon* POCO

Susan Simpson *Anon* POCO

Metaphor, Simile and Image

As *Anon* RR, Green

Winter the Huntsman *Osbert Sitwell* PL, IV; TC I

Locomotive *Shigeharu Nakano* RR, Yellow

This smokey winter morning *Charles Reznikoff* JV, IV.

Silver *Walter de la Mare* PL, III

Night Clouds *Amy Lowell* OB III

The Storm *Emily Dickinson* OB, III

Mexican Song *Osbert Sitwell* OB, IV

Grey *James Reeves* MGR; WS

Slowly *James Reeves* PQ; WS

Poem *Emily Dickinson* TWD

Stuff *Adrian Mitchell* BW

The Candle *girl,aged 10* EW

A Bundle of Old Lead-Coated Electric Cable *Peter Waterfield, aged 10* PC

A Lion *Jane Horlock, aged 12* PC

Grey *Carol, aged 11* WS

Verbs

The End of the Road *Hailaire Belloc* RR, Green; WS

Cabbage White *Christopher Hassall* HJ

Throwing a Tree *Thomas Hardy* HJ; WS

Song *Anon* BS

A Fire *Bruce Middleton, aged 14* PC

Jump or Jiggle *Evelyn Beyer* WS

Rhythm

Night Mail *W.H. Auden* OB, III; ILTP

Bad Sir Brian Botany *A.A. Milne* PL, III

Fire Down Below; Old King Cole RR, Blue

The Rain Dance *Marina Brunskill, aged 14* PC

From a Railway Carriage *R.L. Stevenson* ILTP

This old hammer trad. JV, I

Salt, Mustard, Vinegar, Pepper *trad.* JV, I

Cowboy Song *Charles Causley* ILTP; WSP

Forms

Under this head we would like to consider one or two simple verse pattern which are easily demonstrable. An obvious form, and easily imitable, is the typographical shape of the piece as it is printed.

The second is from *Alice in Wonderland.* It is Alice's idea of a 'long tail':

'Fury said to a
mouse, That he
met in the
house
"Let us
both go to
law: we will
prosecute
you, Come
I'll take no
denial; We
must have a
trial; For
really this
morning I've
nothing
to do."
Said the
mouse to the

cur, "Such
a trial
dear Sir,
With
no jury
or judge
would be
wasting
our
breath."
'I'll be
judge, I'll
be jury,"
said
cunning
Old Fury:
"I'll
try the
whole
cause
and
condemn
you
to
death."'

Ideally the shape of the piece should represent the sense. It is easy to convey this to children. The difficulty is tactfully to restrain them from attempting impossibly complicated shapes which completely obscure the sense. The casiest shapes are diamond, kite,butterfly (two halves of a diamond), snake or worm, catherine wheel or watch spring, staircase, pyramid, wheel and zig-zag path (up the side of a mountain). Before giving examples of children's work perhaps we should say that we would not wish to claim that their English is better in any direct way because of an exercise such as this. All we would claim is that the enjoyment in using words in new and different ways is a valuable adjunct to any English teaching.

ball
The *goes*
hill. *rolling*
steep *down*
very *and*
the *down*
up *the*
and *hill*
up *non-*
and *stop*
up *until*
higher
it
and *gets*
higher *to*
me *Bill*
to *and*
it *then*
throws *Bill*
and *picks*
ball *up*
the

(*Lynne, aged 11 UC*)

The
worm
with
its
long
slender
body
was
slithering
along
the
ground
gripping
with

I
saw a
kite flying
in the sky
blowing, blowing, blowing
high. Flipping and flapping
in the strong wind and struggling
to get free. Then, all-of-a-sudden

its
tiny
bristles.
Suddenly
it
felt
a
movement
behind
it.
although
it
cannot
hear
it
can
feel
the
ground
vibrating.
Its
tiny
mind
knew
the
mole
was
coming
after
it.
The *body.*
mole *mole's*
was *the*
getting *inside*
closer *wriggling*
and *still*
closer *worm*
Then *the*
one *and*
gulp

(Dianne, aged 11 UC)

a gust of wind blew the little kite
out of sight. Shouting I'm
free! I'm fee! I'm
fee! I'm so happy
because I'm free.
It's getting
smaller
in the
dist-
ance
till
three
is
only
a
tiny
speak

(Teresa, aged 11 UC)

Children delight in rhyme and their wish to use it in poems often has the effect of crippling their expression or distorting it in a weakly facetious way. It is as well to give the class a specific outlet for this desire to rhyme and for the pleasure of being funny. Limericks and nonsense verse seem to offer endless opportunities. Most children enjoy limericks and they can make them up without too much difficulty. The teacher should present them with a very simple formula such as that used by Lear in many of his limericks, i.e. begin: 'There was a young man/old man/woman,' etc., then find a place for the character to come from which presents a fair chance of a sensible or amusing rhyme (e.g. Birmingham/learning'em, Bath/laugh, France/dance). Sometimes local place names are a fruitful source of rhyme (Astley/ghastly, Eyemore/buy more, etc.). Then two more lines which rhyme and which say something about the subject of the poem, and a final line which repeats the first with slight modification. Here are some limericks written by children.

There was a young man of Worcester,
Who ate all his meals with a duster.
His porridge and such he ate with a brush,
That silly young man of Worcester.

(Leslie, aged 11 UC)

There was an old bee man of Kidder,

Who went and he married a widder.
He took all her money
Only leaving her honey
That cruel old bee man of Kidder.

(Philip, aged 10 UC)

There once was a student of France
Who taught a canary to dance
He then taught a bee
To sit on a pea.

That clever young student of France.

(Roger, aged 9 UC)

Riddles are another source of much enjoyment. Bright children will see that riddles are usually based upon some paradox or some verbal trick, but it is essential for the teacher to find a riddle in which the device is fairly clearly evident and then to show the children how it works. For example there is one kind of riddle that misleads because the reader expects the answer to be a thing and it turns out to be a letter.

It is in desk but not in a draw
It is in a soldier but not in a war
It is in silver but not in gold
It is in said but not in told.

(The letter S)

(Dianne, aged 11 UC)

It is in apple but not in peach;
It is in lesson but not in teach;
It is in lend but not in keep;
It is not in jump but it is in leap.

(The letter L)

(Julie, aged 9 UC)

It is in cat but not in dog;
It is in clear but not in fog;
It is in cup but not in plate;
It is in cow but not in gate.

(The letter C)

(Lyn, aged 9 UC)

Another kind of riddle works on the principle of ambiguity, since we ascribe human attributes to inanimate things, e.g. the sun has a face, looks down, dies away, etc. Here is a child's attempt to construct a riddle on this theme:

We can rise but not wake up.
We have a face but no body.
We are always hot but sometimes cold.
We are very big but we look small.
We are very old but we go on forever.

(Alan, aged 11 UC)

Here is another on the theme 'Book':
We have leaves but no branches
And a back but no legs.
We have lines but no hooks
And letters but no postman.
We have spaces but no room
And words but we cannot talks.

(Martin, aged 11 UC)

Nonsense verse the children will indulge in quite naturally but it is a good idea to draw their attention to the forms which some of the verse takes and let them try their hands at one particular type, for example the 'If' type:

If elephants were as small as insects
If ants were as big as whales
If sharks could fly
Like mice in the sky
Then horses would run like snails.

(Frederick, aged 10 UC)

If all the world was yellow,
And all the sea was white,
And all the day was rainy,
What would it be like at night.

(Martin, aged 9 UC)

If the earth were as small as a ball,
And the moon was as small as a bee,
There wouldn't be much room
For you or for me.

(Martyn, aged 9 UC)

Poems

Shapes

Dogs round a tree *Edwin Morgan* BW
Wheels BW
The Computer's Spring Greeting *Gary Lewis* JV, II
It's raining *Guillaume Apollinaire* MW
Diamond Cut Diamond *E. Milne* H; CDS
The Ups and Downs of the Elevator Car *Caroline D. Emerson* FBNV
French Persian Cats having a ball *Edwin Morgan* JV, III
in Just-spring *e.e. cummings* TWD
Shaped poems, various WS
Shaped poems, various P

Limericks

Three Limericks *Edward Lear* MGR
Two Limericks *Edward Lear* PL, III
Two Limericks *Lewis Carroll* PL, III
Limericks PC; RR, Green; FBNV

Alphabets

Tom Thumb's Alphabet RR, Red

A was an Archer *trad.* WS

The ABC *Spike Milligan* BW; ILTP

Rabbit and Pork, Rhyming Talk *Trad.* JV, IV

Riddles

Aeiou *Jonathan Swift* MGR

Riddles MGR; RR, Green; RR, Yellow; FBNV; WS; TC, I; P

Nonsense

The Man Who WAsn't There; A Thousand Hairy Savages RR, Red.

On the Ning Nang Nong *Spike Milligan* ILTP

Sense and Nonsense FBNV

Our Brother Bert *Ted Hughes* POCO

Our Sister Jane *Ted Hughes* POCO

Jabberwocky *Lewis Carroll* MGR

Mr. Tom Narrow; Queer Things *James Reeves* PQ

If *Michael Thompson, aged 9* PC

Over the Ocean *Jill Pearson, aged 10* PC

Daddy fell into the pond *Alfred Noyes* ILTP

The Folk who live in Backward town *Mary Ann Hoberman* BS

Centipede's Song *Roald Dahl* BW; ILTP

If... *Anon* BW

The Man in the Wilderness *Anon* WS

Supposing *Alastair Reid* YSH

Supposing *Alastair Reid* RSH

Miscellaneous Forms and Oddities

What is Pink? *Christina Rossetti* OB, I

This is the Key RR, Blue

Things we Love *Elizabeth du Prez* RR, Red

The Twelve Days of Christmas; We Saw a Peacock; Twelve Huntsmen;

Tree on a Hill MGR

We Saw a Fishpond FBNV

Picnic *Hugh Lofting* FBNV

A Nail *trad.* MGR

Pattern Verse

Counting one to twenty *trad,* V, I

We bought our a cat *trad.* JV, I

Knock, knock, who's there *Bob Dunn* JV,IV

Spell of Creation *Kathleen Raine* PMV

The Months *Christina Rossetti* ILTP

I'm just going out for a moment *MIchael Rosen* MW

There was a man, he went mad *Anon* WS

There was an old woman *Anon* WS

Went to the river *Anon* POCO

One old Oxford Ox *Anon* POCO

If you don't put your shoes on *Michael Rosen* BS

Also see:

Penguin English Project Handbook. pp. 77-78 and 86-87.

Images (Teacher's Handbook) *Barry Maybury*, Oxford.

The Puffin Joke Book *Bronnie Cunningham,* Penguin.

2

Teaching Strategies

The emphasis should be put on writing, or on ideas which lead towards writing. There are different perspectives as there are different teachers, different schools, and different needs and abilities of the pupils. Sometimes an idea catches the imagination of a group of children and takes over, radiates outward into Science, Music, Painting, Drama, Design, etc. The following 'flow' charts show how this might be encouraged.

Debating the nucleus idea: The Sea, Me, Games, etc. — will bring to light more specific areas of interest which individuals or groups of pupils can concentrate on and research further. Stimulus material on the specific topics is fed in, and this might then lead to any variety of creative activities (shown at the edge of the charts), including writing. Some of these activities will result in individual 'end products,' artifacts, things made, but others are on-going activities and not necessarily finished. We sometimes think that we are constrained by a need to have children's work polished or on display, when it may be that the process itself is what is important. At any rate, we have arranged the ideas to lead into processes which might be open-ended or might be 'finished.' The treatment of the idea in the flow charts is not intended to be exhaustive. The charts merely suggest patterns of work which have some chance of involving pupils in different and individually interesting activities, Essentially it is a matter of (1) seeing relevant connections with the main idea which can lead to a variety of pursuits—research, making things, designing, experimenting, devising publicity material perhaps, holding competitions; (2) being aware of supporting ideas, stimulus material, etc.; and (3) seeing the possibilities in the various subject areas — Music and Sound, Drama, Science, Painting, etc. — but more importantly, relating all this to the natural interest and fantasising of the children.

We suppose any idea might be made to work in this way, but experience suggests that some ideas have more potential than others. Those we have included in the charts are some that students have found useful in the past, and which seem to appeal to children of this age. Other such subjects are:

Buildings
Journeys
Adventures
Space
Sound
Work
Exploration
Costume
Ships
The Universe
Flight
Food
Trees
Countries
The Future
Stories
Inventions
Songs
Myths
Movement
New Worlds
Memories
Ghots
People

Legends
Heroes and Heroines
Fantastic
Folklore
The Past
Dreams
Sports
Discoveries
Sound
Time
The Environment
Our Town
Machines
Fabulous Island
Motor Cars
Colours
Toys
Horses
Wild West
Humour
Magical Creatures
Mysteries.

As with anthologies, of course, teachers eventually make their own collection of ideas and develop their own strategies for putting them into operation.

Finally, we would like to say that it is very important not to forget the potential in all this for fun. This is why we have offered a flow chart of Crazy Ideas. But, of course, there is reason even in this, in that the creative process itself needs and thrives on the irrelevant, the bizarre, the impossible as well as on the rational, the ordered and the sequential. Anyway, there should be some fun.

General Book List

A Word about anthologies. We have made reference to a wide selection of anthologies in the hope that some at least of the poems, stories and extracts we have recommended will be available to the teacher. A number of these pieces will naturally appear in more than one anthology and in most cases we have indicated where this is so. Books go out of print but copies are still to be found in many schools, so as well as giving more up-to-date references we have retained some of the earlier ones on the assumption that students and teachers will still have access to those books in College Libraries and School cupboards.

Anthologies, etc.

BP *Birthright Poetry,* I-IV, W.T. Cunningham, (Hamish Hamilton)

BS *Bandstand,* Barry Maybury (Offord)

BSH *Blue Story House,* David Jackson and Dennis Pepper (Oxford)

BW *Bandwaggon,* Barry Maybury (Oxford)

CDS *Come Down and Startle,* Jeffrey Aldridge (Oxford)

DT *Drums and Trumpets,,* Leonard Clarke (Bodley Head)

FBNV *Faber Book of Nursery Verse,* Barbara Ireson (Faber)

GSH *Gren Story House,* David Jackson and Dennis Pepper (Oxford)

H	*Happenings,* Wollman and Grugeon (Harrap)
HJ	*Harrap Junior Book of Modern Verse,* Wollman and Grugeon
ILTP	*We Like this Poem* (Chosen by Children), Ed. Kaye Webb (Puffin)
JV	*Junior Voices* I-IV, Geoffrey Summerfield (Penguin)
MGR	*Merry Go Round,* James Reeves (Heinemann)
MW	*Our World* (Poems from Living Language), Ed. Joan Griffiths (BBC)
OB	*An Anthology of Verse for Children* I-IV, James Britton (Oxford)
OBP	*Oxford Book of Poetry,* Edward Blishen
OBS	*The Oxford Book of Stories For Juniors* I-IV, James Britton
POCO	*Poet's Corner,* Barbara Ireson (Nelson)
P	*Poems,* Michael Harrison Christopher Stuart-Clark (Oxford)
PdM	*Poems,* Walter de la Mare (Puffin)
PL	*Poetry and Life* I-IV, Nora Grisenthwaite (Schofield and Sims)
PMV	*Puffin Book of Magic Verse,* Charles Causley
PQ	*Puffin Quartet of Poets*
RSH	*Red Story House,* David Jackson and Dennis Pepper (Oxford)
RR	*Rhyme and Rhythm* (Red, Blue, Green and Yellow), Gibson and Wilson (Macmillan)
SSV	*Puffin Book of Salt Sea Verse,* Charles Causley
TC	*Touchstones* I and II, M.G. and P. Benton (English Universities Press)
TH	*Thoughtshapes,* Barry Maybury (Oxford)
THW	*Thoughtweavers,* Barry Maybury (Oxford)
TW	*Tree in the Wood* I-IV, O'Malley and Thompson (Chatto)
TWD	*This Way Delight,* Herbert Read (Faber)

V	*Voices* I-IV, Geoffrey Summerfield (Penguin)
WS	*Wordscapes,* Barry Maybury (Oxford)
YI	*Young Impact* I and II, Poole and Shepherd (Heinemann)
YSH	*Yellow Story House,* David Jackson and Dennis Pepper (OXford)

Course Books

Passwords (Books I to IV plus Introductory Book), James Rose and Peter Young (Oliver and Boyd)

Poems for Writing (I and II), Sheila Lane and Marion Kemp (Blackie)

Expression (I to VI), Sybil Marshall (Hart Davis)

Ideas and *Young Ideas,* Edward Ramsbottom (Macmillan)

Penguin Primary Project, A range of books and records — this is no longer published, but still tobe found in college libraries.

Books for Teachers

So many useful books have come onto the market since this was first published, that it would take pages to list them all, but here are a few which students have found particularly helpful, together with one or two old stallwarts:

EW	*The Excitement of Writing,* A.B. Clegg (Chato)
PC	*Poems by Children* 1956-61,Michael Baldwin (Routeledge)
LCW	*Let the Children Write,* Margaret Langdon (Longman)
YWYR	*Young Writers Young Readers,* Boris Ford (Hutchinson)

Mirror Poems, William Worthy (Ginn)

Images Teachers' Book to *Wordscapes,* etc.), Barry Maybury (Oxford)

An Approach to Creative Writing in the Junior School, Sheila Lane and Marion Kemp

Teaching Children English, Cedric Cullingford (Ward Lock)

Seeing to the Heart, Marie Peel (Chatto)

Where's That Poem? Helen Morris (Blackwell)

Does it Have to Rhyme: Teaching Children to Write Poetry, Sandy Brownjohn (Hodder and Stoughton)

Children and Themes, Alan Lynsky (Oxford)

An Introduction to Words and Music, Lawrence and Montgomery (Longmans)

Creative Expression in the Primary School, Peter Dixon (Blackwell)

Children Solve Problems, Edward de Bono (Penguin)

A World Book of Children's Games, Arnold Arnold (Macmillan)

Ounce, Dice, Trice, Alastair Reid (Dent)

Puffin Joke Book, Bronnie Cunningham and Quentin Blake (Puffin).

3

Use of Activities and Play

We mean by 'Activities' the physical activities children indulge in for the sheer thrill of pleasure they get out of them, such as running fast, sliding, roller-skating, swinging, tearing downhill on skateboards, etc. In the infant school the children write quite naturally about such things and we see no reason why they should not draw on these experiences in their written work when they get older. Some teachers in junior schools seem not to consider such experiences sufficiently serious for the grownup work of the junior department. We think perhaps we are inclined to make too much of the dichotomy between infant and junior schools. Certainly provision has to be made for the developing interests of the older children but they are not *so* different. They are still absorbed by the activities we have suggested and they still enjoy writing about them. We occasionally feel that the enjoyment justifies the lesson, but at any rate is is unquestionably a vital ingredient in any English period where the teacher hopes for lively, personal writing.

It is sometimes objected by students that such a topic might engender resentment since it is so exclusively personal, dealing as it does with the child's enjoyment of play. We have never actually encountered this resentment either during our own teaching or in the supervision of students on teaching practice, so the objection may be more academic than real. We can, however, imagine a situation in which a teacher who was insensitive or antipathetic to children could make the class feel uncomfortably aware that their privacy was being invaded by someone for whom they had little respect. No worthwhile classroom activities such a teacher could institute without meeting some such resentment. It does happen, of course, that there is in the class one boy or girl who will resist work of any kind and the student should not take this to indicate that everyone feels the same way and that the lesson has been badly initiated (although this may have something to do with it). The student is at a disadvantage here in not knowing the class as well as the regular teacher. If there is a general feeling of antipathy, then either the teacher has cut across the mood of the class (and classes do have moods) or else the lesson has been introduced clumsily. This is where experience counts. The teacher who has had a lot of it knows instinctively how to introduce any topic so that the class is disposed to pursue it with her. There are any number of ways in which this might be done; the simplest is by asking the children about things they like doing in the playground, or out of school, then steering the discussion in the direction in which you want it to go, perhaps with the help of an appropriate extract from a good book.

We have arranged examples of children's writing in order of theme. The pieces are from various classes and the different themes reflect the children's personal preferences. In no case was the whole class expected to write on exactly the same theme.

SKIING, SLEDGING & SKATING

The Sledge

As we come down the hill
Trying to avoid the trees,
Faster and faster as the wind cuts into our faces.
As we go on we can see white all round us
Like a long blanket covering the earth.
Now the snow is coming faster it touches the ground.

(Michael, aged 9 UC)

We should like to go skiing in the snow and in the mountains. The best place to go is Switzerland. There are lots of great big mountains there and you could go skiing for hours without stopping. First we should have to go up the mountain to the top in a special trolley on wires. You are so high up you can see right over the mountains and across all the snow and it takes hours and hours. All the time we are thinking if there should be a break-down and we got stuck on the wire or we fell down. We should dive down like into the water into the snow and be all right in the deep snow. But nothing happens and the trolley keeps going higher and higher until we get to the top at last. Then the fun starts and we fix on our long skis. We start to go down the hills faster and faster like a speed boat in the water. The wind rushes at you at miles an hour and you have to twist one way and then another so as not to go into the trees and rocks. It is thrilling going down the mountains as fast as this, like flying in the air. Then when you come to a big drop you let go high up and shoot out like an eagle. We keep our arms out to get the balance and then falling slowly slowly until we shoot on the ground at the bottom of the mountain at last.

(Alan, aged 9 C)

The Ice Rink

The ice rink was cold but we did not mind that. We kept on skating. It was the best ice-skating I'd ever done we somehow felt free to do what we pleased. We did some turns and then we did a most remarkable thing. We went round the ring skating on one leg. We kept our balance well. Everyone stared at our but we kept on skating and we took no notice of anyone. Soon the ring was cleared so we had it all to myself to stake on we thought it was lovely.

(Enid, aged 10 C)

DOWNHILL

Paul Berna's book "100 Million Francs " has an excellent first chapter which captures the thrill of moving downhill at speed, and this was used to introduce the lesson. Discussion followed in which other activities were mentioned and the children wrote on which-even particular activity took their fancy. For some it was the scooter, for others the bicycle, while for others it was moving fast down a hill:

> *We have a fourwheeler cart which we made with the help of our father. It is made of wood and is big enough for one person to sit in. There are two axles and two wheels on each axle. The front axle can move on a bolt that goes through it so that you can steer with nylon rope. The rope is fixed to the ends of the axle. Now we have painted it looks smashing. It has blue sides and a yellow bottom and it's got a name Flora written on the side like a boat. We don't know why we called it Flora, it was just a name we thought up. We run it down Daisy Bank about eight of us. We have got three carts between us but Reggie Bailey is making another one. Where we go on Daisy Bank there is a path worn down the side and you can only use the carts in the summer because the path gets muddy when it rains and the wheels stick. It is good for sledging though when it snows.*
>
> *You have to pull the carts up the bank, two of you so you can have it in turns. When you start to go down you are so excited and it takes your breath away. It is like going on a bobsleigh in the olympic games. You start to go down faster and faster untilat one place it seems like about 60 miles an hour and it is a job to hold the wheels straight. Then it slows down a bit slower and slower on the level ground and you let it go until it stops itself to get the furthest record for distance. The furthest record is marked by a stone.*
>
> *(Roger, aged 10 C)*

Running down Wind Mill back,
Arms spread out wild,
The wind blowing our coat like a gale.
The children are shouting wee as they run down.
Jumping over the stones
And pushing our hair away from our eyes as we go
And watching the mud and cinders
As we nearly reach the bottom.

(David, aged 10 UC)

The Skateboardist

He looks like an American footballer, or a combat space fighter in his helmet, elbow pads, knee pads and gloves. Bending his leg to swerve, he twists and shoots, skimming the ground like a flicker of lightning, or he leaps from one to another like a skier on a jump. He knows no fear of falling when he moves, though his bones have been broken in many places like a jockey in the Grand National. He only thinks of the excitement and thrill of speed winding past, that one day he might be a champion of the world.

(Boy, aged 10 C)

CLIMBING AND ACROBATICS

Since the introduction of climbing apparatus there are in most primary schools opportunities for climbing and scrambling as officially sanctioned activities, but outside school these exercises still have the attraction of the illicit; boys and girls will climb trees, fences, walls and even greenhouses (see Roethke's poem in list, p. 118).

Swinging High

In the playing field by our house are some swings. When we go on them with our sister we have a race and see who can go the highest. When you swing high you feel as if you were flying forward in the sky. But, alas! you keep flying back as if there were magnets drawing in front and behind you. They keep on pushing you to and fro. One doesn't want you but when you go to the other he doesn't want the other to have you. Sometimes when you are nearly over the bars you can see for miles around, but then you have to come back to the ground.

(Norma, aged 10 UC)

Climbing a Tree

It's great fun to climb up into a tree like an oak or
a chestnut
Then you can run along the branches and
Swing right up and over the top.
A boy can climb right up into the thinnest branches
When you get to the top the wind creaks the tree.
It moans and whistles and you hold on tight.
From the top you can see for miles,
Everything looks so small
The people in their gardens look like tiny insects.

(Alan, Aged 8 C)

On the Apparatus

Our apparatus is fixed to the ground so that we can climb on it without fear. There have only been two accidents on it so far and nothing serious. One boy broke his leg and that was his own fault for getting where somebody else was swinging. We like the low bar best. We will tell you how to do it. The best way is to jump up a bit, turn your hand round and then swing down then you are upside down. You let go if you want to or you might want to swing back up again, then you have to push your legs up in the air and come back to where you started from at the beginning. Or you can hang backwards on your legs upside down then you can just touch your legs with one hand and touch the ground with the other. We like climbing up the ladder as well and hang on the top bar and then drop down. That's very exciting.

(Margaret, aged, 9 C)

SWIMMING & DIVING

A good time to have a lesson on this is after a visit to the swimming baths when the experience is fresh. Some children won't, of course, be able to swim or dive but generally they all like playing about in water, although if some children wish to write about some other activity they are particularly good at then we think they should be encouraged to do so. A difficulty that often arises here is the sense of frustration arising out of vocabulary which is not equal to the experience, so that a brief discussion on words is frequently worthwhile. Here are some words suggested by children in one class:

slide	thrash	pressure	crashing	silvery
slice	flounder	force	plash	misty
glide	chop	power	dull	cloudy
drift	struggle	strength	boom	foggy
float	bustle	weight	trickle	
plunge	flail	velvet	swish	
	lollop			

The grouping of the words is deliberate. The children were asked to think of graceful movements, struggling movements, the feel of the water, the noise made by it and by them, the appearance of the water. Here are some pieces which followed the vocabulary exercise. It is perhaps worth mentioning that some children clung almost obsessively towards they had suggested, while others tended to avoid their own words and use those suggested by other children; we assume there are personality reasons for this. The important thing is to make it clear that they don't have to use words that have been suggested if they don't want to.

Diving and Swimming

Sliding through the air in a swallow dive
The diver sliced his way into the cool green water.
It looks like a green jelly till he plunges into it,
Then he hears a dull booming sound in the water.
For a little time everything is misty and twirling
As he pushes back the green silvering liquid.
He cuts his way through the water like a knife and
Bobs up on the surface, flinging his hair out of his eyes.
His legs kick out violently into the green fluid,
His hands chop the water and turn it back and he
Reaches the side like a wet fish.

(Malcolm, aged 11 C)

We go to the baths every Tuesday and we look forward to it very much especially as we can nearly swim a width now. We used to walk down the steps but now we jump in from the side. It takes your breath away for a minute and makes you excitable. You splash and thrash up and down in the water and probably splash your friends and so your hair gets wet. You jump up and down to get used to the water. Mrs. D. doesn't mind this for a short time but then you get going and swim across the width. You have to force your way through the water with the arms and legs and kick with the feet and when you can do it properly you glide gently through the water without effort. Underneath the water it is all misty like a fog and the noises are all softened and quiet so that when you jump up the sounds are deafening. we like the baths very much and one day we should like to be able to dive from the high stand.

(Janet, aged 10 C)

Suggestions

It is not suggested that each of these items should be the subject of a single lesson, although, of course, some of them might be. Rather it is an indication to the student of some of the activities which are particularly engaging to children and therefore might attract and absorb some of them as themes in writing: swinging on a rope, old tyre or swing; see-sawing; on the roundabout; on the slide; jumping across a ditch or rope, or off a wall; cartwheels, skipping, headstands, racing; walking on stilts; jumping on a pogostick or spring heels; rounders, football. fighting; roller-staking. These ideas might be used as themes for pieces of description, openings for stories, poems, diaries, tape-recorded accounts, 'documentaries,' etc. Or they might be starting points for some imaginary exploit, e.g. climbing Everest, swimming to an island, running to escape. (See Further Ideas for Writing and Language Work page 204 ff).

Poems & Extracts:

The Rascue *Hal Summers* HJ; POCO

Dancing *Eleanor Farjeon* RR, Blue

The Roundabout by the Sea *John Walsh* BP, II

Child on top of a Greenhouse *Theodor Roethke* H; JV, III

School's Out *W. H. Davies* RR, Red

Out of Doors *James Britton* OBS, III

The Flight, from 'There is a Happy Land,' chapter 14 *Keith Waterhouse* WS

Birches *Robert Frost* H

How we Learned to Roller-Skate *Christopher, aged 10* OBS, III

Hard Cheese *Justin ST. John* JV, III

Children's Games *Wm. Carlos William* YI, I

The Blue Ball *John Walsh* MW

Breathless *Wilfred Noyce* WS

The Fight *Gareth Owen* WS

The Gamekeeper *Barry Hines* BSH

PLAY

We often play with our dolls in the garden. We have fifteen altogether but they are not all in very good condition. Some are broken, some have lost their eyes or their hair and one unfortunately has lost one arm and one leg, but this does not make any difference because we love them all just as much. Our best doll is called Janice and she has an embroidered dress in lemon colour and brown hair.We play tea parties with our dolls and we always let Janice do the serving because she is very good at it. She corrects the others if they misbehave. She knows what's what she does. When they have all had their tea they have to get ready for bed, then there is pandemonium and fuss. Janice tells them off and they all soon get ready. They have their nightdress put on and they go to bed.

(Janice, aged 8 C)

We think that in order to introduce a lesson successfully the teacher should have a clear idea of the particular kind of experience she wants the children to deal with so that she can arouse the particularity of their own interest. But naturally, that does not mean that they are put in an imaginative strait jacket when it comes to writing. On the contrary, if the lesson has been properly introduced the children should have a sense of the greater freedom, of exploring a region they know a great deal about already. Pupils might, for example, do some research into games in History, or games in different countries, perhaps contributing to a Book of Games; or they might make up new board games on the model of Snakes and Ladders; or they might take a game that interests them and write a poem, rhymes, or description based on it, e.g. building a raft, flying a kite, cycling, skateboarding, etc.

A poem in which a common play situation is very clearly evoked together with the attendant feeling of a child in that situation in Vernon Scannell's Hide and Seek' (JV, IV; WS). This is good because it has a story interest, there is no language difficulty, and the central experience is one we should think every child is familiar with, and we have fund that it usually sparks off a good deal of discussion of similar situations. To help the student who is uncertain how to develop such a discussion or perhaps extend the lesson into a project on play we shall list below some perennial favourites. The divisions are somewhat arbitrary, of course, since there is a good deal of overlapping.

Imaginative Play

Dolls, Dolls' House, Puppets, Toy Cars, Guns, Bows and Arrows, Tea Parties, Schools, Castles, Tree-houses, Dressing-up, Model-making, Play-acting.

Games

Hide-and-Seek, Statues, TV Series, Mimes, Hopscotch, Skipping, Rounders, Ball Games, Tip-cat, Tops, Jacks (Fives), Marbles, Conkers, Street Games, Board Games.

Constructive Play

Making cotton-reel tank, rubber-band gun,model theatre, raft, Guy Fawkes, Lego, Meccano models, tree house.

Books

A Book of practical Ideas for the Primary School *Redvers Brandling* Ward Lock

A World Book of Children's Games *Arnold Arnold* Macmillan

How to Do Nothing with Nobody All Alone by Yourself *Robert Paul Smith* World's Work

Play in Childhood *Margaret Lownefeld* Gollancz

Something to Do *Septima* Puffin

And here is some children's work:

The cold night with the boys and girls playing
With the moon shining bright
In the dark and cold night

With the stars all shining.
They are playing games
They could be climbing trees,
They could be doing some help for their mothers
They are sowing the dark night with golden stars,
Playing with their love.

(Christopher, aged 10 UC)

When we were small, we used to play dressing-up.
We've get mom's old clothes and hats.
We used to have her shoes that were miles too big
Which always fell off our feet.
We would always trip in our mom's long dress
All her dresses touched our toes.
And all her hats come down to our nose.
We could not see a thing at all
But we loved dressing up best of all.

(Linda, aged 11 UC)

When we were about 2-3 years younger we used to play War. We were mostly a prefessor working for the risestance. We had a German helmit at one time but it got lost. When we were a prof. We would heat up some chemicals and pretend that it was Liquid Nitrogliserine. When a German patrol came round we would through a cob of durt and it would blow up and kill everyone in the patrole. Barry our friend had a set of earfones witch we would plug into the dust bin and send radio messages. Our brother David would put stones in his durt and aim for the German helmet.

Poems & Extracts

In Just — *e.e. cummings* H.

Come out to Play RR, Red.

Song for a Ball Game *Wilfred Thorley* RR, Blue.

Out of School *Hal Summers* H.

Making Raft, chapter 36 (extracts) of 'Bevis: the story of a boy *Richard Jeffries* (Puffin).

The Fantastic Machine *Barry Maybury* BW.

Lovejoy and Tip *Rumer Godden* WS.

The Dress *Joan Guest* TH.

Rainbow Stuff *Joan Guest* WSP.

Fresh *Phillipa Pearce* BSH.

Kite Flying *Vivian Virtue* BSH.

Cricket in the Road, *Michael Anthony* RSH.

The Playground *girl, aged 12* EW.

The Sandcastle *John Walsh* TW, III.

Hide and Seek *Vernon Scannell* JV, IV; WS.

Me in a Tree *D.G., aged 10* JV, I.

Boy Fishing *E.J. Scovell* MW; POCO.

Canoe Song *Geoffrey Summerfield* MW.

Saturdays *Michael Rosen* MW; WS.

Making Pancakes *Paddy Kinsale* BW.

4

Learners and the Course Curriculum

An English langauge teacher should try to answer the question, 'What did the children think of the curriculum?' We believe that this is an important question in at least two respects. First, there is the question of pupil learning, the ostensible purpose of the Education Reform Act. While the debates around the National Curriculum largely concerned themselves with structures, content and assessment issues, we retain a conviction that the motivation of children is also important. Of course, it was precisely this issue that led members the Hadow Committee to publish their 1931 statement that 'the curriculum should be thought of in terms of activity and experience rather than as knowledge to be learned and facts to be stored' (Board of Education, p. 93). Both HMI and Hadow had an essentially practical concern here. They wanted children to learn effectively and they were concerned that the curriculum should connect with the concerns and ways of thinking of young children.

A second reason for the importance of pupil perceptions of the curriculum follows if one views the educational experiences of childhood as worthwhile in their own right, rather than simply as means to later goals in life. Primary education, for instance, may be seen as something much more than a preparation phase for secondary education or the 'realities' of work. It is a significant part of each child's life and, as parents have consistently recorded (Hughes et al., 1990 pupils' perceived quality of classroom experiences is therefore important. Blyth (1984) encompassed many aspects of these issues in his conception of curriculum as 'a planned intervention into the interaction of development and experience' (Blyth, 1984, p. 43). This sentence immediately draws attention to issues such as the physical, social, cognitive and affective development of young children and to the ways in which they learn through interaction with their experienced environment—points that seem to have been discussed very rarely by those constructing the National Curriculum in England.

Further, curriculum is seen as contributing continuously to both the development and the experience of young children as they grow up. However, while development and experience will occur naturally in one form or another throughout life, curriculum is seen as the outcome of deliberate decisions by others about appropriate provision for learners. The curriculum, as Blyth (1984, p. 43) put it, 'is designed to make a positive impact on children.' This, of course, is exactly what the National Curriculum was intended to do: to provide a broad, balanced, system-wise education and to raise educational standards of achievement. The rationale of the National Curriculum, in other words, was that it would, ultimately, be reflected in greater clarity of thinking, more knowledge and gradually developing levels of skill among pupils. It was a 'planned intervention' on a national scale. But what would its impact actually be in the realities of classrooms across the country, far from Whitehall? And, further, how would it appear to the pupils, in whose name it was ostensibly, created? Would they feel motivated by it so that its introduction could contribute to the quality of their learning and of their learning experiences? Our interviews with children were designed to find out.

Major Findings of Previous Research

Research on children's perspectives of the primary school curriculum is relatively scarce, and, where it is available, has usually focused on the process of curriculum delivery rather than on the subject content issues *per se.* There are good reasons for this tendency, because children tend to be concerned far more about the implications of a curriculum subject in terms of 'what we have to do' rather than in terms of the subject matter itself. Meaningful curriculum descriptors for young children are thus likely to describe processes — writing, climbing, sitting, doing sums, reading — or qualities of experience — fun, exciting, interesting, boring, Makins (1969), for instance, suggested that what primary school children learn matters to them less than how they are taught.

Cullingford (1990) vividly conveys many aspects of children's feelings of vulnerability in learning,the involvement of self and the defensive strategies that are often adopted. As he writes,

> *All children want to remain invisible, unnoticed. For their experience is always private. They do not want to be cajoled into learning. They have the general human tendency to be suspicious of being taught. and when they are learning they know that it is their own. Their ownership of learning makes it real, and private. (p. 117).*

These points are interesting, for classroom situations are anything but private. Indeed, pupil experience has been powerfully characterized as being of crowd (Jackson, 1968). It follows that the learning experiences associated with particular curricular subjects may well be evaluated by the balance of psychological and social exposure and challenge they bring, when compared with the interest and enjoyment they offer. Good examples of this are provided in the work of Woods (1987, 1988), where the ways in which primary school teachers create classroom contexts that are conductive to learning are explored. Similarly, Pollard (1990) and Pollard with Filer (forthcoming) provide accounts of pupils' learning strategies and relationships to the social contexts of home, classroom and playground. In this ethnographic case study it was the ratio of risk to enjoyment that seemed to determine how children felt about curriculum activity, rather than the nature of the tasks themselves. Further, the significance of the issue is confirmed by Lewis (1993) in her analysis of the views of schooling held by children with moderate learning difficulties. She argues that, rather the curriculum content per se being important, such children need a curriculum that addresses social and emotional development, and issues such as friendship and coping with conflict.

More directly Tizard *et al.,* (1988) interviewed 133 seven-year-olds about, among other areas, their work at school. In this case, questions were confined to children's attitudes to reading alone, reading to a teacher, writing and mathematics. The most popular subjects were maths, liked by 71 per cent overall, and reading to the teacher (65 per cent). Writing was appreciated by 56 per cent, while reading to oneself was positively viewed by only 51 per cent of children. Tizard *at al.* speculated that the relative unease over writing centred mainly on the tedium of routine writing tasks and spelling difficulties, while concern over reading to oneself was associated with the difficulty of achieving success with self-selected books.

Goodnow and Burns (1985) produce a rather different account with their interviews with 2000 Australian children. Junior school pupils were unambiguously keen on sport, games and playing at school, and also liked subjects such as art, craft and music. However, they had very mixed views on the standard core subjects of maths and English. Goodnow and Burns attributed this to a discrepancy between the expectations of children regarding their education and the realities of school life. For instance, children expect 'to learn everything,' but they are mainly taught basic skills; they expect 'to learn useful things,' but the relevance of the curriculum is only rarely apparent; they expect 'to like the work,' but it is sometimes 'too hard' and is often 'boring'; they expect the school day to provide variety, but it tends to be very predictable and repetitive. Clearly there are also likely to be differences among pupils and at different ages. For instance, the responses of the eleven-year-olds interviewed by Pollard (1985, p. 89) showed that by this age children's evaluation of learning is closely associated with the social identities they have acquired, in this case within peer groups of 'goodies,' jokers' or 'gangs.' Goodies' conformist strategy overrode their feelings about curriculum subjects as they strove to maintain their image in their teacher's eyes. Jokers were likely to try to direct lessons they considered boring into 'more fertile activities,' while gangs would, on occasion, become more directly subversive. Unlike the other two groups, they rarely obtained intrinsic satisfaction from their learning unless they saw direct links with future work—a more instrumental approach.

Public Preceptions of Curriculum Content

We were interested in the children's perceptions of curriculum-related activities in their classrooms, and in the ways in which this related to the findings of our systematic observation of curriculum subject coverage. With this in mind, we showed the children a collage of pictures of 12 common infant school activities that had been extracted from a book by Ahlberg and Ahlberg (1988). We then asked, 'Which of these activities do you do in your classroom?' This question was asked first in 1990, when the children were in Year 1, and it was repeated in 1991, when they had become Year 2 pupils. From among the large number of activities that the children nominated on each occasion, we coded the first two. In Table 1 these nominations have been aggregated and expressed as a percentage of all activities nominated on both occasions by boys, girls and all pupils. We thus have an indicator of curriculum activities as perceived by infant school pupils.

There are several interesting aspects of Table 1 but perhaps the most significant is the way in which it resonates with findings from our systematic observations of curriculum content. The three aspects of English identified by the children as taking place in their classrooms (stories, reading and writing) total 30 per cent of the nominations made, compared with 36 per cent of our total observations in the two years. Maths provided 19 per cent of nominations and 15 per cent of observations, while for science the figures were 2 per cent of nominations but 8 per cent of observations. Such figures seem to show a broad mapping of pupil perception and systematic observation regarding the curriculum of 'the basics' at least, though perhaps a lack of pupil awareness regarding the nature of 'science' as a curricular subject. However, the most striking finding is undoubtedly the fact that no fewer than 24 per cent of pupil nominations concerned physical education, far higher than our combined figure of 3 per cent of observations.

Taken together with findings that are reported later in this chapter, we think it likely that the pattern of children's perceptions of curriculum activities is influenced by subjective feelings that are associated with the experience of these classroom activities. Physical education was seen by many children as a enjoyable source of activity and release from 'work,' as other studies have also found (Mortimore *et al.*, 1988), and while regularly provided, may have been exaggerated in what the children reported. Maths, on the other hand,may have loomed relatively large as a major source of 'work' itself. Aspects of what might be taken as 'play' (sand, 'home corner' play, construction) were, quite accurately, not perceived to occur very often at all, despite the fact, as we shall see, that they were greatly valued by the children.

TABLE 1

Classroom Activities Nominated by Pupils in Response to the Question 'Which of These Sorts of Things do you do in Your Classroom?' (Percentages)

Nominated classroom	Girls activities	Boys	Overall
Stories	11	11	11
Reading	13	12	13
Writing	7	4	6
Maths	16	23	19
Science	3	1	2
Construction	1	3	2
Sand	2	6	4
Dressing up	2	1	1
Play	2	1	1
Painting	10	4	6
Drawing	2	0	1
Singing	9	3	6
Physical education	22	25	24
Missing data	2	7	5

Source: PACE 1 child interviews.
Sample: 54 Year 1 and 54 Year 2 children.
Date: autumn 1990 and autumn 1991.

Pupil Preferences for Curriculum Activities

In both the 1990 Year 1 interviews and the 1991 Year 2 interviews the children in our longitudinal sample were asked to identify curriculum activities they 'liked best' and then those they 'liked least.' In both 1990 and 1991 they were asked to make selections from the set of 12 activities we had presented to them. Since those activities were not fully comprehensive regarding all infant school activities we cannot treat the data we collected as being totally representative. Nevertheless, they do provide powerful indications of children's preferences for different sorts of curricular activities. We will present the basic findings in this section, while the reasons offered by the children are analysed in section 5.

For the purpose of this analysis we coded the activity that was named by each child as 'most liked' or 'least liked. Table 2 provides data on the curricular activities that were most favoured by the pupils. The most consistently favoured activity was physical education. This was liked by boys and girls in both Year 1 and Year 2 and was a first choice for no less than 28 per cent of children. Also clearly favoured were painting and 'home corner' play, though, as for sand, their favoured status was strongest when the children were younger. As the children moved from Year 1 to Year 2, appreciation of maths and singing developed significantly. Girls tended to favour reading, 'home corner' play and painting, while boys prioritized construction activities and sand. Analysis of preferences by pupil attainment showed few differences, though there was a slight preference for lower-achieving pupils to like 'home corner play.

Data on the curriculum activities 'least liked' are presented in Table 3 Overall, the least liked curricular activity was writing, first named by 15 per cent of pupils, followed by maths, science and listening to stories — a finding that made the PACE team immediately wonder about stress on the core subjects of the National Curriculum. The dislike of hearing stories was almost exclusively mentioned by the children when they were in Year 2 and does not undermine the generally positive views of the children when younger. However, there were strong patterns by gender among the activities disliked.

Girls disliked construction, science and stories must more than boys, while boys found writing, reading, maths and 'home corner' play more distasteful than girls. Again analysis of pupil attainment revealed no significant differences.

TABLE 2

Curricular Activities 'Liked Best' by Children Year 1 and Year 2 (Percentages)

	Year 1	Year 2	Girls	Boys	Overall
Stories	7	4	7	4	6
Reading alone	4	7	9	2	6
Reading lessons	0	0	0	0	0
Writing	6	2	2	6	4
Maths	2	17	9	9	9
Science	0	4	0	4	2
Construction	6	6	0	11	6
Sand	13	0	2	11	6
'Home corner' play	17	6	13	9	11
Painting	20	7	19	9	14
Singing	4	13	9	7	8
Physical education	22	33	26	30	28
Nothing liked	0	0	0	0	0
Missing	0	2	0	2	1

Source: PACE 1 child interviews.

Sample: 54 1 and 54 Year 2 children.

Date: autumn 1990 and autumn 1991.

In keeping with the spirit of the early 1990s we have produced a 'league table' of Year 1 and Year 2 pupil preferences. This is based on a rank order of the net score when the percentage 'best liked is set against the percentage 'least liked' for each subject in each year. Table 4 sets out the result of this analysis. There are many interesting features of these league tables of pupil preferences. First, we should note that physical education occupies the top of both tables, while writing and science are at the bottom of each.

Other curriculum activities that record a change of only two places or fewer and painting, 'home corner' play and singing in the upper half, and reading alone, construction and reading lessons in the lower half. The big 'success story' is mathematics, which rose from twelfth position when the children were in Year 1 to second in Year 2. Conversely, sand and stories fell down the list of pupil preferences as the children aged a year.

TABLE 3

Curricular Activities 'Liked Least' by Children Year 1 and Year 2 (Percentages)

	Year 1	Year 2	Girls	Boys	Overall
Stories	4	17	15	6	10
Reading alone	9	7	2	15	8
Reading lessons	7	2	6	4	5
Writing	15	15	6	24	15
Maths	15	7	9	13	11
Science	7	15	17	6	11
Construction	11	7	17	2	9
Sand	2	2	4	0	2
'Home corner' play	6	2	0	7	4
Painting	4	6	6	4	5
Singing	6	9	7	7	7
Physical education	0	2	2	0	1
Nothing liked	13	7	6	15	10
Missing	2	2	2	2	2

Source: PACE 1 child interviews.

Sample: 54 1 and 54 Year 2 children.

Date: autumn 1990 and autumn 1991.

It is, perhaps, just as well that recent government policy has not seen pupils themselves as the prime educational consumers in the new market-based model of education that the Education Acts of 1988 and 1993 have introduced. Had this been the case, the National Curriculum core subjects would have been significantly skewed off balance at Key Stage 1, with the possible exception of maths. Children, on this evidence, would have done a lot of physical education, painting and playing.

TABLE 4

'LEAGUE TABLE' OF PUPILS' FAVOURED CURRICULAR ACTIVITIES

Rank	Year 1 net rank	Year 2 net rank
1	Physical education	Physical education
2	Painting	Maths
3	'Home corner' play	'Home corner play
4	Sand	Painting
5	Stories	Singing
6	Singing	Reading alone
7	Construction	Construction
8	Reading alone	Reading lesson
9	Reading lesson	Sand
10	Science	Science
11	Writing	Stories
12	Maths	Writing

Source: PACE 1 child interviews.
Sample: 54 1 and 54 Year 2 children.
Date: autumn 1990 and autumn 1991.

However, this is too simple, for we have already seen in Chapter 7 that 60 per cent of the observed classroom curriculum was in fact devoted to the core subjects in both years and there was, in fact, *very* little time spent on physical education, painting or play. The children, in other words, seemed to dislike things they were required to do regularly but would have liked to do more of the occasional activities, which in their experience provided respite from the more normal routines and curriculum diet of classroom life. More detailed reason for children's perspectives are explored below.

Why did Pupils Prefer Particular Curricular Activities?

Two sources of interview data were collected by the PACE team regarding this issue. First, following the identification of 'most liked' and 'least liked' curricular activities, children were asked, 'Why do you like (the most liked) better than (the least liked)?' This sought pupil reasoning concerning activities chosen freely but relatively abstractly. A more contextually embedded approach was also used at the start of the pupil interviews in Year 1 and Year 2, when the children were referred to an activity in which they had participated and that the researcher had actually observed earlier. The children were asked whether they had 'liked' or 'disliked' doing the activity and to explain the reasons for their answer. The activities around which these latter questions were based were the same as those from which our systematic observation findings were derived, and they may be regarded as providing a representative reflection of the Key Stage 1 curriculum. In combination, we believe that pupil responses to these two questions provide a strong data source.

Answers to the two questions were analysed using an identical set of codes and in quantitative terms the results are shown in Table 5. These are provided as percentages of the coded responses for each question. Six major pupil criteria for evaluating curricular activities were identified: success/case, interest, fun, activity, autonomy and long-term education. A seventh major coding, like, was used when pupils affirmed but did not adequately explain their preference for a curriculum activity. These data have not been used in the subsequent analysis.

TABLE 5

Pupil Criteria for Preferred Curricular Activities (Percentages of Codings)

Criterion	Overall preferences
Success/ease	27
Interest	24
Fun	18
Activity	13
Educational	5
Other	7

Source: PACE 1 child interviews.
Sample: 54 1 and 54 Year 2 children.
Date: autumn 1990 and autumn 1991.

'Interest' was an important criterion, used by 24 per cent of children in describing reasons for their curricular activity preferences. From the pupil comments, it could be associated with 'fun' but certainly had an obverse in 'boring.' As other researchers have found (e.g. Goodnow and Burns, 1985), boredom is a child concept that seems, to children, to need little explanation. The pupil use of the concept tended to be brief:

> 'Cos science is writing and we have to write a lot.
>
> 'Cos writing you've just got to write things and grown-ups, like my mum, write all squiggly (shows).
>
> I just don't like singing, it's boring.
>
> The stories can be boring if we all have to listen to them.

More positively, on the other hand, the majority of pupil comments noted aspects of curricular activities that were clearly valued. Some were associated with particular subjects, such as those of the core curriculum.

Regarding English:

> Yes, I like it when you can go and read. I like the good stories. We've got the books at home.
>
> Yes, I liked finding out he ideas and I like poems.

Regarding science:

> Easy question? I like doing the things we do like making a light-bulb work with a battery and wire. Writing I don't like because we have to write long stories.
>
> Yes, you can watch and see what happens and learn something.
>
> Yes, because I like playing with magnets and I brought a train to school and the back magnets to the front.

Other subject areas were also mentioned. Regarding technology:

> Because it's making models and trying to make a machine.

> Yes, 'cos it's nice to try and build things.

Regarding art:

> Because it was good when you write down and you draw the pictures I did the grass by — I did light green first and then dark green so it looks like the real grass.

> Yes — I like drawing but not the quiz sheet. Art is my favourite subject and you don't have to add up or write. I like mixing colours and smudging.

More play-orientated activities were also prominent:

> Because you can play schools and stuff in here. Play with all my friends. Because you make things good and you play with the train set.

> Because I like making sand castles when it's wet ....'cos I've been down to the seaside before, and last year I done a big sand castle... and me mum did a big flag so I could do a big flag sand castle and some people played with me and I had a 'turtle' spade and bucket and we dig right to the bottom and we fund treasure and silver.

Egan's (1989) argument, that the understanding of young children should be linked, through curriculum, to their interest and facility in fantasy and imagination, takes on a direct significance with play of this sort. The children whom we interviewed confirmed his priority.

The 5 per cent of occasions when long-term educational reasons were cited by the children is a low figure but perhaps one that would be expected from children so young. Their perceptions were of relatively generalised sort. Something good was being done to them:

> Yes, 'cos I like learning how to add all these things up and I wouldn't know all these things if I don't go to school.

> Yes, I think they're good for you — you learn.
>
> I like painting because you can be an artist when you grow up, and PE because you can be a PE teacher. Some stories take too long.
>
> Because you can work harder and I'm going to go to college. You have to work hard for that. That's why I like maths.

The issues of the sense of fulfilment and degree of success and effort that pupils put into their work were also very major criteria in establishing preferences for curricular activities. 'Success/ease' was the primary coding of 27 per cent of pupil responses and there were four major sub-categories of this code.

First, some children were aware of the problem of understanding the tasks set and teacher expectations of them:

> I don't know what to make and what not to make.
>
> Yes, When Miss tells me to do it, I like it. I like it when I'm doing those numbers
>
> No. because sometimes you don't know what to write.
>
> In science it's a bit hard 'cos sometimes you don't know what you are doing it in.

Second, there was the issue of just how hard tasks or activities were to complete. There was a variety of views across curriculum subjects and activities but the calculation appeared to concern maximizing the product for a given effort. There was a hint of the need for children to meet teacher-set work quotes or targets here, but also the theme of intrinsic fulfilment from learning itself:

> Because you don't have to do new work [Maths better than writing]. Because you can learn to count like 10 and 10 and I find writing more difficult and takes longer.
>
> Maths is easier because if we get our writing really

> spidery we have to write it again. In maths we don't — we just rub out the answers and write them again. Reading is easy 'cos I could read when I was three. I like singing because of learning Christmas songs. Because, well, I like doing maths and they're easy. Writing is more difficult because I have to keep on going to get words from Miss.

> I like sums because they are hard and I have to think. Other things don't take enough time and I get bored when I've done all my 'jobs' and I have to read and you get bored doing that every day.

> Because I sometimes get it really quickly done. I got ten sums done in five minutes which are hard ones. Writing takes me a long time because the spellings trouble me and I can't rush it. Miss wants it done quick.

> The words in my word-building book are hard-like "alphabet, photograph and physical. But I like reading stories' cos most words are easy— and maths has easy answers.

> Maths is more difficult.

> Because you can draw lots of pictures. Science is hard.

> 'Cos you paint pictures, writing is hard.

> 'Cos writing and reading is my favourite things as school. 'Cos at reading you don't have to do any sums, you just write the letters.

Following pupil concern about the process of learning was their awareness of the importance of success. On this, they were concerned with their personal performance in both absolute and relative terms. For instance, some appreciated their attainment in itself:

> Yes, I like adding in my head. Getting the right answer: that's what I like.

> I quite liked it. 'Cos I knew all the answers — one of them was so easy — it was two add two.

> Yes, I like getting on hard books.

Some appreciated completion of work:

> Yes, I like finishing things off.

Others drew attention to their achievements relative to others in their classes, and the status that this gave them:

> Miss said mine was excellent. She gave me one of the hardest — Simon had the hardest. Because it looks like a tortoise.

> Because I like — it isn't really a contest, but I like feeling if you want to win you can do a lot and if you don't win you can say, 'well, I don't mind.'

> Yes, 'cos I'm good at writing.

For some, the problem was completion itself:

> I don't like writing. I feel that I'm never going to get it done.

There was also the question of 'having fun':

> They're fun things and science is good because you learn a lot of things from it. Singing's a bit fun but it's not fun when you're practising for the Christmas Play like now, because you have to keep singing boring songs.

> Yes, because it's funny and I like writing and doing puppets.

> Yes, like sticking and cutting-out. It's fun and painting too.

> Yes,' good fun 'Cos you can paint and stick things and put wheels on and Sellotaping.

> Yes, because it's fun holding the puppets up.
>
> 'Cos it's fun, all sorts of hats and clothes and trousers. It's really fun. I like them a lot. Singing is boring. She has to shout and we are too quiet and we don't know the songs. She thinks we should know them.

Beyond 'having fun,' however, was a point where a degree of classroom disorder actually became threatening, or problematic to children. This was rare in our data, but the following are examples:

> No, because Amanda was getting on our nerves. She wasn't getting on with her writing. Some of it. Sally and David were messing about. They wouldn't .... We didn't do it all.

Autonomy was coded as the main criteria for 5 per cent of pupil answers, though it featured as a factor in many other responses. Children recorded statements such as:

> Because you can play in the sand but you can't in science and writing.
>
> It's fun and you can choose what to do.
>
> Because you can choose what to dress up in and it's fun.
>
> 'Cos you don't have to do so much work and that stuff.
>
> Because I can build something I like doing — I built a really good ark.

Regarding the pupil criterion well called 'activity' (13 per cent of cold responses), many pupils drew a contrast, which gets right to the point, between physical education and story time.

> 'Cos you have to sit down when it's story time and when it's PE you can run around.
>
> 'Cos you can have a lot of running about in PE and 'cos you can't in the book corner.

Sitting down for long periods of time, such as we had observed in the whole-class sessions on the carpet, was not favoured:

> You have to sit down, I get hot, I like to stand up and get cool.
>
> Because you have to sit on the carpet and listen or you get told off and you think "Oh dear, this is boring.'
>
> We sit on the floor and I get squashed.

In contrast, physical education seemed to provide variety, excitement and a sense of challenge and fulfilment for almost all children:

> Because you can run about, go up ladders and swing on the bar and go up the plank. In singing you have to sit still on the floor.
>
> Because we're allowed a crash mat out and you can do hand-stands and can jump on the box and there's a climbing frame and a rope to swing on. Science — we have to do lots of sitting down and writing and going round the classroom looking for things.
>
> 'Cos it's good. You practice and you can run.
>
> 'Cos you do all sorts of things.
>
> 'Cos you climb on things.
>
> Sometimes in PE we have climbing frames, mats, etc. It's like playing, when you read you make mistakes and you don't like it.
>
> Because you do exercises there [points of PE] but I can't get on much there [points to maths].

Our interpretation of these data relates to the context of power relationships between pupils and teachers in classrooms. As one of us has argued (Pollard, 1985),pupils seek to cope in primary school classrooms by juggling major interests-at-hand. Primary pupil interests can be identified as the maintenance of self-image, enjoyment, control of stress and the retention of dignity, and these are satisfied by the enabling interests of peer group membership and learning. All pupils, in other words, have to satisfy three main parties: themselves, their peers and significant adults. Different pupils adopt particular strategies for doing this, as we shall explore fully in future books from the PACE project.

In aggregated and analytical terms, however, we can relate pupil criteria for evaluating curricular activities to the zone of major influence of pupils and teacher respectively — to the power context. This model locates fun sense of humour, mischief and sociability of young children and to the physical energy and developmental stage that set them apart from adolescents and adults alike. Teachers cannot keep up with children as they climb, skip or run about in physical education or the playground, nor can they appreciate their jokes in the same ways the children do. The activities that relate to these criteria are therefore the children's own. They related to being a child and to child culture.

The criterion of success/ease, on the other hand, is located squarely within the teachers' zone of major influence. Curriculum activities in classrooms yield success or failure, ease or difficulty, depending on the nature of the tasks the teacher sees and the assessment procedures that are implemented. The teacher has the power of structuring and decision and the pupil is maximally exposed — hence the very high proportion of children mentioning this criterion. After all, as Blyth (1984) put it, 'the curriculum is an *intervention* in a child's development and experience.' Of course, it comes as no surprise to realise that the most popular Key Stage 1 pupil activities — physical education, painting and 'home corner' play — give relatively large scope for fun and activity, while less favoured curricular activities, such as writing, tend to be seen as difficult and as a potential source of failure.

In what we have called the 'intermediate zone' we have located pupil criteria that identify the 'interest' of the curriculum activity and the degree of autonomy provided. Interest is particularly important for, together with its obverse of 'boring,' it represents a pupil evaluation of the intrinsic and directly experienced worth of educational activity. As such it is also a pupil concern through which teachers can connect with pupil curiosity and imagination, and can thus support them in moving from the pupil zone of fun and activity towards the more staid goals of the adult curriculum. Nor, it should be said, are pupils unwilling travellers on this developmental and educational track, particularly if it is achieved in ways that leave them appropriate dignity and autonomy. This last criterion, although articulated relatively less often than the others, is important for the processual reason. The fact that it was not cited by more than 5 per cent of pupils could, of course, be taken as another indicator that classroom relationships were seen as good by both teachers and children.

Finally we have the criterion that identifies the long-term educational benefits of particular curricular activities. Explicated rarely, it is a good indicator of the extent to which most young pupils do or do not understand the reasons behind the educational experiences to which they are exposed.

How did Pupils Perceive Teacher Intentions?

Research has consistently shown that it is helpful for learning success if pupils understand the specific aims and purposes that teachers have for tasks. However, it has also been shown that such detailed understanding is relatively rare in schools (Bennett *et al.*, 1984) and, unfortunately, our data largely confirm this.

As was described in section 3, following systematic observation of a task the 54 children in our classroom studies were asked, 'Why do you think your teacher wanted you to do (the task/activity)? The question was thus embedded in a real context and was part of the longer interviews that took place in 1990 and 1991, when the children were in Year 1 and Year 2 respectively. The data were coded using seven main codes. These were associated with pupil ideas as follows.

A quarter of pupil answers reflected a belief that teachers set tasks to help pupil learning, in some very general way. For instance:

> 'Cos we're learning to do our letters and write and read. She wants us to learn to read and write.
>
> Because she wanted us to learn a new story and write it out. *Why?* Because she wants you to learn so when you're older you can write.
>
> Because she thinks it's good for us. She used to put them on the board but she thinks we've got so good at that, we could do a sheet.
>
> We're doing it each day. Trying to get better and dead neat and write stories.
>
> I don't know — get good at writing.
>
> I think it was our maths for today so we can be a bank manager if we like when we grow up. As we get older we get nearer to being very old and ready to work.
>
> So we could learn them.

Many children thus trusted their teacher's overall judgement in helping them learn. However, for almost a further quarter, tasks were seen more as things that were simply 'required.' Tasks were set because that was what happened in school and reasoning why did not appear to be an educational question. It was more an issue-of what the routine or structure of classroom organization was or the moods or preferences the teacher herself came up with.

> 'Cos everybody in class had to do one.
>
> 'Cos we have not done it for a long while.
>
> She just said do it.
>
> (Blank, pause) 'Cos it was on the blackboard.
>
> 'Cos I'm on yellow table.

> Because she read us.... Because she read a story and.... when she reads a story she usually has to let us write it.... If she thinks it isn't very good then we have to write it out again.
>
> Because we were doing our news and that and then we done our maths. Because she knows what we were doing and that.
>
> Probably she wanted us to do extra work; she couldn't think of any more work work because we'd done it all.
>
> She thought it was a good idea to do maths.

Among the numerically significant answers given by children was the simple statement that they 'don't know' why activities were set — proffered on 13 per cent of occasions — or that the task was associated with a class topic of some sort.

> Because you've talked about your mums and now you talk about your dads.
>
> 'Cos we saw a barn owl on telly. She wanted us to do the writing 'cos it's a little bit of work.
>
> 'Cos we were doing about colours in the classroom.
>
> Because we're doing water vapour and how it evaporates. A week ago we did a thing with a kettle — an experiment. We put a plate on it and it steamed up and turned into water vapour.

A few children mentioned the 'products' of curricular activities:

> To go on wall.
>
> Wanted it for Mr. Brown's office.
>
> Like to keep models, and let us show our mums. Think mums will like them.
>
> Because she wanted everyone to make a puppet theatre like the one she made.

Others mentioned aspects of 'assessment' as the reasoning behind teacher decisions:

> To see how good I write.
>
> Don't know, but she wants to see how we can read.
>
> To see if we were good at maths.

Just three children believed teachers had chosen curricular activities especially for their enjoyment:

> 'Cos I like it.
>
> Because I liked it.
>
> 'Cos I like it.
>
> Because I liked it.

TABLE 6

Pupil perceptions of Teacher Intentions

	Year 1		Year 2		Overall	Total		Total	
	Girls	Boys	Girls	Boys	(%)	Boys	Girls	Year 1	Year 2
Learning	31	7	31	32	25	20	31	19	31
Required	15	36	27	18	24	27	21	26	22
Topic	15	7	19	14	14	11	17	11	17
Don't know	15	25	12	0	13	13	13	20	6
Product	15	7	4	7	8	7	10	11	5
Assessment	0	4	4	18	6	11	2	2	11
Enjoyment	4	4	4	0	3	2	4	4	2
No answer	**4**	**11**	**0**	**11**	**6**	**11**	**2**	**7**	**5**

Source: PACE 1 Child interviews.

Sample: 54 children in Year 1 and Year 2.

Date: Autumn 1990 and autumn 1991.

We analysed these data by gender and pupil year and some interesting patterns were revealed (see Table 6). When the children were in Year 1 a greater maturity and social awareness in the girls seems to be apparent. While the girls appreciated the teacher's learning intentions, albeit in a relatively general way, the boys either had no idea of teacher intentions or simply received the activities as requirements. This gender difference was not apparent in Year 2. Indeed, the overall numbers of 'don't know' answers fell sharply as the children aged and understanding of links between curricular tasks and 'learning' or classroom 'topics' developed.

There was a clear pattern of increasing awareness of educational purposes as the children got older. However, there were almost no answers in other than highly generalized ways. Children were not able to relate their specific work to personal learning targets.

Summing Up

Overall, our interviews with pupils showed that, while they enjoyed many curricular activities, they had strong preferences. Pupils liked activities that offered them interest, success, activity and fun. They disliked curriculum activities that produced boredom, difficulty sitting, listening and writing. In expressing their concerns in terms of activity and experience the children reflected the meaning of the curriculum to them, as primary school children had also done in previous studies. It is unfortunate that, in general terms and with the possible exception of mathematics, our findings show that the core subjects of the National Curriculum were less favoured than activities such as physical education, painting and play, which give children more scope for movement and autonomy. At face value, this would seem to suggest that pupil motivation regarding the most important subjects of the curriculum was a concern and that the curriculum as a 'planned intervention' was proving inadequate to harness the energy and interest of the children in support of the learning process.

It would be unfair to make too much of this argument about the 'failure' of the core curriculum to motivate children because it has probably always been the case. Indeed, it could be argued that the more significant finding from our pupil interviews is that there is very little evidence that the National Curriculum has made any substantial difference at all to the curriculum as it is actually experienced by pupils. Findings from previous research are not strong enough to enable us to be categorical on this, but the criteria that the children used are very consistent with previous research, and the understanding of the purposes of tasks (or lack of it) is also as expected. While we cannot say that the children have not been affected by the National Curriculum, we cannot show evidence of any dramatic effects. Pupil perceptions and experiences seem to be much the same as before its introduction. As a child once put it, 'School is school and learning is something that they do to you.'

5

Classroom Teaching and Students

Three major issues pertaining to teacher pedagogy are dealt in this chapter, with particular regard to pupil experiences and perspectives. Each of these issues relates to what is a key concern for young pupils: their teacher's use of power. Essentially, teachers have the power and authority to structure the experiences of children at school and, in so doing, to facilitate or compromise the fulfilment of pupil interests. Teachers' use of power is thus crucial to the quality of the school experience that pupils perceive. This is one reason, for instance, why pupils are so careful in 'getting to know' a new teacher at the start of a school year, why they are so skillful at monitoring teacher 'mood' and why much of their knowledge about teachers is organized defensively. From the relatively powerless position of the individual pupil, it simply makes sense to gauge patterns in the teacher's behaviour and to be able to detect what he or she may do next. Pupils also care deeply about what they are 'allowed to do' and about their relation with the teacher.

The three issues are: first, the strength of framing in classrooms as indicated by the scope that is, or is not, offered to children for autonomous choice of activities; second, the nature or teacher-pupil relationships; third, the pattern of observed pupil activity. At the end of the chapter we relate these issues and discuss their consequences. The ways in which behaviour is framed and maintained in classrooms are important classroom control, but they also provide a significant element of the social context in which school learning takes place. That having been said, relationship between learning and control is complex. On the one hand there are documented advantages in pupil exercising self-directed conrol over the learning process (e.g. Rowland, 1987).

In such circumstances they may be more highly motivated and the tasks undertaken may be self selectively geared to existing levels of understanding and attainment. On the other hand, there are also clear advantages in there being greater teacher control over learning experiences. Teacher knowledge, experience and skills can be shated and pupil learning ca be considerable extended by appropriate intervention, diagnosis, structuring and restructuring, so that pupil performance is assisted in its development.

Teacher-pupil relationships is the second major pedagogic issue considered here. How concerned teachers have been to sustain the quality of their relationship with pupils, despite perceived threats from the overcrowding of the National Curriculum and from assessment procedures. The data reported here provide the pupils' perspective on this issue, based on interviews in Year 1 and Year 2 with the 54 children in our sample. We address the issue conceptually in terms of the dimensions of the expressive, instrumental or alienated commitment that children may feel towards their teachers and we also consider the consequences that the quality of classroom relationships may have for classroom life and educational emphaticness.

Thirdly, the major dimension of pedagogy on which we report concerns the nature of pupils' classroom activity. Here we document and discuss the patterns we have found in the relative balance in levels of pupil task engagement, task management, waiting and distraction, as measured for 18 different classroom settings using our systematic observation procedures. In so doing, we have regard to the limitations of this form of data—gathering but also, notwithstanding this, draw attention to the considerable strength of the patterns we discovered. We focus, in particular, on the relationships between what was coded as 'on task' and 'distracted' pupil behaviour, and between what we have termed 'potential teaching-learning time' and 'classroom management time.'

In the final major section of the chapter we investigate the relationship between our systematic observation and interview data from pupils. The result is an important qualification of over-simplified arguments,which assert the value of whole-class teaching and forms of classroom organization designed, unproblematically, to produce high levels of pupil task-engagement. Task-engaged dispositions may not, after all, be quite what they seem, and there may also be more to 'distraction' than meets the eye.

WHAT WERE PUPIL PERCEPTIONS OF CLASSROOM FRAMING AND CONTROL?

There are many ways of engaging with the issue of how behaivour is framed and maintained, for it goes back to some of the basic realities of classroom life: the goals of pupil learning and the existence of relatively large class sizes. Many years ago Waller (1932) drew attention to what he called the 'despotism' of teachers and, even in a more enlightened era, Jackson (1968) talked of 'crowds, praise and power' as enduring features of classroom life. Such analyses reflect different teacher strategies of achieving educational goals in challenging circumstances and, one way or another, they inevitably involve the use of teacher power and authority to set structures and rules for behaviour and to establish specific goals and tasks for learning.

However, teachers know that neither the evolution of a positive and disciplined culture in a classroom nor the achievement of learning target are attainable through their efforts alone. Thus, in primary school contexts there have been sustained efforts over many decades to evolve incorporative ways of managing classrooms, thereby leading pupils into a commitment to classroom rules and to the establishment of a social morality of expectations that can underpin educationally productive classroom interaction. Similarly, teachers have been aware of the significance of pupil motivation on learning and of the inadequacies of simple, didactic strategies of 'chalk and talk.' Thus, despite the critique of the motivational priority that characterized some models of 'child-centred' practice, pupil perceptions and approaches to learning remain issues that cannot be ignored.

From the pupil perspective, as we saw in Chapter 8 and shall see again, there are at least two particularly important aspects of pupil motivation: whether the activity itself is 'interesting' or 'boring' and the extent to which it is framed by constraint or allows for a degree of pupil autonomy.

This brings us directly to 'frame' — one of our key analytical dimensions in recording changes in primary school practices. In this context it refers to the extent to which activities are structured by power relations and expectations. Where frame is strong, then behaviour is bounded. Where it is weak, there is more scope for self-determined and autonomous activity. We attempted to monitor this issue as the National Curriculum was being introduced by identifying indications of change in classroom frame, both from teachers, as reported in Chapter 9, and from pupils.

In each of our two rounds of classroom study, in 1990 and 1991, we asked the 54 children in our longitudinal cohort, 'Do you like it best when you choose what to do or when your teacher does?' Almost two-thirds of the children, in both Year 1 and Year 2, recorded that they preferred to control their own activities. This proportion is, in itself, significant, through perhaps it might have been expected to have been even higher. The other third of children preferred their teacher to select their classroom activities. The two groups of children were asked to explain the reasons for their preferences and their responses had many resonances with the pupil views on curriculum that we discussed in Chapter 8.

Perceptions of Children Preferring Child Choice of Activities

The two-thirds of children who preferred to choose activities themselves gave accounts that were coded as shown in Table 1 The pattern was relatively clear. The children preferred to engage, autonomously, in activities they selected and regarded as both more interesting and easier than teacher selections.

In year 1, the 30 percent of children who emphasized *autonomy* ('my choice') said things like:

TABLE 1

Reasons Given by Pupils who Preferred to Choose Activities Themselves (Percentages)

	Year 1	Year 2	Overall
Because it's easier to do	8	14	11
Because it's more interesting	17	8	13
Because it's my choice	30	39	35
Because it's good for me	2	0	1
Don't know	8	2	5
No answer	2	0	1
Total percentage	67	63	65

Source: PACE 1 child interview data.

Sample: 54 Year 1 and 54 Year 2 children.

Date: autumn 1990 and autumn 1991.

Note: These are percentages of choices made by the whole cohort in each year.

> I like to choose my very best things I like doing.
>
> Because you can do what you want.
>
> Because you don't have to wait.
>
> 'Cos you can choose to play.

Among the comments of the 39 percent emphasizing autonomy in Year 2 were the following:

> I like to choose which games we have and who you are with.
>
> We can't get on with what we want when she chooses. 'Cos she sometimes gives us something that isn't very good, 'cos we can't make something good out of it. I'd like a spaceship that drops down toy bombs or a car with guns that shoot out.
>
> I feel I can do whatever I want and you don't have to do what you don't like.
>
> Because sometimes Miss gives us jobs I don't like, don't

> want to do or am not very good at... because it might be too hard.
>
> Because we can do anything we like. It's better.
>
> Miss don't know what I like best.

The 13 percent who appreciated scope to choose *interesting* things to do, in Year 1, said:

> Because Miss gives us boring things.
>
> 'Cos you can make things.
>
> 'Cos I can choose nicer things.
>
> 'Cos I like it. More fun. I play with dough.
>
> I think it might be because I like playing.
>
> 'Cos you can get at the Polydroms and you can stick 'em together.

In Year 2, children said very similar things. For instance:

> Because you do good things like painting and puppets. It's fun.
>
> 'Cos I can play with me mates.
>
> Because then I can choose Clever Sticks or Polydrons and I like playing with toys.

A further of 11 percent of children overall drew attention to the greater *ease* of pupil-selected activities or the greater difficulty of teacher-directed tasks. They said things such as:

> She just gives us writing to do and it's really hard. She gives us a lot and I get really tired.
>
> Because I don't want to do hard things.
>
> Because we can choose easy work — not hard work.
>
> Because she might just say, 'Go and draw a picture,' like one of those [Tudor] houses and it's hard to do.
>
> Because if I don't like it I might get it wrong and then I won't like it.

Two-thirds of children thus appeared to appreciate opportunities to take decisions, to follow and develop their own ideas, to be creative, to have fun and to 'do things' that were not too difficult. As we saw in Chapter 8, they wanted some success. Their concern for the intrinsic value of activity was also contrasted with their view of many teacher-directed activities as being 'boring' and as 'things we have to do first.' These criteria articulate very closely with those represented, in regarding curriculum and this fact reaffirms their significance to children.

The differences from Year 1 to Year 2 are suggestive of pupils becoming more aware of a prime need to cope with classroom requirements that might, themselves, outweigh the intrinsic value of activities. This possibility of these children gradually adopting strategies for coping with school and 'playing the system' as they mature within it is suggested by the decrease in pupil concern with interest and the increase in references to making choices autonomously and simply making things easier. This could be interpreted as reflecting the development of a form of instrumentalism as pupils strive, one way or another, to satisfy the more structured tasks that teachers reported setting since the introduction of the National Curriculum.

Perceptions of Children Preferring Teacher Choice of Activities

The third of Children who preferred their teacher to select classroom activities for them were also asked to give the reasons for their preference, and the results were also coded and tabulated in Table 2. Then main reason given for valuing teacher choice was consistent in both Year 1 and Year 2: teachers were simply regarded as providing more interesting activities.

On this issue of *interesting* activities, the children said things such as:

> I like it when the teacher chooses 'cos she's nice and chooses good things.
>
> She lets us do good work, colouring, playing on the computer, playing in the Wendy House, construction, Lego.

'Cos she has better ideas. We haven't been taught.

You do more things when Miss chooses.

'Cos sometimes we pick out the boring things, the teacher picks out the better things.

When we go home at night, she sorts something out. It's usually good.

She does fun things.

Sometimes I like a surprise for what I'm doing.

TABLE 2

Reasons Given by Pupils who Preferred their Teacher to Choose Activities (Percentages)

	Year 1	Year 2	Overall
Because it's easier to do	0	2	1
Because it's more interesting	19	24	22
Because it's my choice	0	0	0
Because it's good for me	10	4	7
Don't know	0	2	1
No answer	1	2	1
Total percentage	30	34	32

Source: PACE 1 child interview Data.

Sample: 54 Year 1 and 54 Year 2 children.

Date: autumn 1990 and autumn 1991.

Note: These are percentages of choices made by the whole cohort in each year.

Some 10 percent of Year 1 children took and explicitly deferential view of teacher judgement. They favoured teacher selection of activities on the grounds that it simply was the teacher's decision and clarified requirements.

Well she's the teacher, so if she chooses we know what to do.

'Cos she's the teacher and she's bigger.

Because we won't know what we're doing if the teacher doesn't tell us.

However, in Year 2 this certainty was less evident.

The preference of almost a quarter of Year 2 children for teacher-led activities because of the interest they derived from such work is a very encouraging finding for teachers, many of whom have, as we saw in Chapter 6, put great efforts in recent years into developing both their subject knowledge and the quality of curriculum provision. However, as we indicated earlier, the growing pupil search for 'easier' activities may also reflect pupil recognition of the ways in which learning tasks progressively challenge them, on a day-by-day basis, ass they move through school. Interestingly, we could find no pattern in these results by pupil attainment or gender.

We thus have results that document children's clear preference for autonomy, interest and ease of the selection of classroom activities. Although a significant minority of children appreciated the interest of teacher-led activities, there were also signs of children, as they got older, adopting more instrumental strategies to accommodate the progress challenges they faced in school.

Pupil Perceptions of Teacher Control

Having considered child preferences, we also wanted to consider what, in their view, actually happened in their classrooms. We therefore asked them: 'Do you choose what you do at school or does your teacher choose for you most of the time?' Not unexpectedly, as Table 3 shows, the children indicated a very high degree of teacher control — almost 70 percent across the two years.

The results here are very striking in overall terms, with only 7 percent of children suggesting that they had significant degrees of choice. Of course, directly contrasts with the image of infant classrooms as arenas for 'free play.' Table 3 also suggests the children, like their teachers (see Chapter 9), perceived a tightening of teacher control and direction as they moved from Year 1 in 1990 to Year 2 in 1991. Of course, we cannot be sure of the extent to which this apparent tightening of frame is related to adaptations in pedagogy as the children grew older or to growing pressures of the National Curriculum over the period, but the comments of teachers, reported in Chapter 7, suggest that curriculum pressures were considerable. Our 1991 data thus show that no fewer than four-fifths of Year 2 children recognized their experience of classroom life as being framed by tight teacher control, with only 13 percent drawing attention to joint decision-making.

TABLE 3

Children's Perspective of Who Selects Tasks at School (Percentages)

	Year 1	*Year 2*	*Overall*
Teacher	59	80	69
Children	13	2	7
Both	26	13	19
No data	2	6	4

Source: PACE 1 child interview data.

Sample: 54 Year 1 and 54 Year 2 children.

Date: autumn 1990 and autumn 1991.

As we have seen from the earlier parts of this section and from the discussions of pupils' views of curriculum in Chapter 8, the children were not universally appreciative of this degree of teacher control and frame around their activities. As many of them saw it, teacher control restricted their autonomy, posed more challenging activities than they desired and often required them to do things that were usually less interesting then they would have selected themselves. In a word, despite important exceptions, teacher-framed work was likely to be more 'boring.'

However, whatever their views and preferences, all the children in the sample perceived the necessity of 'doing what the teacher says' while at school. We know this from their answers to the question we put to them: 'Do you have to do what your teacher says?' Over the two years, 94 percent of children's answers confirmed the paramount significance of teacher decisions. A few more aware children, particularly in Year 2, recorded that it all depended on the activity and situation, but no children claimed that what their teacher said did not matter. Sometimes the pupils were explicit about the ways in which teacher power might be used, as the following answers to our question show:

> Otherwise she gets angry and might send you out of the class.
>
> 'Cos if you don't you'll have to go down to [headteacher].
>
> 'Cos if we don't she says we'll get told off.
>
> Because if you don't she gets cross and tells you off and you might feel worried.
>
> Or you'll get told off. If some one is very naughty they have to stand by the wall inside.
>
> Yes, and if you don't do what you're told you have to stand in the book corner and you're not allowed to leave or talk.

Here we see pupil concerns with being shown up, told off, worried and isolated from there peers. Following the analysis of Pollard (1985), these can be interpreted as concerns over the threat to 'self.' The children feared being drawn individually out of the relatively safe anoymity of the class and having their dignity threatened.

Returning to Jackson (1968) and his identification of crowds, praise and power as facts of classroom life, we thus have to say that the children in this study were gery much aware of the power of their teachers. The children knew what they preferred in terms of autonomy, and in terms of making their classroom lives more interesting and less difficult, but they accepted that it was teachers who structured and framed their classroom activities and experiences. In this respect there were no clear differences in our post-National Curriculum findings from those available before 1988. It seems that pupils have always had to take account of teacher power and control in classrooms and they still do.

HOW DID PUPILS SEE THEIR RELATIONSHIP WITH THEIR TEACHERS?

An area central of the PACE research was the question of whether the imposition of external requirements on teachers as embodied in the National Curriculum and assessment procedures would affect the relationship between teachers and children.

In particular, we wanted to investigate whether the close personal relationships, to which primary school teachers have been so strongly committed in the past, would be comprised by the impact of external pressures. If this were the case, we reasoned, both teacher and pupil perceptions and actions were likely to become more instrumental or, perhaps, even alienated. In terms of the analytical dimensions reviewed in Chapter 3, we thus sought to track the nature, of, and change in, the expressive-instrumental alienated dimension of classroom interpersonal relationships.

As we saw in Chapter 9, when asked if they felt that the quality of teacher-pupil relations had been affected by the introduction of the National Curriculum, 31 percent of the 88 teachers interviewed in 1990 said that there had been a change for the worse and that their relationship with children was affected adversely by pressures on teaching time or by feelings of stress on the part of the teachers. Many felt that contact with children had become more formal and artificial. Considering data from our 1992 interviews, we found a significant rise, to 58 percent, in the number of teachers perceiving a deterioration in teacher-pupil relationships. However, though this deterioration was resisted and regretted, there was no weakening in teacher commitment to close and caring relationships with pupils. There did not seem to be a movement by teachers towards instrumentalism.

When we conducted our interviews with the children in our study, in 1991 and 1992, we asked them directly about relationships. First we enquired, 'How do you get on with your teacher?' This was followed up with the question, 'What do you like best about your teacher?' The children's responses did not convey the sense of the worry and foreboding felt by the teachers, but they mapped almost exactly on to the teacher' concerns and also revealed some interesting patterns of response.

In the first place, for the children in Year 1 and Year 2, the quality of classroom relationships was very strongly attested. As Table 4 shows, only 3 percent of all the children's answers were coded as indicating negative responses to the question, 'How do you get on with your teacher?' Most of the children, 53 percent, made positive statements about their relationship with their teacher, and 41 percent of responses were coded as 'neutral': 'quite well,', 'all right,' 'OK.' Certainly, a finding of only 3 percent of answers in the negative is a powerful affirmation of the success of infant teachers in maintaining high-quality relationships with their pupils.

However, there were some other interesting patterns that are worth noting. First, referring back to Table 4, a slight trend away from positive replies and towards more 'neutral' statements can be seen. Table 5 develops this detail by showing the overall distribution of perceptions of boys and girls. It can be sent that boys were considerably less appreciative than girls. Of the latter, no fewer than 63 percent expressed positive feelings about their teachers.

TABLE 4

Year 1 and Year 2 Pupils' Perceptions of Their Relationships with Their Teacher (Percentages)

	Year 1	Year 2	Overall
Positive	57	48	53
Neutral	35	46	41
Negative	2	4	3
Don't know	2	0	1
No data	4	2	3

Source: PACE 1 child interview data.

Sample: 54 Year 1 and 54 Year 2 children.

Date: autumn 1990 and autumn 1991.

The final table in this set, Table 6, shows the same aggregated data by pupil attainment. Here we can see that there appears to be a tendency for higher-attaining children to be more positive about relationship with their teacher than lower attaining children.

TABLE 5

Boys' and Girls' Perceptions of Their Relationships with Their Teacher (Percentages)

	Year 1	Year 2	Overall
Positive	43	63	53
Neutral	52	29	41
Negative	2	4	3
Don't know	0	2	1
No data	4	2	1

Source: PACE 1 child interview data.

Sample: 54 Year 1 and 54 Year 2 children.

Date: autumn 1990 and autumn 1991.

TABLE 6

Children's Perceptions of Their Relationships with Their Teacher, by Attainment (Percentages)

	Attainment					
	High	<—		—>	Low	
	1	2	3	4	5	Total
Positive	12	14	15	5	7	53
Neutral	6	6	12	11	6	41
Negative	0	1	0	0	2	3
Don't know	0	0	1	0	0	1
No data	0	0	1	1	1	3
Total	18	20	29	17	17	100

Source: PACE 1 child interview data.

Sample: 54 Year 1 and 54 Year 2 children.

Date: autumn 1990 and autumn 1991.

The significance of these variations, by age, sex and attainment, is, of course, that they suggest the gradual emergence of differentiated pupil perspectives. As developed through child culture and further school experiences, these could evolve to contribute to more explicit differences in pupil motivation, attitudes to learning and attainment. This is something that will be investigated further in future phases of the PACE research.

As we saw above, to elicit their perspectives and reasoning a little more, the children were also asked, 'What do you like best about your teacher?' Five major categories were used to code the children's responses.

Interaction was recorded for 34 percent of all pupil responses. These were directly concerned with actions of the teacher towards, or with, the child or children. For instance:

> When she says something nice, like 'Well done, Sarah.'
>
> Bestest is that she likes doing things with us. When I can't do it, she writes it for me — helps me.
>
> When she doesn't shout. That's when I like her.
>
> When she's not mad.
>
> She's kind and she lets us go to the toilet when we want to.

Interest was used, for 29 percent of all responses, to categorize comments that referred to the perceived quality of content or activity offered by the teacher. Thus:

> When she does good work with us.
> The way she reads,
> I like her stories.
> when she gives you work you like.
> When she comes and she's doing things with us, like when she had a big table and we have all things to taste and we dip papers in and it goes different colours.

Personal was a code used to classify pupil statements referring to some teacher characteristic of appearance, temperament, dress, etc. It was used for 13 percent of all comments. For instance:

> I like her clothes and when she dresses up.
> It's the way she talks. She's got a nice voice.
> Well, she looks nice.

He's got a beard.

He's handsome. I love him.

Choice, used for 9 percent of all comments, described pupil references to the ways in which their teacher provided them with opportunities to choose activities:

When she lets us play games and read books and go out to play.

If she says we can choose.

'Cos she lets us do painting.

Because she lets me play.

When she lets us go over to dinners and we can sit by somebody.

Finally, *ease* was recorded for 4 percent of statements and was used to categorize reference to teachers reducing the challenges of schoolwork. Thus:

She gives easy work.

When she lets us play games and read books and go out to play.

As with children's overall perceptions of relationships, there were some important patterns in the reasons given by the children when in Year 1 and Year 2 and by boys and girls. Regarding pupil year, Table 7 shows the distribution of categories of things the children liked best about their teachers. There is significant move here in the proportion of children mentioning the nature of pupil-teacher interaction, though the criterion of the interest of teachers' curricular provision seemed less important.

Table 8 Shows that while girls focused on the nature of their interaction with their teacher and on personal factors, boys were far more likely to prioritize the interest, or otherwise, of the curriculum and of the activities that the teacher offered. Having choice, a reflection of the value of autonomy to children, remained important to both boys and girls.

TABLE 7

Child Criteria for Liking Teacher (Percentages)

	Year 1	Year 2	Overall
Personal	11	15	13
Interest	33	24	29
Ease	6	2	4
Choice	11	7	9
Interaction	24	44	34
Don't know	9	4	6
No data	6	4	5

Source: PACE 1 child interview data.

Sample: 54 Year 1 and 54 Year 2 children.

Date: autumn 1990 and autumn 1991.

TABLE 8

Boys' and Girl's Criteria for Liking Teachers (Percentages)

	Year 1	Year 2	Overall
Personal	7	19	13
Interest	41	15	29
Ease	4	4	4
Choice	9	10	9
Interaction	27	42	34
Don't know	7	6	6
No data	5	4	5

Source: PACE 1 child interview data.

Sample: 54 Year 1 and 54 Year 2 children.

Date: autumn 1990 and autumn 1991.

Of course, such patterns in children's concerns are not unexpected. They are very similar, on the one hand, to findings reported by other research studies such as those of Davies (1982), Pollard (1985) and Goodnow and Burns (1985). On the other hand, they resonate with other PACE findings, reported both in Chapter 8, on children's curricular priorities, and earlier in the present chapter. It may be recalled from Chapter 8 that among the pupil criteria for evaluating curricular activities were ease and success, interest, fun, activity and autonomy. In many respects, our findings on pupil perceptions on relationships with teachers echo these curricular concerns. Earlier in the present chapter we also fund that children valued selecting their own school activities — even though they felt that this was rarely allowed. They liked having autonomy, choosing more interesting things to do and making their classroom experiences easier.

As we also saw, there were some signs of the children, as they got older, becoming a little more 'canny' regarding the requirements of their teachers and a little more aware of the exercise of teacher power. The data on teacher-pupil relationships reinforces this impression. Certainly as Year 2 children in 1991, the cohort, particularly the boys, were less positive about their relationships with teachers than they had been in 1991. The overall impression from this may well be that the boys in particular were becoming aware of the contested character of classroom life, and of the tension between their desire to 'have fun' and 'do interesting things' and their teacher's concerns with order and learning. However, we should make clear that, in terms of influences on teacher—pupil relationships, our data provide little evidence that we can specifically attribute to the National Curriculum or assessment procedures.

This seems to confirm the success of teachers in their commitment, reported in Chapter 9, to ensure that relationships did not deteriorate despite the increased pressure to which they felt they were subjected. Pupil experience in this respect again seems to have been one of rélative continuity. What, following this analysis of what pupils said, did they actually appear to be doing?

WHAT PUPIL BEHAVIOUR WAS OBSERVED IN THE CLASSROOMS?

As described in Chapter 4, as part of our classroom studies we classified pupils' classroom behaviour into key categories and used time-sampled systematic observation to measure the proportions of each. In this approach, the observer codes the pupil activity at each sampling point, thus building up a systematic record of researcher judgements of pupil activity. We used four pupil activity categories — 'task-engaged,' 'task management,' 'distracted' and 'waiting for teacher' — categories that, though important and well established, also require relatively high levels of researcher inference or judgement.

Evidence from research studies of the 1970s and 1980s that have adopted this approach to studying pupil behaviour has consistently indicated that, for about 60 percent of their time, young children were judged to be directly involved in their work (e.g. Galton *et. al.*, 1980; Tizard *et. al.,* 1988). Findings from the PACE study show very similar results, as Table 9 shows.

Despite their different ages, the children in the PACE project were judged to be 'task-engaged' for roughly the same amount of time as the Key Stage 2 children studied by Galton *et al.* (1980). They were also deemed to be 'managing tasks' and 'distracted' for roughly similar amounts of time. More time was spent by the PACE children in 'waiting for the teacher,' and this probably reflects the younger age of the children. A similar comparison with slightly adapted data from the Tizard *et al.* study of infant children yields results that are not drastically different, although the Tizard *et al.* children seemed to be coded as distracted slightly less often.

TABLE 9

Main Types of Pupil Activity in the Classroom (Percentages)

	Year 1 1990	**Year 2** 1991
Task-engaged	56.9	59.5
Task management	11.8	13.5
Distracted	19.3	21.5
Waiting for teacher	8.0	5.6
Other	4.0	0.0

Source: PACE 1 child systematic observation.

Sample: 9 Year 1 and 9 Year 2 children.

Date: autumn 1990 and autumn 1991.

Overall, the results are fairly consistent. Children in English primary schools are likely to be regarded as task-engaged for about 60 percent of their classroom time. They may be seen as distracted for up to 20 percent of the time and are likely to be organizing themselves to complete the task or waiting for the teacher for the remaining 20 percent of the time. The aggregated pupil 'time or task,' in getting organized or working, is just over 70 percent of classroom time.

DID THE CLASSROOMS SEEM TO PRODUCE VERY DIFFERENT LEVELS OF PUPIL TASK ENGAGEMENT?

The observation data produced interesting variations in levels of pupil task engagement, and in the following two sections we shall discuss some of the factors associated with different levels of time-on-task across classrooms. However, these results and their possible implications need to be treated with some caution. Clearly the amount of time pupils spend task-engaged in interesting and important educationally. Equally clearly, however, it does not in itself tell us anything about the amount of quality of learning going on. This has been well put by Karweit (1984), who wrote that 'Time is necessary but not sufficient condition for learning.' Time-on-task cannot be used as a surrogate measure for classroom effectiveness and the analysis here cannot tell us how pupil learning actually takes place or which classrooms produced the 'best' learning outcomes. Nevertheless, we do have some interesting and challenging findings about patterns of variations in a major feature of classroom life.

Our results for each of the four categories of pupil activity in each of the 18 classrooms in which data were collected. Looked at another way, our classification of the activity of the same target children, in Years 1 and 2 of their school careers, within nine primary schools.

The basis of descending percentage of recorded pupil task engagement. This creates a dramatic visual impression of one of our key findings of classroom variation. Expressing exactly the same data in more aggregated, statistical terms yields the rank order correlations contained in Table 10.

In discussing classroom variation we will use particular combinations of the four variables of observed pupil activity to produce three indicators: 'classroom management time,' 'teaching and learning time' and 'time on task.'

Classroom Management Time

This indicator is based on the combined pupil time spent in task management and waiting for the teacher. Our use of this combination of variables is based on the argument that such data will record pupils who are more, or less, dependent on teacher guidance, depending on the routines, procedures and overall management system that exist in their classroom.

TABLE 10

Pupil Activity in the Classroom (Correlations)

	Pupil task-engaged	Task manage-ment	Wating for teacher	Distracted
Pupil task-engaged	1.00			
Task management	– 0.56	1.00		
Waiting for teacher	– 0.38	– 0.35	1.00	
Distracted	– 0.75	0.33	0.28	1.00

Source: PACE 1 systematic observation.

Sample: 9 Year 1 and 9 Year 2 classes

Date: autumn 1990 and autumn 1991.

Our first finding of note is that there is a tendency for task management and waiting for teacher to vary together. Where task management is high, waiting for teacher tends to be low, and vice versa. This pattern must be slightly qualified, for both variables were low for a few classrooms, classrooms that also had relatively low levels of distraction and high levels of task engagement. Overall figures for classroom management time in Year 1 classrooms were also slightly higher than our Year 2 findings, perhaps reflecting greater time taken by younger children in learning classroom procedures.

Notwithstanding these slight variations, over all the classrooms, task management was coded for almost 13 percent of pupil observations and waiting for teacher for just under 7 percent, a total of almost 20 percent.

This classroom management figure of 20 percent of observed pupil time is important. While it can evidently be reduced in some circumstances, we believe that it is realistic at present to accept that this is the sort of proportion of time that is likely to be spent by pupils on classroom management, *whatever* the teacher strategy. Perhaps an approximate commitment of 20 percent of pupil time is simply a necessary time commitment, given the range of class sizes and task, group and resource organization to be found in English primary schools.

Of course, having noted the overall 20 percent figure for classroom management, we must look at its composition. What is the ratio of 'waiting for teacher' to 'task management' that may be undertaken without the teacher? This has implications for both use of teacher time and the development of pupil independence.

Teaching and Learning Time

The use of teaching and learning time is our second indicator of classroom variation, and is arguably the most significant. We define teaching and learning time as the time that remains once classroom management issues have been dealt with. Putting this another way,if we allow 20 percent of observed pupil time for classroom management of one sort or another, how do pupils use the remaining 80 percent of time?

The codes that related to teaching and learning time are 'task-engaged' and 'distracted,' and clearly they are likely to map against each other in some way. Children who are not task-engaged could well be distracted, and distracted children will certainly not be task-engaged. However, in our comparisons of classrooms we were not expecting as strong a pattern as the one we found. The correlation in Table 10 show, there is a very considerable difference in pupil activity within the classrooms and a very strong relationship between task engagement and distraction.

Classes that have high levels of pupil task engagement do tend to have relatively low levels of pupil time used in waiting for the teacher and in task management. Proportionately, however, as we would expect, they have even lower levels of pupils distraction. Conversely, classes with relatively low levels of task engagement tend to have much higher levels of distraction. The correlation on the latter relationship, –0.75, is very strong indeed. These variables are not, of course, independent of one another, for if more time is spent on-tasks then there is less time for other activities. However, the correlations show which of the tasks co-vary with task engagement.

Thus, in terms of the question 'how do pupils in different classrooms use the 80 percent of classroom time that is available for teaching and learning?' the answer has to acknowledge huge variations in the level of task engagement rather than distraction. Interestingly, the extreme cases are Lawnside Primary School, serving a relatively affluent commuter village near a large Midlands city, with its 'Year 2 class figure of 72 percent of observed pupil time on task engagement and only 14 percent of time coded as distracted, compared with the Year 1 class at inner-city Meadway Primary, serving a community with severe socio-economic problems, where task engagement was down to 47 percent and distraction was up to 28 percent, twice the Lawnside figure.

Time on Task

A further, and more commonly used, way of exploring the relationship of these variables is to monitor the total 'time on task.' Thus the time in which pupils are 'task engaged' and involved in 'task management' is added and compared. Table 11 shows the results of this procedure, classroom by classroom, for the two rounds of PACE data-gathering.

There is some variation here from year to year and between classes in the same year. The extremes are again the over 80 percent 'on-task' activity of Year 2 pupils at the village school of Lawnside and the figure of less than 60 percent recorded for pupil 'on task' activity at inner-city Meadway. These cases having been noted, the degree of consistency is perhaps surprising, with almost all the other 16 classrooms producing pupil on-task figures of between 65 and 75 percent. It seems that, despite what one may occasionally read in some newspapers, in most classrooms at Key Stage 1 pupils work on-task for the bulk of their time. The real question seems to be not whether the children are on-task in itself, but whether on-task activity is educationally productive. Certainly some classes, such as that studied in both years (though with different teachers) at the small rural Orchard Primary, had unexceptional figures for time on task overall, but unusually high levels of task management concealed within them.

The averages of time on task for all classes are once again worth considering. For Year 1 the figure is just under 69 percent but for Year 2 classes there is a rise to 73 percent. Further phases of the PACE research will enable us to monitor this possible trend of increasing task focus as children get older.

There was also substantial variation between the classrooms, and between the average percentage of pupil time devoted to forms of classroom management for each year,. Thus, for instance, classrooms at Lawnside, with the highest recorded figure of whole class interaction (50 percent), produced significantly lower classroom management figures for each year than those at, say, the small, rural Orchard Primary which, with mixed-aged classes, had the highest figure for individualized work (67 percent).

WHAT PATTERNS OF TEACHING WERE ASSOCIATED WITH PUPIL TASK ENGAGEMENT?

We looked at how total time on task varied according to different teaching contexts and some interesting relationships emerged. The issue was investigated by calculating correlations between the four main categories of pupil activity and the three main categories of teaching context. Table 12 conveys the results. This is a fascinating and challenging table. It shows that classrooms where high levels of class interaction were recorded are also likely to have been coded with relatively high levels of pupil task engagement, low levels of pupil task management and fairly low levels of pupil distraction. Classrooms with high levels of individual work are likely to have relatively low levels of task engagement and waiting for the teacher, but higher levels of pupil time taken through task management or distraction. Group work falls between these two patterns on each variable. These results echo those reported by Croll and Moses (1988), based on 32 junior-age classrooms.

TABLE 11

Total Pupil Time on Task (Percentages)

	Law-side	Valley	Green-mantle	St. Bede's	Mead-way	Ardley	St. Anne's	Orchard	Ken-wood	Aver-age
1990 Year 1	74.9	67.8	72.4	63.2	56.7	73.7	71.1	68.4	70.1	68.7
1991, Year 1	82.6	75.7	74.2	74.4	74.5	66.6	69.6	73.2	65.8	73.0

Source: PACE 1 systematic observation.
Sample: 9 Year 1 and 9 Year 2 classes
Date : autumn 1990 and autumn 1991.

Of course, time on task is not in itself an indicator that learning is taking place, although it may well be a pre-condition for it. Indeed, a number of earlier studies have indicated a positive association between time on task and pupil performance (Brophy and Evertson, 1976;; Soar, 1977; Stallings, 1980). Southgate *et al.* (1975) found that teachers of pupils who made the greatest degree of progress in maths, language and reading tended to make use of whole-class or group instruction, whereas in classrooms where there was a high level of individual attention children tended to spend less time concerned with the task. The ORACLE study (Galton et. al., 1980), which attempted to identify teaching styles most closely associated with pupil progress, named one group of teachers as 'infrequent changers.' These teachers engaged in a high level of whole-class interaction not, as the stereotype would have it, in order to drill pupils, but to provide a high level of challenging questions and statements. Such teachers also used praise more often than other teachers and encouraged a positive climate in their classrooms. In particular, they were able to switch their organizational strategy to take account of particular circumstances in the classroom, for example for individual to whole-class work, in response to their judgements of the children's needs.

TABLE 12

Patterns of Teaching Associated with Pupil Task Engagement (Correlations)

	Pupil task-engaged	Task management	Waiting for teacher	Distracted
Class interaction	0.57	– 0.74	0.09	– 0.21
Group work	– 0.23	0.21	0.20	0.03
Individual work	– 0.42	0.58	– 0.24	0.20

Source: PACE 1 systematic observation.

Sample: 9 Year 1 and 9 Year 2 classes

Date : autumn 1990 and autumn 1991.

HOW DID PUPIL PERCEPTIONS OF TEACHERS RELATE TO CLASSROOM VARIATIONS?

At first sight, from an adult perspective and despite our cautions on interpretation, our other findings appear to show that the range of classroom effectiveness is considerable and that more effective classrooms are characterised by greater proportions of whole-class teaching and by more efficient classroom management. We wanted to relate such impressions to pupil experiences and perspectives.

We investigated for a pattern of pupil perspectives by sorting the 18 classrooms from our two years of study into two groups of nine classrooms each. The first groups of nine were those in which we had recorded the higher levels of pupil task engagement, and the remaining classrooms had lower levels. Our pupil interview data were than reanalysed with the data from higher and lower task engagement classrooms being treated separately.

We investigated for a pattern of pupil perspectives by sorting the 18 classrooms for our two years of study into two groups of nine classrooms each. The first group of nine were those in which we had recorded the higher levels of pupil task engagement, and the remaining classrooms had lower levels. Our pupil interview data were than reanalysed with the data from higher and lower task engagement classrooms being treated separately.

One question that was analysed in this way was that in which we had asked the children what they liked best about their teacher. It may be recalled from previous chapters that the largest proportion of children's answers to this question, 34 percent, had made reference to the nature of teacher action and the effects of it. We coded such answers as *interaction.* Many of the answers showed acute awareness of teacher power and of the potential threat it could pose to pupils if they were seen to be failing to comply with teacher requirements. Children thus 'liked her when she is nice to us,' or thought 'she is best when she does not shout.' The second largest coding category, at 29 percent overall, was *interest.* Most of the pupil statements coded in this way related to the perceived value of pleasures of activities that teachers provided. Children noted that 'she reads good stories,' or that 'it's quite interesting when he gives us an experiment to do.' Of the other codings, *personal* related to personality or physical characteristics of the teacher, *ease* to the difficulty of the work that was required and *choice* to the degree of autonomy that was allowed.

Table 13 shows the results of plotting these codings of pupil reasons for linking their teachers in the nine classrooms with higher levels of observed task engagement and the nine classrooms with lower observed levels. The patterns here are very noticeable.

Pupils in classrooms with higher levels of task engagement, which we also know to mean classrooms that tend to have high levels of whole-class interaction, evaluated their teachers primarily in terms of how they interacted with them. No fewer than 45 percent of answers from children in these classrooms were of this type. The children's answers, showing particular awareness to teacher power and of its potential use, are perhaps to be expected if the frame in such classrooms is strong. Expectations of pupils may thus be relatively specific and, in the public setting of whole-class contexts, compliance is relatively easily monitored.

TABLE 13

Pupil Reasons for Liking Their Teacher in Classes of Higher and Lower Levels of Pupil Task Engagement (Percentages)

	Higher	Lower	Overall
Personal	11	16	13
Interest	22	36	29
Ease	2	5	4
Choice	7	11	9
Interaction	45	22	34
Don't know	7	5	6
No data	5	4	5

Source: PACE 1 child interview data.

Sample: 54 Year 1 and 54 Year 2 children.

Date: Autumn 1990 and autumn 1991.

Pupils in classrooms with lower levels of task engagement, and lower levels of whole-class interaction, tended to think of their teachers in more diverse ways, but with particular attention to the interest of the curricular activities that were provided by them. Pupil criteria had a stronger focus on the quality of curriculum activities, with reference, in particular, to what they intrinsically offered in terms of enjoyment and experience. They were also more inclined to make reference to personal characteristics of their teachers and to comment on the ease or difficulty of work and on the degree of autonomy they enjoyed.

We carried out a similar analysis focusing on pupils' perceptions of curriculum subjects, reconsidering the children's views reported in chapter 8. The results of this are reported in Table 14. Here we see another facet of the same pattern being repeated. Children in the classes with higher recorded levels of task engagement and whole-class interaction more aware of the need for success and were concerned to evaluate the relative difficulty of activities. They seemed to be a little more sure of their evaluations of curricular activities (there are fewer 'don't know's and they seemed to expect less classroom 'fun.' In classrooms where task engagement and whole-class interaction were lower, the children were more inclined to evaluate the interest and fun of curriculum activities, but also tended to be more uncertain in their views of curricular activities. Perhaps of particular note, they also seemed to be less concerned with achieving success.

TABLE 14

Pupil Criteria of Evaluating Curriculum Subjects, by Level of Task Engagement (Percentages)

	Higher	Lower	Overall
Fun	12	18	15
Activity	12	11	12
Interest	20	27	23
Autonomy	5	3	4
Education	5	2	4
Success/case	33	19	26
Don't know	12	19	16

Source: PACE 1 child interview data.

Sample: 54 Year 1 and 54 Year 2 children.

Date: autumn 1990 and autumn 1991.

In one sense then, pupil experience in the classrooms with lower task engagement seemed to produce pupil views that, compared with the classrooms with high levels of task engagement, were broader and more focused on intrinsic aspects of classroom life and curriculum experience. Such pupils also seemed to be more relaxed about their learning — less sure of their curriculum evaluations and less concerned with success, but more aware of the intrinsic interest of the curriculum activities they experienced, of the personal qualities of their teachers and of 'having fun' at school.

Summing Up

The findings reported in this chapter require careful interpretation and some caution. Pupils, we have seen, would like more control in classrooms, though they do not really expect to have it. Their answers to our questions on classrooms control and on relationships with their teachers tended to reaffirm their concern to experience interesting classroom activities, thus avoiding boredom. However, their awareness of the extent of teacher control and power was considerable. In this, they also repeated the major themes of their views of curricular activities.

In terms of the analytic dimensions, pupils recognized constraint but preferred autonomy; they recognized teachers' rights to impose requirements but preferred negotiation; they were very aware of the strength of frame in different classroom contexts and of the ways in which this influenced their activities; they showed signs of the emergence of differentiated responses with varied strategies for action and with different degrees of commitment to teachers' classroom goals. We have also reported findings that there was a considerable range in levels of appartment task engagement in different classrooms, according to our systematic observations, and that pupil perceptions varied in patterned ways. In terms of the analytical dimensions, the classrooms in which higher levels of task engagement were observed appeared to be more concerned to teach established knowledge than to provide conditions in which pupils could construct their own. Pupil perceptions implied that teachers in such classrooms tended to be more categoric than provisional in their assessments. However, they also seemed to be more constraining and tended to produce more instrumental attitudes on the part of the children. From the pupil perspective, they were less 'fun' and less 'interesting.'

Remember, be cautious about these results and they will be investigated further in later phases of the PACE research, but they do raise some important issues about the priorities of infant schooling for children. For instance, is it possible that the majority of parents, who, as Hughes *et al.* (1990) found, prioritize social aims for their young children, would actually prefer their children to attend the ostensibly 'less effective' classrooms because of the reduced pressure that seems to be indicated and th greater intrinsic satisfaction of the experience that is suggested?

On the other hand, if it is essential to focus children's attention on learning objectives and provide a tight frame around their efforts, as seems to be provided in the apparently 'more effective' classrooms, should we be concerned by the indications that the children seem to be more aware of the power of the teacher in evaluating their work extrinsically rather than concerned about the intrinsic educational goals to which teacher efforts are supposedly directed? In other words, is tight teacher control appropriate for six-and seven-year-olds, whether it be inspired by government, 'wisemen' or others? Of course, teachers, curriculum providers and educationalists are not simply charged with making life enjoyable for children, though childhood remains a unique phase of life, of value in its own right. The point is to strike some sort of balance between the classroom structuring that is necessary if teachers are to offer children appropriate support in their learning and the provision of psychological space and opportunity for children to learn through more self-directed experiment and experience. Much psychological research suggests that for successful learning to take place, whether the teacher or the pupil initiates the activity, it is important that the learner retains a degree of control so that new knowledge and understanding gained can be incorporated into pre-existing schemata and frameworks.

Motivation remains vital in this whole discussion and our findings have some important messages of offer. First, to those who address curriculum content while ignoring pupil motivation, it simply asserts their short-sightedness, More constructively, it confirms the views of many teachers that classroom control or whole-class teaching are unlikely to be sufficient to produce high-quality learning gains. Certainly, as we have seen, they can produce pupil awareness of the need to comply with teacher requirements, but the connection with learning has to come through an engagement with and interest in the curriculum itself. However, the potential is there, for a significant minority of children do value teachers as a source of 'making classroom life interesting.' Nevertheless, there is arguably much more that could be done. While affirming the importance of teacher-pupil relationships in providing positive social contexts in which learning can take place, we are back to the need for teachers to have a rich resource of subject knowledge and a wide repertoire of pedagogic strategies to convert their expertise into productive pupil activity. A successful and popular teacher should always keep these mind and opt for these while teaching a language, specially the English.

6

Classroom Pedagogy

We an speculated that teachers might increase the extent to which they sought to control and structure pupil time and behaviour, in response to the curricular constraints and pressures they faced. This, of course, relates to another of the analytic dimensions, that of the strength of the 'frame' within classrooms. Following Bernstein, 1975, a strong frame reduces 'the power of the pupil over how he (*sic*) receives knowledge' and increases 'the teacher's power in the pedagogical relationship. On the other hand, weak framing increases the options open to both teacher and pupil in the 'selection, organization, pacing, and timing of the knowledge transmitted and received in the pedagogical relationship'.

A strengthening of frame in classrooms would thus mean that there was more constraint and greater specification over the pedagogic roles of both teachers and children. There would be less scope for self-directed and flexible activity for both.· However, it is also possible that the strength of curriculum classification and frame could vary independently of one another and that pedagogy could remain relatively unaffected by a tightening of curriculum content. This chapter explores this relationship empirically. A wide range of issues is involved in a consideration of whether constraint is increased and choice reduced in the classroom. These include the selection of work and tasks, the organization of classroom activities in terms of the use of space and resources, and the grouping of pupils, as well as the contexts in which teaching takes place and its timing. Many of these issues are discussed in current chapter. We explore teacher perspectives on pedagogy and on relationships with children, and we consider the extent to which these changed, drawing upon interviews carried out in 1990 and 1992 with our larger sample of 88 and upon interviews and discussions in 1990 and 1991 with our 18 classroom study teachers. The current chapter is based mainly upon the systematic observation carried out in 18 classrooms in our nine study schools.

First, however, in order to establish a baseline prior to the introduction of the National Curriculum, we examine some of the research findings of the 1970s and 1980s.

Teachers Approaching Classroom Teaching and Organization in the Past

In terms of teachers' beliefs about children's learning, the progressive movement that led up to and culminated in the Plowden Report (CACE, 1967) had a profound and long-term influence in England. For instance, the teachers in King's (1978) study of infant schools took child-centred approaches as being axiomatic, some even regarding the move to the junior school as the end of 'real' education. Key elements in these teacher's perspectives about the nature to children's learning were ideas about developmentalism, individualism, play as learning and childhood innocence. Closely related to learning through play were ideas about the importance of child interest, happiness and busyness. Similarly, Berlak and Berlak (1981) emphasized infant teachers' perspectives in terms of seeing childhood as unique and as a special case, in contrast to the alternative view of childhood as continuous and of children as mini-adults.

However, it is of the the case that there is a difference between the ideals to which people aspire and the actions that turn out to be possible. This has also been true for primary school teachers. Thus many of the research studies of the 1970s and 1980s documented a gap between commitments and ideologies and practical realities in classrooms (e.g. Bennett, 1976; Bassey, 1978; DES, 1978; Galton *et al.,* Alexander, 1984). A key play, while some that did still limited pupil use because of the potential difficulties of wet or sandy floors.

One of the most common teachers strategies was to allow choice to children only when they had finished their designated 'work.' 'Choosing' was thus used as an inducement to complete tasks, and the range of activities that could be selected was often delineated on a day-by-day basis. Often this might be limited to activities that were regarded as requiring little teacher support, thus enabling the teacher to target her attention towards children who had not completed their tasks. Of course, with this arrangement, slower children only rarely got a chance to choose.

This use of choice as an inducement to complete 'work' increased as the children became older. However, a balance was still sought. Thus Year 2 teachers said:

> Children ought to have some choice, especially as they get older and more self-reliant. But 1 do think you need to give them a grounding to start with and then also have the opportunities open for them around the classroom so that they can choose *(Year 2 teacher at Meadway).*

> I think children need enough choice to be able to give them a sense of their own importance, but not to go overboard because we have to remember that they are still children. They need to be guided and taught, but certainly there should be times when you give a child a plan and say 'you can choose,' but this again needs to be thought out by the teacher as to why she's doing it and how she's doing it and not just free for all *(Year 2 teacher at Lawnside).*

It was apparent from teacher interviews conducted both through the classroom studies and in the two major interview rounds that teachers had found it progressively more difficult to reconcile their belief in the value of some child choice of activity with the demands of the National Curriculum. We reviewed some of the data that bear, where, among other things, we reported a 1990-2 increase from 20 to 55 percent of teachers perceiving the curriculum to be overcrowded and no fewer than 85 percent of teachers in 1992 saying that the National Curriculum had been the biggest influence on their recent pedagogic changes. Taken overall, there was a strong feeling from our findings that teachers felt they were being forced to prescribe more and more classroom activities and thereby restrict scope for pupil autonomy.

In terms of the tension between the perceived nature of six- and seven-year-old and required educational purposes, this was seen as resulting in requirements that were both 2 class explicitly stated that her freedom to allow child control was now more limited: 'There's no longer the freedom to go away and write a story about what you want. Even with the very young ones, free writing is now curtailed somewhat because we're doing "my family" and it's all geared to getting ready for the attainment targets.' This was perceived as a significant change: "It didn't used to be. Before, every child would write on subjects they chose and I would be their scribe helping to express their great needs.' Another Year 2 teacher said: 'In the last two years I've had to cover as much as possible, such as science. So I've chosen more and more of what we have to do. For instance, I aim to cover the attainment targets for science and this has rather dominated.'

Lest any reader has images of 'golden days' of the past, we should remember that, despite some popular impressions, research studies of the 1970 s and 1980s consistently found that actual teacher control of primary classrooms was tight and that child choice was relatively limited. However, it appears from our data that, since the subject content of the National Curriculum and the assessment procedures have been introduced, teachers have felt it necessary to take more control and direction of children's activities. They have done so largely despite their better judgement and with concern over the imposition of a degree of curriculum overload, resulting in pedagogic constraint, which they feel to be inappropriate for such young children.

Our evidence suggests that not only had the choice of learning tasks become more restricted since the introduction of the National

Curriculum, but levels of teacher intervention during tasks had also increased. Of course, the latter could well have been beneficial, if more subject matter teaching and encouragement were being offered so that children became more 'interested.' However, as many teachers feared, it could also have been detrimental, if so much control was being taken away from children that their motivation and commitment to school and learning was compromised.

How did Teachers Perceive Changes in Their Pedagogy Following the Introduction of the National Curriculum and Assessment Requirements?

In this section we draw on data from two rounds of interviews with teachers, conducted in the summers of 1990 and 1992. The data thus reflect teacher perceptions in the early stages of the implementation of the National Curriculum and at a point when its impact on classroom practice was becoming apparent. We asked about teachers; classroom practice and how this was being affected by the National Curriculum and Assessment.

In particular, teachers were asked, 'How would you describe your approach to teaching?" Their responses were coded in broad categories. The result is shown in Table 1. One notable feature of these data is the fact that the vast majority of teachers, over 70 percent, stated that they adopted 'mixed' teaching methods. Even in 1990, only one fifth subscribed exclusively to forms of 'child-centred' pedagogy, a fact that somewhat belies the senzationalism about progressivism that has sometimes filled the media in recent years. One teacher, whose response was fairly typical, said:

I try to be a co-learner with the children, I try to increase my skills and be a more reflective teacher and I try to use the principles of really looking at the children's work and following through the stages in their learning. I think I use a range of styles, depending on what I'm working on with the children. There's a tremendous range of different levels with the children and there would be a more relaxed informal style when the children are composing writing, and spellings might be a more formal situation. When the children were planning and reviewing their work, there's quite alot of discipline so that they listen to each other. Music has its own inherent discipline and then they're playing with construction, where they might have a task to do but there will be an informal atmosphere in the classroom where they're all doing their own activities.

However, by 1992 there was a significant fall in the number of teachers declaring themselves to endorse child-centered approaches and a corresponding increase in those whose responses were coded as 'traditional' or 'formal.'

The pattern is clear, but it was made even more apparent when we coded teachers' comments made in respect of an open-ended opportunity to amplify their previous response. Table 2 presents these data. Some of these figures are dramatic. For instance, there was a fall in teachers mentioning forms of integrated day, from 29 to 8 percent, and a rise in teachers mentioning whole-class teaching, from 4 to 29 percent. Both these changes are highly significant statistically. The continuity in emphasis on group work and on the curriculum 'basics' is also notable, while there was no perceived decrease in the prominence of topic work. The latter finding somewhat contradicts the patterns found through our classroom observation, but this may reflect continuing attempts to provide integrated work despite the difficulty of actually doing it.

TABLE 1

Teacher Perspectives on Their Approaches to Classroom Teaching (Percentages)

	1990	1992
Child-centred/informal	22.7	16.1
Mixed	75.5	72.0
Traditional/formal	5.7	10.8
Other	1.1	1.1
Total	100	100

Source: PACE I teacher interviews.

Sample: 88 teachers in 8 LEAs.

Date: Summer 1990 and summer 1992.

Lest the origins of such changes be doubted, over 85 percent of the teachers interviewed in 1992 attributed them to the introduction of the National Curriculum, while 55 percent identified new assessment requirements. Only 12 percent spoke of other changes in school and just 3 percent mentioned personal sources of change. The 1990 figures were very similar. The teacher quoted above cited particularly the demands made by the National Curriculum in terms of classroom management: 'I'm finding that the demand of organizing and managing the children has changed a tremendous amount. I'm trying to maximize on time.'

TABLE 2

Open-ended Comments by Teachers on Approaches to Teaching (Percentages)

	1990	**1992**
Group based	50.0	50.0
Class work	3.6	29.1***
Individual work	20.2	32.6***
Emphasizing basics	31	34.9
Integrated day	28.6	8.1***
Topic work	16.7	20.9

Source: PACE I teacher interviews.

Sample: 88 Key stage 1 teachers in 8 LEAs.

Date: Summer 1990 and summer 1992.

Note: Figures do not total to 100 percent because of multiple coding of open-ended responses.

This perceived change in teaching approach and philosophy was also reflected in changes in classroom practice. Most teachers (87 percent) felt that the advent of the National Curriculum had resulted in significant changes to their working day and for 38 percent in 1990 and no less than 62 percent in 1992 these changes were seen as major. The most important areas of change involved more time spent on assessment-related record keeping, with over 60 percent mentioning this in both rounds of interviews, and more time spent on planning and preparation, with this being mentioned by cent on both occasions (see Table 3).

Even in 1990 there was certainly evidence for the 'intensification of teachers (in the sense of chronic work overload)) (Lawn and Ozga, 1981; Apple, 1986), teachers either having to work longer hours or having to work in a more cot less relaxed way in order to discharge their responsibilities. There was general of being swamped by change. 'Too much has happened too quicklywas the teachers put it. While they were developing new ways of working, particularly of record keeping and assessment, more information would arrive that supersing reqirements, meaning that they had wasted their time. For example, with the documentation that accompanied the National Curriculum was sector as 'simply overwhelming.' Far too much to assimilate. I have just had to go for the time being,' as one teacher put it.

Many teachers expressed frustration and even anger over the amount of tution apparently demanded by the NCC and SEAC for record keeping and assessment were fears that this was beginning to 'take over from teaching,' that the heavy demanded in time and effort left too little time for planning, for responding to for display work, for all the things that were seen by many as 'real teaching.

TABLE 3

Teachers Identifying Changes to their Working day (Percentages)

Type of change	1990	1992
More record keeping	62.8	63.3
More assessment	33.7	18.9
More meetings	29.1	15.6
Change in curriculum content	34.9	41.1
Change in teaching methods	12.8	23.3 **
More planning and preparation	46.5	42.2
More pressure	not coded	64.4

Source: PACE 1 Teacher interviews.

Sample: 88 Key Stage ' teachers in 8 LEAs.

Date: Summer 1990 and summer 1992.

Note: Totals do not equal 100 percent since teachers identified up to three changes.

We thus have clear signs, from teacher accounts, of tighter classroom structures, tighter teacher control and heavier workloads in response to the National Curriculum and assessment. In the nest section we consider how the tightening of 'frame' and the increased pressure experienced by teachers were felt to be influencing teacher relationships with the children in their class.

How did Teachers Perceive the Changes to have Affected their Relationship with Children?

In 1990 only 31 percent of the teachers felt that the National Curriculum had a negative effect on teachers' relationships with children. By 1992 this proportion had increased to 58 percent, partly as a result of the impact of the introduction of national assessment, but in particular because of a perceived increase in pressure on teachers' time, leaving them both less relaxed and less able to spend time responding to children. Most teachers had strong feelings about the importance of defending their relationship with the children, feelings that were closely tied to their own sense of identify as primary teachers (Nias, 1989).

Time and again they mentioned the National Curriculum as a definite pressure on the close relationships they had formerly enjoyed with children. Contributing to this was the loss of fun and responsiveness to children in the teaching and the feeling of a need to justify everything in terms of the attainment targets. In 1990 one teacher argued:

> There isn't anything that you do now that you don't feel, 'Can you actually justify this, what educational guide are the children getting out of it, how can you tie it up with an attainment target or programme of study?" All that sort of thing. Or can you, like you used to be able to, just do it for the pure fun and enjoyment of it?

This feeling of pressure was almost universal among the teachers we interviewed. The Valley Year 1 teacher agreed:

> I think on a bad day I'm definitely more 'crabby' because

> I do feel under pressure all the time. Hen the children do something, instead of looking at it and thinking only 'Has this child tried hard, is this good for this child?' I'm thinking, 'Does it fulfil certain criteria?' And if it doesn't, my anxiety .... shows through. I think because of the pressures at the moment I'll be more likely not to have been so nice and loving as might have been.

Closely related to this was a sense of loss of the close affective ties many teachers had developed with the children in their class. As one teacher put it:

> I think there is a tendency to be so pressurized by the demands of the National Curriculum that there isn't so much time to spend discussing emotional and personal issues with the children. It's 'Right, let's get on. Tell me about it later.' And those issues are just as important as the more academic issues.... So many of the very nice aspects of being with the children have been lost. And I think the children feel it. I feel they feel very tired and pressurized at the end of the half term.

The feeling of stress and a loss of relaxed, enjoyable time with the children seemed, if anything, to have intensified between 1990 and 1991. As another Year 2 teacher put it. 'I'm very aware of that close contact time, that personal connection that makes the children happy and at ease with you. You don't have time for that and you can't teach an unhappy child.' As she put it, the making of a trusting relationship with young children aged between four and seven was all-important and it would be lost: 'They'll see this horrible women who makes me do this, this and this, through the day, and that's not right.' Another teacher agreed:

> We are not so relaxed in the classroom now. Teachers are more worried. 'Are we doing enough? Are we giving children enough experiences? There is constant planning and record keeping. Some of the children in my class would be so much better off with a motherly teacher who

> had time to sit with them on her knee and do things with them but it's impossible now with all the pressures.

Such feelings were intensified where teachers felt there was a particularly strong conflict between the demands of the National Curriculum and the needs of the children. The Year I teacher at St Anne's, working in a socially disadvantaged area in the north of England, felt a conflict between

> knowing the kind of work you should be doing and which the National Curriculum encompasses and the restrictions imposed by the kind of children they are. I feel that I'm not able perhaps to take things as far as I would like, it has to be a very simple level, sometimes I'd like to take it one step further and I'm not able to do that.

In 1990 there was evidence of a strong determination among teachers not to allow the changes to destroy their relationship with the children, and this protectiveness was still strongly in evidence in teachers' responses a year later. As the Year 2 teacher at Valley put it,

> When I feel those frictions I lay off the National Curriculum. When I feel those I say, 'I don't care, we will do something completely different,' and I change my tack, and I go back to being myself the 'proper' teacher and I don't care. Angela [the head] backs me up on this. When I feel those tensions come back into the classroom I stand back. I make an assessment, make a sensible judgement, and think, 'Enough's enough'

In spite of the perceived pressures, the responses of these teachers expressed a determination to try to protect their relationship with the children and to mediate the demands of the reforms to acceptable professional ends. Nevertheless the figures suggest that, as the implementation of the reforms progressed, an increased proportion of teachers felt this relationship to be under threat.

In the sections that follow, we draw upon both teacher interviews and our observations of 18 year 1 and Year 2 classrooms to examine directly the changes in teacher's classroom practice.

What Were the Main Teaching Contexts in the Classrooms and How Have These Changed?

In monitoring changes in classroom practice, we were concerned particularly with the extent of whole-class, individual and group teaching. On this, we have two main sources of data. First, we have the findings of systematic observation by the PACE team in the 18 classroom studies during the autumns of 1990 and 1991. Our second data source comes from interviews with our wider sample of 88 classroom teachers, conducted in the summers of 1990 and 1992.

Table 4 shows the results of the systematic observation of teaching context. It is apparent that a wide range of teaching contexts are used in infant classrooms, with approximately two-fifths of the time being spent in each of whole-class interaction and individual work, and the remaining fifth being used for group work. We should emphasize in this context that our observational coding of 'whole-class interaction' included all teaching time spent together as a class: discussions and story time, for instance, as well as more didactic teaching sessions.

Interesting our data record a slight fall in the proportion of whole-class interaction from 1990 to 1991, though we are unable to say whether this was caused by an absolute change in teaching approach or by teacher adaption to the age of the children. It will be recalled that our 1990 observations were based on Year 1 children but that these same children were in Year 2 for our 1991 observations. It is possible that whole-class sessions are used more for induction and socialization purposes with younger children. In any event, the decrease in whole-class interaction does seem surprising, given the pressures that were mounting externally at the time.

Data from our interviews with the wider sample of teachers also raised some interesting questions about changes in teaching contexts. In both 1990 and 1992 teachers were asked to say whether they felt they were doing 'more,' 'the same' or 'less' of whole-class, group or individual teaching. The results are shown in Table 5. This table shows the absolutely clear perception by just over a fifth of teachers in 1990 and a quarter in 1992 that they were increasing the proportions of whole-class interaction in their classrooms. While this increase was matched by a rise in groupwork in 1990, teachers believed that their use of groups had fallen back by 1992. Individual work was felt to have decreased in 1990 but had begun to stabilize by 1992.

How, then, can we account for the apparent discrepancy between what we observed as a slight fall in whole-class interaction and the repeated teacher perception that there had been a rise?

We believe that the problem is essentially methodological and that the data can, in fact, be reconciled. The key question is 'What is seen to count as whole-class teaching?' We believe that the main teacher reference point on this, when answering our interview question, was likely to relate to explicit whole-class teaching sessions they had specifically planned in relation to the content of a National Curriculum subject. Indeed, our field note data confirm teacher perceptions that, in the light of the demands of the National Curriculum, the extent of explicit subject-based whole-class teaching was increasing. However, our systematic observation data record a much wider range of whole-class interaction, much of which, such as 'news time,' 'review time' and 'story time,' is traditional and commonplace in infant classrooms. We think it unlikely that teachers were thinking of these in response to our question on whole-class teaching.

Our overall interpretation, then, is that there has been a steady increase in explicit, teacher-planned, whole-class teaching sessions while the overall number of whole-class interaction sessions has decreased. We thus need to ask, 'How are whole-class sessions actually used?" as well as, 'What proportion of whole-class sessions are there? We believe that our data suggest that although there may have been slightly fewer whole-class interaction sessions in 1991 than in 1990, a greater proportion of them were being used for explicit teaching purposes.

TABLE 4

Main Teaching Contexts: (Percentage of Observe Time: Column Percentages)

	Year 1, 1990	Year 2, 1991	Difference, Year 1 to Year 2
Class interaction	39.5	35.9	−3.6
Group work	18.4	19.2	+0.8
Individual work	39.5	41.0	+1.5
Other	2.6	3.9	+1.3

Source: PACE 1 systematic observation.

Sample : 9 Year 1 and 9 Year 2 classrooms.

Date: autumn 1990 and autumn 1991.

TABLE 5

Teacher Perceptions of Changes in Teaching Context (Column Percentages)

	Whole-class teaching		Group work		Individual work	
	1990	1992	1990	1992	1990	1992
More	21.6	25.8	28.4*	9.7	9.1	9.7
Same	64.8	67.7	65.9	74.2	65.9	77.4
Less	12.5	5.4	3.4	12.9	23.9*	10.8
Other	1.1	1.1	2.3	3.2	1.1	2.1

Source: PACE 1 teacher interviews.

Sample : 88 teachers.

Date: summer 1990 and summer 1992.

In terms of teaching the curriculum, teachers were, arguably, using the available time more effectively. However, few teachers actually saw it like that, and for most the increase in whole-class teaching was something that was forced on them by the subject specification of the National Curriculum. Indeed, it was often seen as potentially damaging to social, affective and some cognitive aspects of children's learning.

A rough comparison may be made between the PACE findings and Tizard *et al.*,'s (1988) study of children of the same age in

London inner-city infant schools. In Tizard *et al.*'s study, Year 1 children spent 61 percent of their time in individual work. This increased to 66 percent of the time in Year 2. The proportion of group work in both years was relatively low. Interestingly, children had direct contact with the teacher for only 20 percent of their time in the classroom compared with 43 percent of the time in the PACE study in 1990 and 41 percent in 1991. It would appear that, since the introduction of the National Curriculum, the proportion of time children spend in group work has remained low and the proportion of time children work as individuals has decreased. However, compared with earlier research, whole-class interaction has increased and the overall proportion of teacher-led situations has grown significantly.

On What Criteria Were Classroom Groups Established?

Although, as we have seen, the proportion of time spent by children in group work has declined, the children we observed sat in groups for most of the time in which they worked as individuals. How teachers seat children in groups for different activities and how much choice children have over their seating arrangements can be one indicator of the strength of frame within classrooms. For example, if children were grouped by attainment for more activities now than in the past and were less likely to be allowed to sit in friendship groups, this would suggest a tightening of teacher control in the pedagogical relationship, and a reduction in the power of the pupil.

We asked teachers during the 1990 and 1992 interviews what criteria they used when they grouped children for different classroom activities. The results are shown in Table 6. In both 1990 and 1992, the results show a repertoire of grouping methods in use, with each being adopted for particular purposes. The method declared by the largest proportion of teachers, four-fifths, was attainment grouping (often inaccurately called 'ability grouping'). This was particularly used for specific curriculum activities, such as in maths, where differentiation by task was needed. However, its use often seemed to be generalised to apply to all work within subjects, such as maths and English, in which differentiation of tasks was seen as being particularly important.

TABLE 6

Types of Pupil Grouping Declared by Teachers as a Basis for Classroom Organization

	1990	1992
Attainment groups	79.5	82.8
Mixed-ability groups	55	72
Friendship groups	62.6	67.7
Gender groups	13.7	9.7
Age-based groups	44.3	16.1

Source: PACE 1 teacher interviews
Sample: 88 Teachers in 8 LEAs.
Date: summer 1990 and summer 1992.
Note: Totals do not equal 100 percent because of multiple coding of open ended responses.

One teacher described this:

I'm having to switch more and more to ability groupings, which I don't like with such young children because I don't think it's appropriate.... Because of the pressure to cover all the activities that they need to, it's just impossible not to formalize the work more, and I do a lot more of dividing the class into high-ability groups, middle range and lower-ability groups just to teach them a lot more formally.'

Mixed-attainment grouping and friendship grouping were also used by most teachers for at least some of the time and such groups seemed to be used where it was more possible to differentiate tasks by outcome.

The decrease in the percentage of teachers using age as a basis for grouping is interesting. Such grouping was most prevalent in small, rural schools with mixed-age classes and there was a slight decrease in the number of mixed-age classes in the 1992 sample. On the other hand, the finding could reflect greater teacher efforts, even in small schools with a wide attainment range in each class, to provide differentiation between learners in terms of attainment. The percentage of teachers using gender as a basis for grouping remained very low. Gender-based groups tended to be used for specific purposes and with awareness of equal opportunities issues.

These findings articulated closely with research on grouping before the National Curriculum, which indicated that many teachers grouped predominantly by attainment. In Bennett and Kell's (1989) study, for example, a little over one-half of the teacher grouped children by attainment. A little over one-third of teachers used age or intake, and a similar proportion claimed to use flexible grouping. One in four said they used mixed-ability groups, and one in six used friendship groups. However, the reality was a little more complex than this, since many teachers used more than one criterion; for example, grouping by both age and attainment.

This comparison suggests that while attainment grouping has long been a significant form of classroom organization, its use has increased since the introduction of the National Curriculum and assessment.

Were Different Groups of Children Being Taught in Different Ways?

Overall, the children we observed in the PACE study were the focus of teacher attention (i.e. were observed to be intracting with the teacher) for 43 percent of the time 1990 and 41 percent of the time in 1991. This figure includes whole-class, group and individual teaching contexts and compares with a figure of 20 percent of the primary observed by Tizard *et al.* in 1988. This difference suggests that after the introduction of the National Curriculum and assessment, teachers began to intervene far more in children's activities. However, this overall figure conceals significant variations in the way teachers allocated their time with children.

The PACE systematic observation data provide some interesting insights into the judgements being used by teachers in differentiating their pedagoic provision. For instance, focusing on data of pupil observations only, we were able to compute the proportions of time in which children of different attainment levels were contact with the teacher in each of the three main teaching contexts: whole-class, group or individual. Attainment, in this context, was based on teacher records, with particular reference to reading attainment. The results are given in Table 7

As one would expect, pupil attainment made very little difference to the contact offered by teachers when pupils were observed in whole-class contexts. The teacher interacted with the children in such circumstances whatever their level of achievement. However, teacher involvement with groupwork was heavily directed towards supporting lower-attaining children. Higher-attaining children seemed to receive only half the teacher attention that was invested in supporting weaker children. Teachers again offered most individual attention to lower-attaining children but also spent time, on an individual basis, with higher attainers. Children attaining at average levels received slightly less individual attention from the teacher.

These patterns show the ways in which the teachers studied resolved the acute dilemmas they face regarding the deployment of their scarce teaching time. It appears that teachers routinely direct whole-class interaction largely at the majority of children with average levels of attainment. They then support lower attainers, in groups, who might otherwise have difficulty in making constructive progress. Finally, they provide differentiated support to particular high-and low-attaining individuals.

TABLE 7

Total Pupil Time in Contact with Teacher in Class Interaction, Group Work and Individual Work by Pupil Attainment (Percentages)

	Teaching context		
Attainment	**Class**	**Group**	**Individual**
Higher	30.5	7.5	3.0
Medium	28.4	9.6	2.1
Lower	29.7	15.4	3.6

Source: PACE 1 systematic observation.

Sample: 9 Year 1 classrooms.

Date: Autumn 1991

A typical way of working was described by the Year 1/2 teacher at Orchard:

> *I talk to the children all together first on what I expect them to achieve during the day and then I generally extract a group for either maths or language and I give the other children the chance — the ones that I'm not gathering together — usually I give them the chance to choose, within those things that I talked about first thing in the morning. So for instance, maths will generally be in their maths book and if a child says, 'Can I do maths first,?' I say, "Well, wait until after play because I want to talk to your group about what they are going on to next. So at some stage during the week I would have expected to see all the maths groups and have taken them on to something new so that on other day in the week they can continue, perhaps getting slightly more difficult, but on the same work that they've been doing. Then, after I have worked with the children as a group, I go round from group to group, helping individuals where I am needed.*

Table 8 elaborates these issues by showing patterns in the experience of children of differing levels of attainment, social class, gender and sociometric status in terms of their total interaction with their teacher and their total interaction with other pupils, It tells us a good deal about teacher pedagogy and, in particular, how teachers resolve the problem of to which pupils to direct their time.

Regarding social class, it is striking that pupils of manual and non-manual parental backgrounds received almost exactly equal amounts of teacher contact. However, children of manual backgrounds spent a little more time interacting with other pupils. Of course, these quantitative data say nothing about the nature of what they were doing in either case, but there is an immediately apparent balance in the distribution of teacher time. Social class made no difference.

Similar statements could be made regarding gender, where again there are very small differences in interaction times. Interestingly, the very slightly higher figure for total *et al.,* (1980). While the overall differences are very small, for individual pupil interaction with their teacher, girls received 25 percent more than boys (3.9 against 2.9 percent of teacher-pupil interaction).

TABLE 8

Patterns of Teacher and Pupil Interaction by Attainment, Social Class, Sociometric Status and Gender

	Interaction	
	Total teacher interaction with pupils	**Total pupil interaction** with other pupils
Attainment		
Higher	41.0	29.5
Medium	40.1	29.6
Lower	48.8	24.7
Social class		
Non-manual	43.6	25.6
Manual	43.4	29.7
Sociometric status		
Very high	33.0	36.0
High	41.2	31.7
Medium	47.9	•24.2
Low	49.0	20.8
Gender		
Boys	40.3	26.8
Girls	42.2	26.1

Source: PACE 1 systematic observation.

Sample: 9 Year 1 classrooms.

Date: autumn 1991.

Note: This represents the percentage of total pupil time in contact with teacher and in contact with other pupils. Therefore percentages do not add up to 100 percent.

Regarding the interaction patterns of children of differing attainment and socio-metric status, teachers, appeared to be making clear judgements about where to direct their time among pupils. There was significantly more teacher interaction with lower attaining children and with children of low socio-metric status. A probable consequence was that low attainment and low socio-metric status were associated with less pupil to pupil interaction.

This evidence highlights one result of the exercise of professional judgement in the deployment of time. Teachers had repeatedly told us of their commitment to meet individual pupil needs and here, it appears, we have a resulting pattern in terms of observed interaction. As one Year 1 teacher argued, 'The kind of children I have in my class can make the National Curriculum approach difficult. It requires diversifying away from the basics and they actually need a lot of help with basic skills. I have to make that my top priority and make time to work with individuals.' Another teacher said:

> Some children in my class need a lot of help. I'm very aware that working with the whole class myself—very often I have to give that over a part-time teacher when I really need and want to do it myself, so that I can fulfil the needs of individuals.... But in doing that you lose that joy and that two-way communication with the class which you also need to fulfil the work and activities as it were. So you lose the cohesive stance between class work, individual work and group work because you're having to fragment that all the time.

As one example of this exercise of professional judgement, the Year 1 teacher at St Anne's adopted a strategy of making sure that she introduced difficult new work to lower-attaining groups of children on Mondays, when there were other adult helpers present in the class to work with other groups. This enabled her to spend longer with lower-attaining children and to concentrate completely on their needs. On one of the days we observed her, she was working with, and moving between, two maths groups doing work with dice, while one helper (a volunteer and grandmother) worked with children constructing and painting model plates of food as part of their topic work on 'our bodies, ourselves.' Another helper, a classroom assistant, worked with children making weather charts, and one group worked alone using worksheets.

Of course, plotted patterns of aggregated data can conceal a great deal of individual variation. As an example of this, a scattergram showing the position of each of our 54 target children in Year 2 in terms of total interaction with other pupils and with their teacher. The spread is very considerable, from one child (top right) who managed exceptionally high levels of contact with both teacher and other pupils to others (bottom left) who had low levels of contact with both. The classroom experience of such children was inevitably very different indeed.

How varied were Differences in Teaching Contexts for Teachers and Pupils?

In this section, we consider differences in pedagogy in each of our nine study classrooms in 1991, taking as one indicator of difference the proportion of time in which different teaching contexts were used.

The predominant teaching contexts were whole-class interaction and individual work and that these were used about twice as much as forms of group work. Teachers were particularly aware of increases in explicitly planned, whole-class teaching. However, these overall aggregated figures conceal striking and significant variations in the experience of teachers and pupils in each of the our nine study schools. Table 9 gives some idea of the range of difference, in which, in 1990, whole-class interaction varied from less than 7 percent of the time in the small rural Orchard Primary School with its mixed-age classes to 69 percent of the time in Lawnside Primary School, although for most schools the variation was somewhere between 30 and 50 percent. Similarly, the proportion of time spent on children working in groups varied from 4 percent in Greenmantle School, situated in a southern market town, to 42 percent in Audley in the industrial North.

In 1991, the greatest variation in whole-class interaction was still between Orchard and Lawnside, but the difference between them was not so great (16 and 50 percent respectively). The variation between most of the other schools had also fallen to between 30 and 40 percent. The variation in group work was about the same in 1991 as in 1990, but the variation in individual work was less. This suggests that one effect of the progressive implementation of the National Curriculum might have been to move schools towards slightly greater uniformity of teaching context, although it is possible that the shift from Year 1 to Year 2 classrooms also made a difference.

Nevertheless, the divergence was still considerable, and, this divergence in classroom organization was matched by a wide variation in the proportion of time spent on different areas of the curriculum. It is evident from Table 10 that those schools which spent a high proportion of their time on whole-class interaction were not necessarily using this time to concentrate on the basics. In Lawnside school, for example, where nearly 70 percent of the time was spent on whole-class interaction, only 19 percent of this time was actually spent on the basics, while 70 percent of group time and 80 percent of the time children worked as individuals was spent in this way. These data directly on tract the common stereotype of chalk and talk, whole-class teaching of the basics.

In summary, the wide variations indicated here suggest that, in these early stages in the implementation of the National Curriculum, there was still considerably diversity in children's experience in English infant and primary schools, in terms of variations in time spent on different areas of the curriculum and on different teaching methods. A number of writers have contrasted the heterogeneity of the English child's experience in this respect with that of the typical French pupil (DES, 1991a; Sharpe, 1992; Broadfoot and Osborn, 1993). However, there was some evidence of a slight move towards greater uniformity in teaching context, possibly as the implementation of the reforms progressed.

TABLE 9

Main Teaching Contexts in Classroom Studies: Percentage of Observed Time (Row Percentages)

	Class work interaction		Group work		Individual work	
Teaching Year 1 (1990)	**Year 2 (1991)**	**Year 1 (1990)**	**Year 2 (1991)**	**Year 1 (1990)**	**Year 2 (1991)**	**context**
Greenmantle	51.1	34.4	4.3	3.1	42.6	56.3
Kenwood	20.5	27.1	20.6	43.8	51.3	29.2
St. Bede's	37.7	40.0	17.0	21.7	39.6	31.7
St. Anne's	34.1	32.7	24.4	3.8	41.5	57.7
Audley	31.3	29.6	41.7	24.1	27.1	46.3
Orchard	6.8	15.6	20.4	17.7	70.5	66.7
Lawnside	69.1	50.0	16.3	15.7	14.5	31.3
Valley	41.5	41.7	5.7	23.3	49.1	26.7
Meadway	50.9	43.1	20.7	15.5	28.3	37.9
Average	39.5	35.9	18.4	19.2	39.5	41.0

Source: PACE 1 systematic observation.
Sample: 9 Year 1 and 9 Year 2 classes.
Date: Autumn 1990 and autumn 1991.
Note : There was also a small 'other' category of teaching context, which was used for just over 3 percent of observations overall.

TABLE 10

Proportion of time Spent by Pupils on Basics (English and Mathematics) in Different Teaching Contexts, by School (Percentages)

	Whole class	Individual	Group
St Bede's	26.0	79.0	30.8
St Anne's	17.6	96.7	75.0
Greenmantle	54.6	72.2	0.0
Kenwood	61.5	92.8	55.6
Audley	56.3	44.0	0.0
Orchard	14.3	53.3	83.4
Lawnside	18.8	80.0	70.0
Valley	16.0	72.5	42.8
Meadway	28.0	22.7	33.3

Source: PACE 1 systematic observation.
Sample: 9 Year 1 classrooms nationally.
Date: autumn 1991.

Summing Up

There were very clear indications that the strength of frame in classrooms was increasing. Teachers were experiencing more constraint and the options open to children to select, organize, pace and time their work were considerably reduced. The teachers, in response to the pressures of the National Curriculum and assessment, appeared to be adapting by tightening their classroom control and by providing more direction to children's activities. There was apparently more frequent contact between the teacher and the children than in Tizard *et al.*'s (1988) study before the Education Reform Act and teachers perceived themselves as using more group and whole class teaching, although our observations did not bear out the predominance of group teaching situations. More group work was becoming based on attainment levels in particular subjects as teachers sought to organize the provision of a differentiated curriculum. There was considerable variation between the schools we studied in terms of patterns of classroom organization and teaching context, but there was evidence that the variation was slightly reduced in 1991.

Debating over teaching methods in the primary school, our data suggest that, apart from the schools at either end of the spectrum, the 'balance' between different types of classroom organization suggested as desirable by Galton *et al.* (1980), Mortimore *et al.* (1988) and most recently Allexander *et al.* (1992) was already being practised by at least half the teachers in our sample. In schools that did not achieve this 'balance,' teachers were often adopting coping strategies to take account of particular circumstances, where the teacher found it virtually impossible to teach a mixed age group of four-to seven-year-olds as a whole class.

7

English through Fantasy

Two good reasons are there for using this as a theme: the first is the simple pleasure the children get out of such things and the second is the opportunity it offers for the evocative use of language. An excellent opening to such a lesson is provided by a poem such as e.e. cummings' 'Hist Whist' or 'Three Witches' by Edith Sitwell (see list). These induced plenty of discussion with classes of 9-10 and 10-11-year-olds, discussion about words and about the sort of things they regarded as ghostly or fantastic. Here are some examples of their writing:

Twitching in the moonlight
The terrible witches go
Out and about and in and out
They weave a spell you know.
They dance like tricketty insects,
Whirling and spindling
Edging and nudging:
Through the filthy air.
You must not look
Or they will get you
With their sharpened nails,
So move away slowly and do not be seen
And leave them to dance alone on the green.

The Meeting

In the eerie glade I saw

Witches one, two, three and four!
Dancing, prancing, always chancing,
Round and round you see them go,
A wart on their heads there's one on her toe.
All of a sudden with a swish and a wail,
They jump on their broomsticks and away then sail.

Eerie Gathering

Up come the broomsticks landing silently on the dark shadowy ground. Up flutter ghosts transparent in the clammy air. The gastly ghosts glow as they howl and wail.

Gloom is all round, the twitching things start singing a horrible sound, phantoms flutter and fitter amongst spiders and toads. Wicked goblins, wizards and witches discuss the latest wicked spells.

No mortal would dare to go anywhere near the gloomy forests when the ghosts, witches and wizards, phantoms and other unbelievable creatures are gathering on Midsummer Night and if they were to have courage enough it would be very unlikely if they would ever be seen again.

> First a leg, then an arm, then a lean thick body and a head come through the door in the wall. The bats flutter away, angry at being disturbed. A rat scatters into a hole in the wall. The mansion comes to life with screams, chattering, croaking, and other such noises. Silence falls as the grandfather clock strikes twelve. After that from everywhere comes unimaginable beings. For the creatures of the mansion know it is the bewitching hour. The noises of the mansion echo over the lonely house to reach the ears of timid, simple people in a distant village who know not about the supernatural.

Apart from witches, ghosts and other spectres are a continual source of interest and writing about them sometimes seems to offer the vicarious indulgence that allows for the release of secret fears. Here are some examples:

In the night when it is very dark and if it is windy and raining a lot it makes you wake up and then it's a long time before you go to sleep again. You think of all sorts of things like there might be ghosts or spirits floating about outside trying to get in and then you wonder if you do believe in ghosts. Every time there is a creak in the house or in the stairs you think there might be some moving spirit climbing up the stairs. Then I put my head under th sheets and say my prayers very fast and I think If I do that I'll be all right.

In a cave with great stalagmights and great stalagtights as ghosts spell them. A great white claw rose about a rock, and the ghost appeared and slid down the rock, then a ghost bird with two heads and another ghost and a great claw spranged out of the bird and three more claws and fore knives for arms and a bird which was red and tan claws and tan knives. Stinky Nit said the Read ghost. Kink said the bird with two heads. Plive sit. And they all turned tiny. Hold your tong said the rock. It was a ghost as well. Suddenly there was a noise like a bear. Then the ghosts were so frightened that they all ran away.

My grandad told me a story about when he was young and had to go to take the horses across the field and one night he went with his friend when it was very dark. They only had one horse to take and when they stopped they heard the sound of horses' hooves and then they saw a white horse rush past galloping, and the next minute it has disappeared, not just run away. They they heard it again all of a sudden not coming near but close to them and they ran home for their lives. My grandfather has told me this story a lot and sometimes in bed I can't stop thinking about it, these horses charging through into the dark and all white. They scare me the thought of them so that sometimes I think I can hear the sound of the hooves galloping through the night.

The way in which this theme is tackled will depend largely upon the age and understanding of the children. With many classes it is a good idea to play up the humorous side in the fashion of Wilde's 'The Canterville Ghost' (edited according to age), or 'Jimmy Takes Vanishing Lessons' in BSH; with others it might be better to emphasise the vocabulary interest. The suggestions below are intended to offer a variety, of possibilities to children of different ages and abilities. There are opportunities for story writing here and I have tried to indicate this in the selection.

Further Suggestions

1. Listen to record of 'Ghostly footsteps' on BBC sound effects record REC 269. Try some free writing.
2. Write an adventure for a good witch or bad witch or an old wizard who gets his spells mixed up.
3. Listen to 'The Sorcerer's Apprentice' by Dukas. Write about another unfortunate adventure the apprentice has.
4. Suppose you came into possession of a fragment of Aladdin's lamp on a tip or dump. There is only enough magic in it for one wish. Write about your adventure.
5. Read 'Robin Good fellow' by Ben Jonson (see list). Write a poem or story about one of his tricks.
6. The teacher might tell the story of Shakespeare's *The Tempest* perhaps emphasising the magic and Ariel's part. Children write a description of An Enchanted Isle or make up a story about Ariel's activities after the mortals have left the island.
7. Make up some spells or charms, e.g. to cure a stitch or a wart or a cold sore, to improve your skill in football or tennis or to turn a cat green, make a pig fly, etc.
8. Write a story about a clumsy, frightened or incompetent ghost.
9. Describe in detail a deserted building (house, castle, chapel, ruins) which has an 'uncanny' atmosphere.
10. Make a tape recording of sound effects and music if you like called 'A Ghost Story.'

Poems, Stories & Extracts

Sprites

Robin Goodfellow *Ben Jonson* MGR.

Hist Whist *e.e. cummings* MGR.

Overheard on a Saltmarsh *Harold Munro* ILTP; JV, I.

Witches

Three Poor Witches *Edith Sitwell* OB, II.

The Witches' Cat *Ian Serraillier* H.

The Two Witches *Robert Graves* H.

The Witches' *Chant John Wilson* RR, Blue.

Witches *Linden, aged 9* BW.

Thrice the brinded cat.... *William Shakespeare* PMV.

Ghosts

Colonel Fazackerley *Charles Causley* PMV; ILTP.

The Old Wife and the Ghost *James Reeves* PL, II.

The Haunted Mansion *Jennifer Beard* PC.

Ghosts *Boy, aged 13* EW.

A Ghost Story *Celia, aged 12* OBS, III.

The Cold Duke *James Thurber* YI, I.

Jimmy Takes Vanishing Lessons *Walter R. Brookes* BSH.

Night at a Cottage *Richard Hughes* Images; WSP.

A Ghost Story *Gaius* Pliny WSP.

Spells

Spells *James Reeves* PMV.

Spell of Creation *Kathleen Raine* PMV.

The Witches' Spell *William Shakespeare* ILTP; WS.

Ominous

Voices *Frances Bellerby* PMV.

The Listeners *Walter de la Mare* PL, IV; ILTP; YI, I.

Spookey Girls *Alison Ann Hunt, aged 9* BW.

Graveyard from *'Tom Sawyer' Mark Twain* WS.
The Old Lock Factory *Paddy Kinsale* WSP.

Strange and Enchanted
Disappearance *Algernon Blackwood* WSP.
In the Strange *Michael Roberts* TH.
Night Shapes *Paddy Kinsale* TH.
The Enchanted Island *William Shakespeare* TH.
Island *Paddy Kinsale*TH.
The Alice Jean *Robert Graves* JV, I; TW.
The Bermuda Triangle *Charles Berlitz* THW.
Voyage *James Elroy Flecker* THW.
La Belle Dame Sans Merci *John Keats* POCO; PMV.

Fantastic
A Small Dragon *Brian Patten* MW; TH.
Far Over the Misty Mountains *J.R.R. Tolkien* ILTP.
The Thing *Michael Baldwin* YI, I.
The Magical Mouse *Kenneth Patchen* JV, II.
Long Broad and Sharpeyes *Anon* BS.

8

Writing and Language Work

One hundred ideas are there to involve children in some kind of creative language activity. They are not offered as arbitrary tasks to be imposed on pupils, but depend on the build-up of interest and involvement in writing suggested throughout the book. With many of the ideas, it is obvious that some discussion might take place before writing: for example, 'if you had the Midas touch,' what would be the consequences of turning everything into gold? or, 'if you were invisible,' what would be the consequences of that? would people bump into you? would anything you touched also become invisible? would your food be invisible as soon as it passed your lips? etc. On the other hand, there are ideas which pupils might find immediately inviting in themselves, and then they will want to be left on their own to let their imaginations move freely over the subject. It is for the teacher to decide which approach to use, on the basis of her understanding of the children. Many of the ideas are based on the children's immediate experience, and thy are deliberately limited to the process of getting what can be observed into satisfying verbal form. The ideas which follow move outwards from there, in order to extend the imaginative possibilities of those starting-points. So there is more opportunity for fantasy, for exploring new worlds, for dealing in magic, the remote, the zany, the bizarre; more for pupils to play with, more to take them away from their immediate world of experience—although there are some suggestions which still keep to the immediacy of the ordinary day-to-day world. Here are some general suggestions about technique and form and the presentation of work.

Many of these ideas can be treated in the form of short stories which pupils might like to draft out in class, modify, work out in a rough form and then perhaps write out at home or in other lessons, if the story turns out to be longish. It is very frustrating to have to leave the story unfinished because the lesson has come to an end and not to have an opportunity to continue it. A lot of the ideas might be treated as reportage: 'Now, from our reporter in Islington/Bombay/ Buenos Aires/Kingston comes news of....' Some might be treated as letters to X from Y. Some might be written in direct simple prose, purely factually; some in a more elaborate metaphorical way. Some might be treated comically, some seriously; some in the form of film, or TV sketches; some in the form of comic strips; some in the form of documentaries on tape using a dialogue procedure; some in the form of ballads, perhaps using the old ballad form with contemporary themes; some in the form of limericks or nonsense poems; some in the form of free verse or what I've referred to as a 'sequence of images,' perhaps after the fashion of the Japanese haiku.A three-lined form, properly with five, seven and five syllables, and dealing with single evocative image. Some of the material might be presented in the form of a frieze like the Bayeux Tapestry, or in the form of poster-poems. or as items for a class magazine, or a tape anthology of poems and stories. A story might be told in a particular dialect or patois, perhaps with old words and word forms side by side with a translation. Sometimes it is appropriate to treat the story in the form of a diary, or a log, or letter, or a 'found' manuscript, or perhaps in the form of notebook. Some of the ideas might be approached as parodies: for instance, one could parody the old ballad form; one might take off an interview with a conceited footballer, or the player who has won the word tiddlywink championship, the butcher who has made the biggest sausage, or the confectioner who has made the longest stick of rock, etc. Ideas might be used as sketches, pantomime, bits of drama, improvised dialogue, using sound effects or music as appropriate. The approach will depend on the capacities of the children and the ingenuity of the teacher.

Sometimes teachers ask me how much choice children should be given in the matter of deciding on a subject or a type of presentation.

Clearly, if you know the children well, you'll know how much choice to offer and how much is relevant to their needs. For some children a great deal of choice is just bewildering. In such circumstances it is better to make a single clear, positive suggestion for work. Another group might respond to the challenge of variety of options. We cannot refer teachers to any laws laid down for matters of language teaching with children of this age. We can only suggest what, in ideal circumstances, it might be beneficial for the children to encounter.

We have offered an Index of themes to the ideas on pages 218-19, since many of them may be seen as appropriate in several categories.

1. Your uncle arrives from China. He makes you a fabulous kite and teaches you how to fly it. The kite rise up in the air taking you with it, over houses, trees, fields, rivers. Describe the ascent and eventually the descent.
2. You are on a picnic with your parents when you become separated from them in a wood. Here you encounter the very last unicorn who tells his story. Your parents find you asleep under a tree.
3. Boy or girl visits crazy inventor uncle in house in town, country or abroad. He introduces the child to his time machine. Visit to past, or future.
4. Watching Test Match at Lords. Your favoured side are losing. Somebody hits a six into the crowd right into your hands. You manage to swap the ball for a ball which is charmed...
5. You have an invisible companion who goes with you everywhere.
6. King or Queen for a day.
7. You are poor at athletics. Sports Day comes and suddenly you find you have remarkable powers.

8. Your utterly marvellous uncle from Japan, Greece, India Cyprus, West Indies or wherever comes to visit you and brings with him the most amazing box of conjuring tricks.

9. While experimenting in the kitchen one day when your mother is out you invent a completely new sweet which, when you chew it, makes you enormously strong/small/ thin/clever/invisible/green/electrified, etc.

10. Design some new fabrics and some entirely new clothes. Give a radio reporter's account of a fashion show in which these clothes are paraded.

11. You exchange places for the day with the headmaster of your school.

12. You paint a picture with paints which your old aunts has brought back from abroad. Your picture grows bigger, or you grow smaller. You fall into the picture. Describe the adventure you have.

13. Your uncle is a Radio Ham. You visit his house and while listening to the receiver you hear a message from someone in outer space....

14. Someone gives you a skateboard for Christmas. The skateboard has special properties...

15. Write the story of a waterdrop.

16. You have an ambition to be a conjuror, but when you get on stage all your tricks go wrong.

17. Your weird aunt Jemima teaches you how to cast a spell on toads / tennis balls / popstars / TV announcers / politicians / teachers...

18. You are in the cup final at Wembly and your side is losing 5-0 when a miraculous thing happens....

19. Consider 18 What might the miraculous thing be? Your

energy increases a thousand-fold / the ball is charmed / all the other players fall asleep / your opponents' goalkeepers develops hiccups...

20. There is a story about a soldier in the First World War called Alf who had a button on his uniform made from a bit of Aladdin's lamp. At the end of the story the button falls into the Channel. Supposing it was washed up on the shore and you found it...

21. You think you are the last girl or boy on earth, and then....

22. On a journey to visit your grandmother in Australia, Jamaica, Hawaii, India, etc., you are accidentally washed overboard in a terrible storm without the knowledge of the others on the ship. In a desperate struggle you manage to swim to a deserted island. You have a day and a night before the ship returns to rescue you. Describe your adventures to a reporter.

23. The dentist visits the school. Some laughing gas escapes.

24. The Wonderful Ice Cream Cart. An ice cream man visits the school and charms the headmistress into letting all the children and teachers have a free ice cream. It happens to be very special ice cream...

25. Write a song, lyric, or jingle to advertise your favourite sweets, food, soap, toys, washing-up liquid, furniture polish, etc.

26. Write a song, lyric, jingle or advertising blurb for the wrost sweets in the world, the worst soap, polish, etc.

27. Write a letter of complaint to the manufacturers of the worst soap, sweets, toys, etc.

28. You go to a garden centre to buy some runner-bean seeds. What you don't know is that one of them is left over from Jack's beanstalk. You plant it in the school garden.

29. Write a poem about an encounter between two bulldozers.

30. Design and write publicity material for a completely new toy / model / bike / sketeboard / ball game / computer / tennis racquet, etc.

31. Write a sequence of images or a poem called 'Night.'

32. Write a poem or a story called 'Wishes.'

33. You are a radio reporter reporting on severe snow conditions, a heatwave, landslide, violent storms at coast, plague of greenfly, wasps, flying elephants, etc. Try to feature a human story, e.g. How Fred Smith survived in a snowstorm, How Mary Brown fought off a plague of Flying Elephants, etc.

34. The most remarkable character I've ever met. Fact or fiction.

35. Describe in detail an object or ornament at home.

36. Spiders' Webs. Look at them in summer, autumn or winter. in garden sheds, on factory walls, in nooks and crannies or wherever they are, and write some poems, some images or a 'notebook' account of them simply called 'Spiders' Webs.' If you like,make a story of it, from the viewpoint of the spider, a fly, or a butterfly who escapes, etc.

37. You are wrongly imprisoned by an enemy. Describe your escape in detail.

38. You escape over a mountain, through a wood, across a river, in heat, ice and snow, etc. Describe your journey in the first person, dwelling on one of these experiences.

39. Write a piece with the title 'Alone.'

40. Write down all the things you can remember about your first day at school. Make it into a straightforward descriptive account, or into a sequence of images or impressions called 'First Day.'

41. 'The School we would Like.' Describe in as much detail as you can what kind of school, and what kind of school work you would really like.

42. Write a letter to a descendant of yours two hundred years from now. Or to an ancestor a long time ago.

43. Do some writing about your journey to or from school, either as a description, or as a story or as a poem.

44. Make a collection of words about water, lakes, rivers, etc. and then arrange them into a typographical poem, or a poster poem, or just write a poem called 'Water.'

45. Listen to 'The Sorcerer's Apprentice' by Paul Dukas or the 'Danse Macabre' by Saint-Saens and then tell your version of the story. Or dramatise it.

46. Start a notebook of your thoughts, each beginning with a title such as Thoughts on... (e.g. Thoughts on School Uniform, Thoughts on Bicycles, Thoughts on Being Alone, Thoughts on Grown-ups, Thoughts on Playing with Friends....).

47. Write some conversations between animals in the zoo after the visitors have left, then dramatise them.

48. Everybody has a hidden talent of some kind. Write about a boy or girl who one day finds out what his or her hidden talent is.

49. Write a fairy tale, or a tale of adventure, or a science fiction story using one of these ingredients or all of them—a shepherd boy, three brothers, three sisters, a princess, an evil wizard, a magic potion, an iron tower, a flying horse, a dwarf with immense strength, a lance-proof cloak, a friendly robot, an unfriendly robot, a sparrow who can talk, etc.

50. You find a capsule containing an assortment of tablets. You unwisely eat one and are immediately reduced to the size of an ant. Describe your ant's-eye view of the

world and your adventures before finding the capsule again and nibbling on one of the tablets which restores you to your proper size.

51. You are in a small boat when a fierce storm blows up and you are thrown overboard and floundering in the sea until you are rescued by a lifeboat. Concentrate on the sense of being in the storm-torn sea.

52. You go with a school party up a mountain. The mist comes down suddenly and you are separated from your companions. Describe how you find your way down the mountainside.

53. With or without the aid of a rope you climb down a well to rescue a puppy who has fallen and broken a leg.

54. Write about something that happened to you under the title 'The Most Memorable Thing in Our Life.'

55. You are down a mine or in a cavern underground when there is a rockfall and all the lights go out. You crawl to safety out into the light.

56. Carnival. Draw and paint and design costumes for a carnival. If you have time and material make them, dress up and have a carnival parade with reporters. Write poems or poems posters for each of the costumes.

57. Make a movie of birds in flight, with some words, a commentary or poems to go with it. Or make a movie of the sea or clouds, factory chimneys, roofs, leaves in autumn, busy traffic, machinery, etc.

58. Jokes. Collect jokes and put them into a class book of jokes with drawings, cartoons, illustrations, etc. Then have a laugh-in.

59. You try another experiment in the kitchen when your mother is out. You put into a saucepan all kinds of ingredients. The concoction begins to overflow the saucepan, the floor go up the stairs, out into the street, etc.

60. You are a poor girl or boy living in a far-off country a long time ago. While digging in the fields you find treasure / a jar of magic ointment / an iron dog / a clockwork bird a magic fish / a silver thimble / a golden ring / a rusty sword, etc. Write a story about how this object helps you to find your fortune. If you prefer, write a poem about the object itself. For instance, call it 'A Magical Fish,' etc.

61. Visiting a museum, you stand looking at a Viking ship. You are left alone and as you move around it, the ship seems to kell you what it was like sailing the seas so long ago.

62. Call it 'The Ship Speaks.' Or use the same idea for a flint, a coin necklace, a dress, a pen, a letter—or any exhibit in the museum.

63. Write a haiku for each of the seasons so that each begins with the words: Spring, or Summer or Autumn or Winter.

64. Write a ghost story and dramatise it as a radio play with sound effects and music if you like. Then make a tape recording of it.

65. Collect some local folklore (stories, events that happened or are believed to have happened in the past, ghostly manifestations, brave deeds, etc.) and write them up for a school reference book, or turn them into a tape-recorded documentary with sound effects and music if you like. Or collect the stories on tape as told by local speakers in local dialect.

66. Make a Collection of words most often used by people in the class, at home, on TV, etc.

67. Make a collection of names — names of places, names of people, surnames and Christian names. Then look up their origins in a dictionary of British place names, or a dictionary of surnames, etc.

68. Write a story from the past as it might appear in a modern newspaper.

69. Design a flying object. Make the object (could be a balloon, parachute handkerchief, glider, rubber-propelled aircraft, boomerang, etc. See Michael Bond's excellent little book 'How to make Things.' Studio Vista Books). Have a flying competition. Make posters to advertise it. Have 'BBC reporters' to describe it, etc.

70. Design a robot. Proceed as above (69). For ideas see 'How to Make Robots' by Gerry Downs which is also a Studio Vista book. See others in the same series on How to...

71. Look at doors. Notice the different colours, shapes, woods, etc. Then make up some images to describe the differences. Try the same thing in another lesson with fences, or windows, or chimneys, or roads, or bottles, etc.

72. One day a boy or girl finds a magic flute in a junk shop. The flute can charm animals and even things. Make up a story with flute or recorder music if you like and dramatise it for a 'tape performance.'

73. Donkey Serenade. Donkey is ridiculed for his voice. Lark takes pity on him and teaches him to sing. Voice becomes so beautiful that he is invited to Italy to sing in opera at the Arena di Verona. Tell the story of his adventures with characters (e.g. Donkey, Lark, Owl, Snake, Impresario, Critic,Film stars, etc.) and with music if you like.

74. Describe your ideal island.

75. Write a story or poem entitled 'The Ghost Ship.'

76. Design and make hats out of 'paper, material, cardboard, string, whatever is available. Give each hat a character. Hold a series of competitions for the most elegant, the craziest, the most fashionable, the most useful, the ugliest,

etc., and make up commentaries about the hats and the people modelling them. Write poems or stories for 'Hats.'

77. Make up some masks with cardboard and crayons, papier mache and paint, glue, straws, milktops buttons wool, etc. for various characters in a story, e.g. Boy, Girl, Monster, Robot, Bird, Rabbit. Make up a story-drama using the various characters with appropriate sound effects and music if you like.

78. Write a poem or a set of images or a story about shadows.

79. Write a poem or a story about a garden shed. It could be your own shed or somebody elses'. It could be full of ordinary garden tools, or junk, or....

80. 'Said the chair to the table....' Well, what do you think it said, and what did the table reply? Or kettle to saucepan, or hat to coat, or window to door, or pen to pencil, or dog to cat, or piano to drum, etc.

81. 'Journey of a Snail,' Watch a snail closely. Write some images or a poem or story about its journey.

82. 'The Journey of a Road.' The road starts as a little track in the mountains. Tell the story of its journey. (Use your imagination or a map or both).

83. 'The Poor Carpenter.' The tools in his workshop take pity on him. (Use the same idea for the Poor Pianist, Poor Stable Boy, Woodcutter, Welder,Weaver, Fisherman....).

84. Make up some music for Wind, or The Sea, or Clouds, or Machinery, or A City, etc. using cymbals, chime bars (on pentatonic scale if appropriate), recorders, and sound effects. Then record your music and write some poems to go with it.

85. Write some riddles to which the answers are a three-wheeler bike or car, a helicopter, bulldozer, roundabout,

wedding-cake, jam-sandwich, daisy, snake, monkey, parsnip, cricket-bat, guitar, etc.

86. John's dad is out of work. John does a good deed for someone and gets a job for his father.

87. Janet's mum has to go into hospital. While she's there Janet has to stay with her strange aunt Serpentina in the country. One day while her aunt is out Janet explores the old house. In the cellar she finds a thick book covered with cobwebs and dust.... What can it be? a diary? a history of the house? a book spells? When you've decided, write a story about it.

88. Make up some images and sounds for children playing, or a storm, a forest, a stream, soldiers, mountains, clear sky, home. If you like, put them all together to make a story in words and music, using chime bars, recorders or whatever instruments you have available.

89. 'The Traveller.' Who could it be? a mysterious stranger? a wandering knight? a ghost? a tramp? a time traveller? a magician? a princess?

90. Write a story about a boy or girl who's always in trouble, and then one day something happens that makes everything right.

91. Take the initial letters of, say, five words and use them as the initial letters of five other words to make up a sentence. Make up as many sentences as you can with the same letters.

For example, take the sentence by which some people remember the lines of the treble staff; Every Good Boy Deserves Favour. Use the same initial letters to make up sentences like news headlines: e.g. Elks Grow Bunions Dancing Fandangoes; Eggs Go Bang During Festival; Estraordinary Gale Brings Disastrous Floods; Energetic Gallop Brings Down Fences; Eager Gnome Bites Dozy

Fairy; Eccentric Granny Bites Deceitful Frog; Electronic Gobstopper Bowls Dapper Fox; etc. Use the dictionary to find interesting, meaningful, or crazy words.

When you have made a variety of sentences, pick one you like and write a story explaining it.

92. Changing one letter each time, how many words does it take to change Foot into Shoe? (Foot, soot, shot, Shoe). Now try changing Song into Bird, Cash into Bank, Coal into Fire, etc. Make up some more.

93. Some words are made up of other shorter words that make sense in themselves, e.g. Donkey, MagPie, BlueBottle. Collect some more and illustrate them e.g. draw the picture that the words might conjure up in the mind of somebody from another planet who didn't understand the language very well. Or, make up a fable about one of them.

94. Make up some sentences using only words that begin with the same letter, e.g. Ample aunty angers an alligator. (You'll need a dictionary.) Then write a story using one of your sentences as a title.

95. Have a competition writing down all the words beginning with A which are made up of other shorter words, e.g. 'acknowledge' gives: 'a,' 'know,' 'now,' 'owl,' 'led,' 'ledge' and 'edge.' Then try the same game using B. Try first without a dictionary, then with one.

96. Make up some anagrams, e.g. 'ant' is an anagram of 'tan,' 'loop' and 'polo' are anagrams of 'pool.' How many more can you find?

97. Collect words for the largest animals, buildings, objects, etc. in the world, and also for the smallest (e.g. mastodon, sky scraper, ocean, etc.; microbe, comma, droplet, etc.). Then find words to describe what they do, how they move and what they're like. Put the two groups of images together so you have a poem of contrasts.

98. Adjectives through the Alphabet. Start with a phrase such as 'an angry dog.' Next pupil substitutes a different adjective beginning with 'B,' e.g. 'a bounding dog.' Next: 'a curious dog,' and so on. See if you can get through the alphabet. Or play the game privately. Or use dictionaries.

Try it with verbs, e.g. 'the angry dog ambles,' 'the angry dog barks,' 'the angry dog dances,' etc. Make it more complicated by altering both the adjective and the verb.

All sorts of variations to this game are possible. Invent some.

99. 'Once upon...' Teacher writes opening words of story on top of a long sheet of paper, folds the paper over to cover the words and passes the paper to the first pupil who adds a sentence beginning with one of the following words (written on the blackboard), or a smaller phrase:

And then...
But...
Still...
Then along came a...
Nevertheless...
Turning the corner....
While....
When....
And yet...
Afterwards....
However....
Meanwhile...
And so....

100. Build a story. Teacher begins, e.g. 'Once upon a time a traveller was walking through the woods....' Pupils take turns to add one phrase or sentence. Go round several times if necessary to resolve the story.

Variations are possible. More or less direction might be given by the words the teacher writes on the board. Pupils might be left to add such conjunctions as they think appropriate. Or the opening might be more specific, e.g. 'It was midnight and the wind howled about the deserted farmyard....'; or : 'Merrily rowing his boat across the river Septimus / Oliver / a brown bear / Molly / a yellow tailed baboon, etc...

Considering variations of this idea—and of many of the others in the list and, indeed, in the whole book—is a creative challenge in itself. Pupils might, for instance, use the idea as an opportunity to invent their own fantasy, crazy fairy tale, SF yarn, etc. The teacher might use the idea to draw attention to the way sentences may be joined up. On the other hand, it might be an opportunity for some to notice how effectively sequences in a story follow on. It's up to the teacher and the pupils to seize on any idea as a creative challenge, twist it, change it. combine it, adapt it, reorganize it, distort it, etc., so that it makes something meaningful or interesting and also if possible becomes a learning point. Or may be just a memory of a happy time?

A general word about games. Most pupils will get great pleasure and fun out of playing games with words. A skilful teacher will also see opportunities of using a game to practise or draw attention to some aspect of language. For instance, the teacher might feel that some of the children's writing lacks vigour, may be because the verbs used are cliches, or have only limited meaning. Or she may want to demonstrate that the children have more words to call on than they realise. This might be put across in a kind of game, e.g.;

He bit the sausage.

Variations?

He gnawed the sausage.

He chewed the sausage.

He bolted the sausage.

He nibbled the sausage. Possibly discuss

He devoured the sausage. shades of

He ravaged the sausage. meaning

He plundered the sausage.

He pulverized the sausage.

He shattered the sausage.....

Obviously, I've let this encounter with the sausage go beyond what might be considered reasonable, but I've done that in order to suggest: (a) how the idea might be limited to alternatives for 'bit'; (b) how the idea might be used to distinguish variant meanings and perhaps degrees of intensity; (c) how an extended choice of words can create an entirely different impression; (d) how the words can extend the idea into metaphor, into fantasy, etc. All this, of course, depends on the age, abilities and responsiveness of the children, as well as the interest, understanding, and linguistic awareness of the teacher.

We hope student and teachers will see the possibilities here. Sometimes pupils themselves will invent games, variants, new rules, new lines of approach. The important thing is that they enjoy playing with language and consequently exercising and developing their abilities in using it.

9

Story Writing

Undoubtedly, it would be inexcusable in a book on creative writing not to say anything specifically about stories, and we have left the subject until last because, although it can be the simplest form of writing, it can also be the most demanding.

Children love writing stories and the able child who reads widely, under discriminating guidance, will tend to write freely and naturally. The less well-read child will find the narrative element more difficult to control; it will either be too unwieldy with too much happening so that it never gets well under way (e.g. 'A Voyage Around the World'), or the concern for the narrative will swamp any imaginative involvement, and we all know the kind of work that results in: 'He went down the street, and he turned the corner and he saw his friend and they went to play in the park, and they went home to tea and they went to bed,' etc. The child is writing a synopsis of a story lurking somewhere in his mind and we think it is possible to encourage the story to get out.

We think the first thing to establish is what qualities we expect a good story to display or what qualities are to be found in stories. Well, there are usually characters in the story; we generally find these absorbing according to whether we can identify with them or, at any rate, understand them, and to understand them we expect them to be clearly presented in terms of personality as well as appearance. We urged that by concentrating on a particular character the writer might be induced to describe the sort of person he was, not just what he looked like, and some of the children's work showed that this was possible. If this can be carried over into the story there is bound to be a proportionate gain in quality. Apart from the literary gain there may also be a social gain in that the more children can be encouraged to share the feelings of others, the more their understanding will be enlarged. However, this is clearly problematical at the junior level, although it should be one of the principal concerns of English teaching with older groups.

Besides the narrative line, which may or may not be very strong, another important quality is that of the use of detail, which may be concerned with setting the scene, evoking the atmosphere or describing the action or any number of other things. The sensitive use of detail can carry us right into a story; consider, for example, this short extract from Ted Hughes' story 'The Rain Horse' (Faber):

> The horse was almost on top of him, its head stretching forward, ears flattened and lips lifted back from the long yellow teeth. He got one snapshot glimpse of the red-veined eyeball as he flung himself backwards around the tree. Then he was away up the slope, whipped by oak twigs as he lept the brambles and brushwood, twisting between the close trees till he tripped and sprawled. As he fell the warning flashed through his head that he must at all costs keep his suit out of the leaf-mould, but a more urgent instinct was already rolling him violently sideways. He spun round, sat up and looked back, ready to scramble off in a flash to one side. He was panting from the sudden excitement and effort. The horse had disappeared. The wood was empty except for the drumming, slant grey rain, dancing the bracken and glittering from the branches.

Or the description of the ride on the lion's back from C.S. Lewis's 'The Lion, the Witch and the Wardrobe' (Penguin, chapter 15) which seems to appeal to children of all aged:

> That ride was perhaps the most wonderful thing that happened to them in Narnia. Have you ever had a gallop on a horse? Think of that; and then take away the heavy noise of the hooves, and the jingle of the bits and imagine instead the almost noiseless padding of the great paws. Then imagine instead of the black or grey or chestnut back of the horse the soft roughness of golden fur, and the mane flying back in the wind. And then imagine you are going about twice as fast as the fastest race-horse. But this is a mount that doesn't need to be guided and never grows tired. He rushes on and on, never missing his footing, never hesitating, threading his way with perfect skill between tree trunks, jumping over bush and briar and the smallest streams, wading the larger, swimming the largest of all. And you are riding not on a road nor in a park nor even on the downs, but right across Narnia in spring, down solemn avenues of beech and across sunny glades of oak, through wild orchards of snow-white cherry trees, past roaring waterfalls and mossy rocks and echoing caverns, up windy slopes alight with gorse bushes, and across the shoulders of heathery mountains and along giddy ridges and down, down, down again into wild valleys and out into across of blue flowers;

We think if children have already been disposed in their writing to use the minutiae of their experience they will be well-equipped when they come to write stories to exploit the use of detail, as well as being concerned to tell the story.

As we have said, given a free choice, some children may tend to adopt narrative lines which are beyond their ability to handle, so that we think a little direction on the part of the teacher is justifiable. An easy way to do this is either to read them a simple story or ancedote by a child of their own age or to suggest the kind of story they might tackle: for example the theme of Vernon Scannell's Hide and Seek' (ws) has the right qualities; it is simple and well within their experience; it is also easy to hold in the mind so that most of the writer's attention can be devoted to describing the detail of the place and the thoughts and feelings of the main character. We are not suggesting that all children be expected to write on the same theme but that such an outline would make it clear to them the kind of thing they might attempt.

Here are some examples of writing by children of average ability:

> One day we got sent to the shop to buy some things. We had to get some sugar, some butter and some flour. We had it written down on a piece of card. Our mother gave me a ten-shilling note and we held it tightly in our hand. It was such a fine day when we went out to the shop. There were some children playing hopscotch in the street. They called me. They said, 'Come on and play, Billy.' So we went over the road to have a look. They were all having a good play and we joined in for a bit. Then we went and stopped to watch some kids playing marbles. They had some new ones with brown and green stripes in them and they let me play with them for a bit so we had a talk about it and we said we'd swap two big ones for a green one. Then we played leap frog for a bit. All of a sudden we remembered what we'd gone ou for and we'd been playing for ages and we expected mom to come looking for me any minute. Then we should be for it if she found out we'd been playing all the time. We had to run off to the shop fast. When we got into the shop it was full of customers all talking and they keep you waiting. We thought we'd never get served with all the women talking. It gets on your nerves when they all keep you waiting. We could have got served ourself if they would let me. Well in the end we got served and we put the things in the bag and we looked for our money in our hand, And it was not there. We felt in our pockets and It was not there. We started to cry a bit because we had lost it. We must have lost it when we were playing in the

street. The shop-keeper said, 'What's the matter, sonny?' and we told him we'd lost the money in the street and he said, 'Well, you'd better go and find it.' We ran all the way to where we were playing and we were crying a lot. We saw one of the big boys had got our ten shillings and we said, 'That's mine. We left it playing.' And he wouldn't give it me so we said, 'If you don't give it me we'll tell pour uncle Sam, he's a policeman. And the girl said, 'Give it him back, Roger.' After a bit he let me have it and we were so glad we couldn't stop laughing all the way back to the shop.

Billy, aged 9 C

When we were about nine we lived down by the river and there was one place where the water from the river formed a pool. Sometimes this pool was deep and sometimes it was shallow and then the sludge and the mud showed up through the water and the water got cloudy very easily. We sometimes still go and swim there is the hot weather but when we were younger we used to go there often because we lived quite close to it. One day we made a raft with two other boys. We had got part of an old shed wall with all the planks coming off it and the nails sticking out rusty. It was easy to nail all the planks down again and then we had got quite a big raft, big enough to lie down on. All we had to do then was to find a long enough pole to stick in the water. That didn't take long to find because we used our mother's prop. We sneaked it away because we knew she wouldn't miss it on a day she wasn't washing.

We got the raft afloat all right and pushed it out with the prop. There were two boys with me. Jackie Robinson and Billy Marsh. It was smashing on this raft on the pool because it was a big pool. We went right across the middle and then we got stuck in the mud. We tried to get

> off the raft and push it but we kept on sinking into the mud and we had to get back on to this raft and there was nothing we could do except wait for the pool to fill up so that we could get off again. We had to wait a long time and when we got back our mom played war with me because we'd still got her prop and it had got mud all over it. She said to me, 'If we ketch you on that pool again we'll give it to you,' she always says that.

Some children—usually those who read a great deal—will want to write a series of stories dealing with the same character or characters; others will want to write stories with several chapters. Clearly they should be encouraged to do this. But often the models they use are of the worst kind, such as those found in many comics and in the trash syndicated for children, where the lowest common denominator of response is appealed to. No great harm may be done by this, but no good is done by it since such literature fails to extend the children, and although it is reasonable that they amuse themselves at home the school ought to be an enlarging not a limiting influence. We would suggest that if an able child is writing to such models she—and it often seems to be girls who do this—should be encouraged to follow more stimulating guides such as those suggested in *Young Writers Young Readers* or those in the Puffin book list.

Further Suggestions

1. Retelling famous stories, Nothing wrong with this; it is what most authors do anyway (cf. Shakespeare).
2. Myths and legends provide a fund of material for story-retelling, e.g. Midas and the Golden Touch, Phaeton who wanted to drive the sky horses of the Sun God, Apollo, the fight between Bellerophon and the Chimera—to mention only a few of the Classical myths. Teachers whose memories of these are hazy might consult Bulfinch's *Mythology* (Mentor Books).
3. The quest is a good idea for a longer story with separate and to-be-added-later advaentures. Our hero sets out to

find his fortune, a princess, his fabulous Uncle Charlie, or all three, and on the way he meets ..... The story can be set in the legendary past or the present.

4. Just suppose .... you had a wrist-watch that told you what people were thinking, or that you could journey into the future/past, or that you could turn yourself into something else, etc., etc.
5. Tell a 'tall story' like those of Baron Munchausen (see BW, page 78).
6. Try a Science Fiction (or Science Fantasy) story, perhaps based on some film or T.V. series, e.g. you might write an episode for 'Star Trek.'
7. Familiar events: a fight, rescue of cat/dog, tyre puncture, earning money on paper round, etc.
8. Special occasions: visit to circus, farm, coach trip, ride on a horse, school trip, almost lost, etc.
9. Fantasies and magic (consider the structural implications of the Mary Poppins stories): magic scooter, hat, cupboard, etc.
10. Adventures: climbing, camping, losing the way, in a boat, fishing expedition.

Stories

Teachers will find the 'Story House' books most useful (Red, Green Blue and Yellow), edited by David Jackson and Dennis Pepper for O.U.P.; also the same editors' collections for Penguin entitled 'Story' (3 books). And for those who like to mine the rich seam of traditional stories, the books of Andrew Lang, published by Dover Books ('The Blue Fairy Book,' 'The Green Fairy Boom,' etc. — 12 books in all), will provide seemingly endless material. See also the Penguin Listening and Reading Project, Stages I and II, together with cassettes and records.

The Fight from 'There is a Happy Land,' chapter 14 *Keith Waterhouse* Penguin WS

Whitewashing the Fence, chapter 2 of 'Tom Sawyer' *Mark Twain*

A Visit to Grandpa's from 'Portrait of the Artist as a Young Dog' *Dylan Thomas* Dent WS

First Day at School from 'Cider with Rosie,' chapter 3 *Laurie Lee* Penguin

The Secret Life of Walter Mitty from 'The Thurber Carnival' *James*

10

Direct Stimulus through English

Most teachers who have attempted some exciting science experiment, such as a jet balloon, or perhaps a lesson on volcanoes using a model filled with ammonium dichromate, will have had the disconcerting feeling that the children are enthralled, not so much by the scientific implications of the experiment but by what might be called the magic. The balloon rises slowly into the air or the flame burns a sinister green and the imagination of the class begins to stir. That air has weight and can be compressed is an irrelevance when the child is steaming towards Mars. Of course, the sensitive teacher will find a way to utilise the interest so that the 'magic' enhances the science, and it is not my purpose here to enlarge on this. The point is that spectacular lessons of this kind are a very good way of providing stimulus for creative writing. We want the imagination to be aroused and there is nothing like the unusual or the unexpected to stir it. In *Free Writing* Dora Pym describes how a teacher, tried of the lack of response in English lessons, threw a knife into a desk and said to the astonished class, 'Now write!' While I would not encourage students to alienate long-suffering headmasters by disfiguring desks, I do suggest that dramatic and unexpected stimulus of this kind can be an excellent way of inducing personal and imaginative work. Because it is in the nature of a shock and tends to release all kinds of feelings and a wish to impart them, and 15 minutes silence with pencil and paper provides the children with the opportunity they need, the writing can become intensely 'real.' Shock tactics and spontaneous writing are not always desirable, of course, Sometimes the teacher will want to spend time considering suitable vocabulary, and at other times the stimulus might lead to a quite different theme (as crystal gardens might lead to a piece of writing on Under the Sea, for instance, or a picture of a Health Robinson machine might suggest designing, making and writing publicity material for their own machines).

Here are few examples.

Fire

It is curious how a match struck in a classroom immediately arouses everyone's. I suppose this is because it is something alien to the classroom situation and it becomes a little daring and exciting. This is why a lesson in intensive writing which begins with something bursting into flame is usually very successful. Sometimes just to stand silently waiting with a metal tray and crumpled newspaper is enough to get full attention and concentration. The teacher sets fire to the paper and tells them to write what they like about it. Example:

> Miss brown set fire to some paper in the classroom and it started to burn with yellow and golden flames. The flames curled and twisted like tongues of fire round the paper and the blue smoke rose up in the room. The paper crackled when the flames devoured it and flickered all over. Slowly the paper curled and changed colour to brown and then to black. At the end it just looked like a heap of black eggshells and if you touched it it cracked into a hundred pieces.

(A boy, aged 9)

This came from a class of lively children who had become used to free writing and who were ready to write without much explanation. With a different class it would be better to approach it another way. The teacher might set fire to the paper and then ask the children what they notice about it, if necessary drawing attention to its different aspects, e.g. flames, smoke, colour, shape, smell, sound.

They then might offer their own words, which the teacher writes on the board, commenting on the best and perhaps suggesting one or two of her own, e.g. *flicker, ignite, lick, conflagration, kindling.* The kind of words one offers really depends on the degree of improverishment of their vocabulary. With a class of 11-year-olds, words like *incendiary, lambent,* etc., would be seized upon by some, whereas with 7- or 8-year-olds the word *flicker* might be useful. After the vocabulary discussion the teacher might burn some more paper, asking the children to notice colour, shape and movement of the paper, flames and smoke. They then write immediately. Sometimes the initial impact can be extended, so that 'Fire' rather than 'Burning Paper' becomes the theme. The pieces given below show how the child's imagination has enlarged on the primary experience:

A fire crackles and sisels. And it is also
Bright and colourful and gay.
When a fire is nearly out it smoulders.
And when a fire is big it sometimes rores.
When a fire is really going it thres sparks all
over the place. Sometimes it starts another fire.
It is also very hot and when you
Are sat by it makes you tired.
And it looks gay when it is a good fire.

(Margaret, aged 9)

Bush Fire

Fire is powerful and destructive. It can destroy whole forests and cities and towns crushing everything in its wake. It roars and crushes and crumbles, its flames shoot up hundreds of feet into the sky, orange, yellow, purple, green, red and blue. It lashes like a whirlwind and eats up houses and people. A great monster murderer. It crackles and crunches and splinters as it comes nearer. You can

> feel it choke you in your throat and taste it in your mouth when it makes you cough and choke, spitting blood. It leaves behind a waste with black buildings, burnt trees and cinders and ashes. It has destroyed all life.
>
> *(Philip, aged 10 C)*

The second passage was written a few months after the disastrous bush fires which swept Australia and which were featured on T.V. The child saw the programme and the burning paper seems to have triggered the memory off. In this instance the television influence was beneficial; at other times it might have had the effect of inhibiting the imagination. The point is that the child's imagination was released by the simple stimulus.

While paper is the simplest thing to burn, there are other materials which provide a more startling effect, such as potassium nitrate, iron filings, magnesium ribbon and ammonium dichromate. The last item is most effective when used in a model volcano which can be made out of clay or papiermache with a tin-can core.

For the effect of a volcanic eruption it is best to add a *very* little magnesium powder (i.e. a pinch to a couple of tablespoonfuls of ammonium dichromate). Important warning! Students should try out these materials on a piece of abestos or a tin tray in the open so that they can judge the quantity and decide how best to use the idea in a classroom. Here is an example of writing arising out of this stimulus:

> There was a terrible noise when the volcano exploded. It blew the ashes into the air for miles and gigantic flames shot upward. Then over the sides of the dreaded mountain came the lava, crawling like molten fire down the sides of the volcano, slowly flowing down on to the houses and the people so that all was destroyed. The animals, plants, trees and people were all eaten up by the boiling hot terrifying fire in the lava. All were dead, the houses filled up with lava. Nothing was left.
>
> *(Michael, aged 11 C)*

If the teacher wishes to extend the volcano idea further, she might display some photographs or use marbling pictures (oil and coloured inks) as a stimulus. Here are some examples of writing begun in this way:

> One painting gives me the impression of lava. Melting hot lava. Creeping menacingly down the mountain side. Sliding into a hot lake of lava. Pulling and tugging as though it is fighting for freedom. A hot lava lake that could petrify anyone who dared to approach it. A savage lake in the middle of the earth. Hungry for violence but never getting any. Then suddenly becoming calm and clear, lonely and sad. All the colours of the rainbow blending into one deep, dark, sad, lonely lake of hot lava. Then again it becomes savage, fighting, fighting, fighting like a lion in a small grove. Space, space, space, space.

(Caryn, aged 10 C)

> The first picture looks like a great roaring red hot fire with colourful flames. The fire looks as though it is in a cave with gignatic stalactites hanging from the ceiling of the cave. The cave walls are dull yet bright brown. The cave has got a torch with leaping flames on the wall. The next picture looks like red hot lava creeping to its death. For beyond the lava is a river evaporating with the red hot feel of the lava. The lava is sliding down a hill with a bright flame leaping from it, destroying everything in its path. Burning trees, houses, people and vegetation.

(David, aged 9 C)

Further Suggestions:

The above ideas are possible starting points. Of course, they might be used during the course of some work of a thematic nature. Fire might become a topic or project extending into several other lessons, and this might give rise to work on the following lines:

1. A forest fire.
2. The Great Fire of London.
3. A visit to a blast furnace.
4. Fire in the evening in an industrial town.
5. A coal fire (things I can see in it, etc.).
6. The fiery furnace into which Shadrach, Meshach and Abednego were thrown.
7. Images of fire in the form of haiku, riddles, typographical poems, etc.
8. Stories involving or beginning with descriptions of fire.

Poems and Extracts

Schoolhouse Chimney on Fire, from 'Cider with Rosie' *Laurie Lee* Penguin

Coals *Walter de la Mare* PdM

A Fire *Bruce Middleton* PC

A Candle *girl, aged 10* EW

Bonfire *Elizabeth Stucley* BW

The Furnace *boy, aged 11* TH

Extract from 'Lord of the Flies' *William Golding* TH

WATER

The easiest way to begin a lesson using water is, I suppose, to pour water from a large jug into a bucket. Things to notice about it are the changing shape, light, movement, sound and perhaps the feel of it. The water can be coloured, or a further refinement is to have an electric light bulb or torch shining through it. Again it can be used as a direct stimulus or the writing can be preceded by discussion and vocabulary work. I suspect that many children find water one of the most difficult things to describe and some suggestions from the teacher are usually necessary. Possible words prompted or introduced by the teacher, are: clear, opaque, sheer sheen, shapeless, translucent, trickle, flow, plunge. A good deal will naturally depend upon the age of the children. Inevitably the subject arouses memories and extended ideas, for example:

The water is like a waterfall
Flinging down then slashing on the rocks.
It is a jet plunging down to crash at the bottom.
It flows smoothly like silver.
It is full of light like glass
Streaking down
Plunging down like a torrent.

(Paul, aged 10 C)

A running tap in the classroom can be used to similar effect. The tap can be left on while the children are writing:

> The water from the tap reminds me of a fast flowing waterfall with jagged rocks sticking out.
>
> A place which is in the country. There is moss and grass around a waterfall. At the bottom wild ponies are drinking from the swirling pool of water.
>
> In a place of warmness there lived a river which was just an ordinary river but it so wanted to be a waterfall. But one day men came from the village in the valley and they came with hammers and shovels and they dug away the rocks by the river and now it is a waterfall.

These are representative pieces from a class of 7-8-years-olds to whom creative writing (at any rate, writing stimulated by this kind of device) was new. It might be argued that this is not much to show for a half-hour lesson (actually they were writing for about 10 minutes) and the children would have done better to have spent the whole time writing. Well, of course, the teacher would never get a whole class of children of this age writing for half an hour, anyway. But apart from this the degree of concentration revealed in these simple pieces is at least equivalent in value to that of a page of diffuse and generalised writing. I often feel that we are inclined to develop a quantitative standard of judgement of children's work, which tends to militate against critical discrimination. The teacher has it at the back of her mind that a page or two pages is an acceptable length, provided that it is neatly written with no spelling mistakes and an absence of grammatical solecism; if it conforms to this standard then everything is all right. This may arise from the teacher's having to mark writing in which the content and language are usually pretty much the same in each case and generally dull. I do not suggest that the teacher should refrain from encouraging good handwriting, spelling and usage; rather that she should ask herself if these are the criteria she employs and to what extent they affect her judgement and attitude to the content and to the teaching of English generally. If they do have this importance, just what are the children learning from the lesson in which these criteria are goals in themselves? Those who can satisfy the requirements enjoy the commendation of the teacher and those who can't (about 75 per cent) learn a few correct spellings and develop a revulsion from, if not hatred of, the English lesson, It is the content and the child's involvement in it, not quantity, that the student should be principally concerned with.

In the extracts shown above an interesting feature is the way in which the idea of a waterfall occurs regularly. Probably the idea was inescapable if one considers the running tap which was the stimulus. But a good way to round off this lesson, or perhaps to introduce it, given a different class, would be to offer a poem about a waterfall, such as Southey's poem, 'The Cataract of Lodore' (Oxford Standard Authors):

Dividing and gliding and sliding,
And falling and brawling and sprawling,
And driving and riving and striving,
And sprinkling and twinkling and wrinkling,
And sounding and bounding and rounding,
And bubbling and troubling and doubling,

And grumbling and rumbling and tumbling,
And clattering and battering and shattering,
Retreating and beating and meeting and sheeting,
Delaying and straying and playing and spraying,
Advancing and prancing and glancing and dancing....etc.

—which is not particularly inspiring as a piece of poetry but is very useful as an exercise in simple form. The children will probably notice that as the fall gathers momentum and increases in size so the number of words on a line increases and they might like to try this for themselves in a poem rather longer than they usually write. This generally serves to add interest in form to the interest in expressing the idea (see page 158 ff and 160 ff).

An extension of the direct stimulus of the water in the classroom is writing on 'rivers,' 'pools,' 'the sea.' Here, if it is possible to arrange one, a visit is helpful. Another approach is to use the school aquarium as a stimulus. Here are some pieces written by a class aged 7-11 after a few minutes spent looking into a small aquarium:

My Favourite Fish

I have got a favourite fish, his tail is scarlet red.
He darts and is quick at the move.
I love to go near his tank and look.
His body is greyish or fawn,
I expect that you know, there are other fish in that tank.
But the red tailed one is my favourite.

(Caroline, aged 9 C)

Fish in the Tank

The fish they dart all over the place
They have gleemy silver colours.
The weeds hang as if in shame
The fish they rest now and then.

They look cheerful and happy
The place looks like the sea
And the water gleams so shiny
The colours would cheer you.

The water sends wavy ripples
They make a form of bubbles.
A Kind of weed is twiny
And the snail moves slowly.

The water looks slimy and gr[illegible]
And looks as if it shakes
It quivers and sparkles around
The weeds grow ever so tall.

There is a lot of reflections
They shimmer and move about
As if they were playing hide and seek.

(Margaret, aged 10 UC)

To one child this experience suggested a picture of the sea-bed:

> At the bottom of the ocean there are rocks and sea weed. The rocky bed is rough bumpy and lumpy. In the ocean it is dark and very slow but if there is a wave the water goes fast in the ocean and makes a rushing sound. The fishes in the ocean are red, yellow and orange. Most fishes are golden or silver. The ocean bed is slimy and green. The sea weed is like dust and is a very light green.

(John, aged 8 C)

It has already been suggested that a natural development of a lesson like this might be some writing on the theme 'Under the Sea.' This can be reinforced by direct stimulus such as looking through coloured glass (a green glass bottle will do), green cellophane, taped sound effects, music (see page 85), or, if the school has a well-equipped stage, a spotlight with rotating device can be used most effectively. Most people, however, will find the results from looking through coloured glass quite encouraging:

Under the sea the water is still
Millions of fishes dart and twist in the great caves
There are great waves and fast sharks
Under the sea.
The huge shiny octopus slides about
The rocks in and out.
Everything is quite and misty like clouds floating in a green sky
A diver can only move very slowly in the water.
He can see shells and caves and twisty seaweed
Under the sea.

(Robert, aged 10 C)

And here are two pieces written following the reading of one or two of the poems listed at the end of this section, together with tape-recorded sound effects of the sea (see page 91):

In the sea you can hear the echoing in the deep dark caves. The water is very calm and still for all the waves are far above. There are a thousand fishes darting here and there and there are lots of colours, blues and greens, coral and yellow. The sea-weed sways and tangles around the great rocks. Some places are dark and some places are light but all is calm under the sea.

(Michael, aged 10 C)

At the seaside where the sea is blue,
People bask and swime

But in the rock pools
You can see the feeble lobster ask himself
Shall I swim or shall I eat.
The coral crab is always scurrying across the sand.
Limpets suck rocks and whelks suckle their young.
A sea horse frolics in the brine
While a mackerel green and white
Sways through the weed.
Star fish sail while the small children wail.
A prawn is a small creature but it has a cousin
Who nips a bite with all his might.
Bottle green coral, red silver and blue
All make the reef.
Down in the caverns beneath
The billowing brine pearls are scattered
Hither and thither
All make the floor seem like coral.

(Markson, aged 9 UC)

Like fire, the sea is a fascinating theme because it has limitless possibilities — power, violence, calm, storms, sea-creatures, it is eternal, shapeless, etc., and most children respond very readily to its compelling qualities.

One final poem by James Stephens which precisely characterises a single powerful impression is extremely effective in opening or closing a lesson of writing about the sea:

The Main Deep

The long, rolling,
Steady-pouring,
Deep-trenched
Green billow;

The wide-topped,
Unbroken,
Green-glacid,
Slow-sliding,
Cold-flushing,
On—on—on—
Chill-rushing,
Hush-hushing,

Hushing-hushing....

The number of lessons spent on this topic is a matter for the individual teacher to decide: if the interest is really there it can be used over several lessons and, of course, can be incorporated into a project (see page 220).

Further Suggestions:

1. Diving or swimming at the baths or in the sea.
2. Submarine journey.
3. Suppose you are a river. Describe your journey to the sea.
4. You are in a rowing-boat and a storm comes up.
5. Imagine you are a deep-sea diver or a skin-diver. Describe your experiences.
6. Imagine you are a seal. Describe your activities in the water.
7. Write a story called 'Escape from the Deep.'
8. Write about the exploration of a sunken wreck.
9. Write a sequence of images or a 'shape' poem (see page 160 ff), describing a waterfall.
10. Make a tape recording of poems about water with accompanying music, either home-made or from records.

Further Suggestions for Direct Stimulus:

1. Crystal gardens. Children can make their own or if an unused aquarium tank is available the effect is more striking. Into a solution of one part water-glass to three parts water sprinkle some or all of the following crystals: copper chloride, copper sulphate, copper nitrate, lead nitrate, manganese sulphate, aluminium sulphate, ferrous sulphate, ferrous chloride, nickel sulphate, alum, cobalt chloride and cobalt nitrate. Most of these chemicals are available from a chemist and only a small quantity of each is necessary. It is not essential to use all of them.
2. Coloured inks in a large glass jar of heated water. Alternatively crystals may be used.
3. Stage smoke or vapour. This can be produced by putting dry ice into a jar of cold water or by burning glycerine.
4. Fragments of mirror stuck to a ball of clay, plaster or plasticine on to which is thrown a spotlight. This provides a ballroom effect.
5. Blowing bubbles with liquid detergent provides attractive stimulus.

Poems and Extracts

Angry River *Ruskin Bond* RSH

The Pool in the Rock *Walter de la Mare* PL, III; CDS

The Shell *James Stephens* RR, Yellow; SSV

Ghost Village by the Shore *Raymond Wilson* RR, Yellow

The Sea *James Reeves* PQ

Pacific Fish, in 'Across the Pacific' *Ian Serraillier* PQ

Full Fathom Five *Shakespeare* Two; TC, I

The Kraken *Alfred Tennyson* TWD

The World Below the Brine *Walt Whitman* JV, IV; SSV; WSP

Water Picture *May Swenson* MW, SWP

Dewdrops *John Clare* WSP

The Scullery *Laurie Lee* WSP
Spray *D.H. Lawrence* MW; TC, I
At Dunwich *Anthony Thwaite* POCO; BSH
The Sea at Night *Kevin, aged 7* BW

Note. The subject of the sea has been dealt with here rather than in a separate section in an attempt to show how it might develop out of direct stimulus. There is no reason, of course, why it could not be treated as a completely separate item using any of the foregoing material.

SPACE

The use of sounds on tape and music to suggest the sea has already been mentioned. The same techniques can also be used to evoke ideas about space. Now that space travel is a fairly common occurrence, even very young children — one sees it in the writing of infants — are avid for information about space and very easily disposed to write and draw pictures about it. The interest is ready at hand and it only needs a jerk of the imagination for all sorts of ideas and images to be generated.

When they get out of the space ship
Everything is beautiful to behold.
There are golden flowers, blue grass and happy
trees
Which bend down to give you fruit and drink.
The sun shines brighter than on earth
The air is dazzling and clear like lemonade,
And everyone is happy like the garden of Eden.
There are little animals dancing about
Lions and tigers playing with the children
And no one comes to any harm,
For everything is wonderful.

(John, aged 11 C)

Hesperian fables indeed! An interesting thing about the appeal of space fiction is that in a world where everything is explained or appears to be explainable it offers the kind of imaginative scope that the world offered geographically in the Renaissance—the world of the Anthropophagi, the enchanted isle of *The Tempest.* Consequently a lesson offering imaginative freedom, licence even where the child can indulge his fantasies usually meets with a ready response.

One way to begin is to ask the children to close their eyes and imagine they have just stepped out of a space ship on to a distant planet or into space. What to they imagine they see and hear, and what do they feel? What would they like to see? What do they imagine they would like to do? Then the teacher might play them a little music (while they have their eyes closed), for instance 'Venus' from The Planet by Holst, or perhaps a band from '2001 A Space Odyssey' or 'Out of this World' (BBC Rec. 225), or a bit of 'Sinfonia Antarctica' by Vaughan Williams: or the sounds can be made by the teacher and pre-recorded on tape (see page 91). Alternatively the teacher might use a visual stimulus, such as slides of non-representational painting, to extended the imaginative response.

Here are some examples of writing triggered off by 'home-made' sound effects:

In Space

The twinkling of the stars, the sun giving out fearful heat. The icy blasts outside and you heat streams of meteorites flying past. Then suddenly the sun is cut off from view by the moon. The moon is black and dismal. You can just see the craters which rise up from the flat surface of the moon. Then you see a lone meteorite coming at you. The meteorite is red and is burning savagely. Luckily it changes course and misses your rocket and goes soaring into space.

(Vivian, aged 9 C)

We have just got out of our rocket ship. It is suspended in space ten thousand four hundred miles away from the earth's surface. Everything is very dark all round us but we can see the planets and the earth shining like a star. We can float about in space up and down if we like but we have our jet guns with us. I close my eyes and I can hear strange noises in space. They are not like any noises on earth, they are effervescent and pop like bubbles. We think that they come from strange electrical creatures with brains made of wires and glass tubing talking to each other. We are not scared because we have our own ray guns which dissolve everything even if it is metal or stone or if it is gas. We are floating silently in space tumbling and turning very slowly. We hope that we shall be able to return to our homes.

(Paul, aged 10 C)

Further Suggestions

1. Using all your senses, describe your first walk on to the surface of an imaginary planet.
2. Remembering what it is like in the swimming baths when you try to move under water, describe your first walk in space.
3. Find out as much as you can about one of the planets in the solar system. Imagine you are Captain Scott and you are exploring this planet instead of Antarctica. What would you write in your diary?
4. Imagine that you are the first person to go right out into distant space and to return safely. What would you be thinking as you came back to earth?
5. Make up some space music and write a documentary or a reporter's account of a space journey.
6. Devise a dialogue between an astronaut and the Earth Control Unit.
7. Draw and write a comic-strip story of a space adventure.
8. You encounter an alien space ship. Write a story describing the events that took place.

9. Plan a series of adventures for a crew of space voyagers.
10. Design, draw and describe a space machine. Make one if you can.

Poems and Extracts

A plane *Stuart Sepple, aged 8* BS

Let's send a rocket *Kit Patrickson* BS

The Unending Sky *John Masefield* ILTP

Destination Jupiter *Nicholas Britten, aged 11* THW

THINGS

By 'Things' I mean objects interesting in themselves or objects which suggest other things. Usually the interest is independent of the proper function and the thing becomes interesting at the inappropriate time. I expect most people will have had the experience of looking in an untidy drawer for something and lighting on some completely irrelevant object which for a while has completely absorbed them. It is this 'day-dreaming' which children, especially, succumb to; they are fascinated by 'things.' Ask any boy to empty his pockets and you are likely to find some at least of the items in Tom Sawyer's hoard:

> He had ..... twelve marbles, part of a jew's harp, a piece of blue bottle-glass to look through, a spool cannon, a key that wouldn't unlock anything, a fragment of chalk, a glass stopper of a decanter, a tin soldier, a couple of tadpoles, six fire-crackers, a brass door knob, a dog-collar, but no dog, the handle of a knife, four pieces of orange peel, and a dilapidated old windowsash.

It so often happens that when the teacher is talking about x or y, something requring the attention of everybody, some boy at the back of the room is absorbed in contemplating a bit of useless pencil or a coloured pebble. Give a child a building set and you find him using the pieces for anything but what they were intended for. The reason is clear: the object becomes absorbing because the child's imagination has got to work on it. The pencil becomes a submarine, the tin lid a doll's bath. it is this intense imaginative involvement one would like to see channelled into writing and it is sensible to use the cause to achieve the effect. In other words let children write on those things they find absorbing.

In a boys' school a good starting point might be to ask the children to empty their pockets and write about any or all of the things in them. Most State Primary Schools are mixed and girls usually do not carry about with them the junk boys have, unless they are in the habit of bringing handbags to school, in which case they will most likely have a good deal more, but the teacher should be prepared to provide the material. Any curious, not strictly functional object can be used—the twisted root of a tree, a cankered branch, an oddly-shaped piece of stone, scrap metal, a loofah, distorted glass, anything in fact that most people consider rubbish. (Students who are in doubt should visit the art department!) A sufficiently large and unusual object can be used as a stimulus for the whole class, since they will all be able to see it plainly. Or a collection of interesting objects might be made over several days and some of these may provide 'incidental' stimulus.

A word about establishing the congenial atmosphere for writing. Some students do this quite naturally and it is, of course, a question of the extent to which the children are used to you, but I know that occasionally students get on the wrong side of a class and the whole thing degenerates into a farce. If the student is having this kind of trouble then it is likely to happen whatever kind of lesson she is doing, but obviously if she is trying something a little out of the ordinary she tends to think the idea was wrong in the first place. Of course, it may be wrong for a particular class at a particular time. It may be that the class needs encouragement to accept one particular teacher's way and time to get used to her. There are all sorts of possible classroom difficulties that affect lessons, and certainly as far as students are concerned teaching practice is an occasion when many of these difficulties should be clearly assessed if not solved. There is no universal remedy for these problems but my experience of teaching and of watching students teach suggests that a lesson goes wrong when the teacher loses the class, i.e. when a mood develops in which she is not a participant. Some teachers crush this mood by the sheer weight of authority; this has the effect of keeping the class quiet but is not exactly conducive to free expression. A good teacher, if she find herself in such a situation, should it arise, will take over this mood and make it her own until either it dissipates or it has been channelled in the direction of the lesson. This is control as compared to domination. Most students should not expect to develop this control straightway, but whatever the difficulties I think they should aim for it.

The reactions of the children will vary, of course: some will try to describe the thing itself, others will tend to pursue whatever ideas the thing suggests to them. Some examples will illustrate this and perhaps they will also serve to show differing kinds of response to the different items. The first two pieces are by children in an infant class.

Lump of Iron Ore

Our lump of iron ore is a picky [pretty] dull colour with ringkuls all over it with Black and grey and Brown and it spareculs a very lot and it Looks like a preety caresull [castle] with the grore brig [drawbridge] up and the spicks are like guns sticking out of something but I do no what it is a funny shape and it is qight lage pese of Iron ore.

(Girl, aged 7 UC)

Lump of Coal

I am a Coal Miner

I am going down the downcast shaft and down the mine I have checked my battery's and all set and reade to go down the min I have got my safety lamp the mining is open all day and all night the mine is full of coal wen the minus finished we go up the upcast shaft and then have a shaowur and go home way the other minus go to the min and wack check thya battery's too and they help us and help us the coal minus help the world.

(Nigel, aged 7 UC)

Chunk of Broken Green Glass

It is green and shining like a green diamond. You can see into it right inside. It could be a rock from the sky with electricity inside it, or little creatures made out of light small as tintacks. It could come through space at thousands of miles an hour. They would be able to see but it is so hard that nothing would be able to break it open. It would land on earth and nobody would know what it was.

(Clark, aged 9 C)

Shrivelled Gourd

This is horrible all covered with pimples and knobbles like a monster. It might come from under the sea. It is a fawn colour with patches of yellow and lines down the sides and little knobs are between the lines. It is smooth in places and it feels like a hideous skin. It is soft in parts like a toad or a frog except that a frog is slimy and this isn't. It is dry. I don't know what it is and I don't like it. It is haunting.

(Angela, aged 9 C)

Piece of Twisted Rusty Scrap Metal

Out of the dark wood
Comes a twisted evils creature
Covered by scales of rust.
He is thousands of years old
An iron creature currugated all over and flaky.
He crawled up sliding and groaning
Clanking and tinkling as he went
Tearing through the undergrowth.

He rose up out of the dark black sea
Long, long ago in the age of reptiles.
He was an outcast made of iron
Had to leave the sea
And crawl with his ugly legs
On land. He has been hiding here for
Many generations.

(Peter, aged 11 UC)

This is particularly vivid piece which displays some attempt to achieve form as well as sharp visual imagery. It may be derivative—it suggests to me the sort of idea that one sometimes comes across in children's comics, although I do not think it is any the less valuable for that. It is after all a successful attempt to convey something sharply imagined which is one of the purposes of the exercise.

Another idea which could tie up with art and craft lessons is to let the children make their own 'thing' or 'things.' With most children of junior age the word 'thing' seems to have taken on a more precise connotation than it usually has, for it can mean a special kind of object which is not clearly identifiable. Such an object can be made with wire, clay, paper or any other material, then painted with strong colours and perhaps varnished, thus using a variety of techniques and offering plenty of scope for the imagination. Here are some pieces describing such an object:

Our thing is all shapes and is black and brown and gold. It sometimes looks like a lot of boxes stuck together. It is. But it looks fearsome as well, a strange thing. It looks as if you could get in it and explore all deep passages and steps and cellars. There could be lots of rooms and dungeons.

(Alex, aged 8 C)

The great place towers up into the sky

Like a great city built in the far future.
It is a city built by the all powerful
The mighty king Kreon ruler of all the Universe.
In the palace there are beautiful rooms
Spacious and high, covered with silk and silver
There are swimming pools with scented water
And goldfish that shine in the transparent waves.
In the pool the beautiful princes Ariadne
Bathes all day with her handmaidens who comb her hair.
There are balcony winding corridors and stairs
Which reach up to the stars in the mysterious palace
Of the all powerful, the might King Kreon.

(Joan, aged 11 UC)

Poems and Extracts
A marble *Cynthia Bodley* MW
A Sea Shell *Martin Drummond, aged 8* BS
Peeling an apple *Linda Piesley, aged 12* WS
My Dad's Thumb *Michael Rosen* BW; MW
Relic *Ted Hughes* TH

SOUND
(Music, Tape-recorder, Drum)

My own experience has been that music has to be used judiciously. It may, of course, be a very effective adjunct to the movement lesson which can be successfully linked to writing. Although music can be used by some students to encourage good writing, I think it is better to delay using it until the teacher knows the class well and the children have become used to a free approach. Having said that, I must now qualify it by saying that sometimes a class which has been used to a severely formal approach may respond very well indeed to the novelty of writing in response to music. Probably it is wiser, if the class is inexperienced, to ask them to listen to the music, to consider what it suggests to them and how it makes them feel; then, after playing a little of it (two or three minutes), the children make their own suggestions before writing. If this is not done, the less responsive children may find themselves left high and dry with no idea of what to write. If it has been generally well received the teacher might play another extract, this time allowing the children to write without discussion, or this might be left for a later date, the teacher referring back to this particular lesson. Sometimes it is enough to play the music and let the children respond in their own way orally with no intention to write.

Here are some examples of children's work. The first comes from an infant class taken by a student, who had played them an extract from 'Mars' from Holst's 'Planets' Suite.

Knights in Armour

In 1991 the english and the french went to wore they did not yous guns they had sords and lances it was horbele people got woondid and pepale got killed and they were left to rot, they were on horse back and some of them were on the ground and then the french ran out of amunishan and so the english wune the wore and so they all went home and they all got marid.

(John, aged 7 UC)

I am in a dark passage and I'm running. There is no way out as I go deeperin to the passage it gets darker and darker. I am now coming to lightness but I still cannot get out because it is only a small window on a mountain top. If I could get out I would not have survived on the steep cliffs. It's all like a dream, but not one at all it is definately true. Then I come to a door. I open it and there is another passage I keep on running then I come to another door. It opens and I am at the bottom of the cliffs. This is all a mystery to me.

(Michael, aged 9 UC)

We must hope the mystery was in the vision, not in the lesson. I have found that the music most likely to induce concentration is that which avoids regular rhythms and classical patterns in theme if not in harmony. What might be called 'mood' music seems to make the greater impact since it tends to be more evocative.* If a hall is available, it is a good idea to try out some of the music on the children where they can move freely to it first. This is especially worthwhile if the music being used is insistently rhythmical, as is 'In the Hall of the Mountain King' from Grieg's Peer Gynt Suite, which is evocative but is also irresistibly motivating. Here are some examples of children's writing inspired by extracts from the following works:

FIREBIRD SUITE — STRAVINSKY

The Sea

The sea is a wild force
Crashing over the rocks
Shattering water into a million fragments.
It runs a wild race to the shore
Hurling itself against the cliffs
Tormenting the sand and shingle,
Pounding like thunder on the mountains
Striking like rain in the shattering fountains.
The sea is like a wild race of bulls
When they thunder through the streets
Scattering the screaming people
Knocking down weak houses
Destroying the town in a wild anger,
The sea is terrible to behold.

(Stephen, aged II C)

This piece, incidentally, brings up the question of sustained metaphor (see page 151 ff.). This boy has, quite naturally and successfully, worked his poem out in terms of two metaphors, the sea as a force and the sea as a heard of wild bulls. This device is something that can be explained and deliberately used by older children. And it is better if this explanation is offered incidentally, and better still if it can arise out of a child's contribution such as the one given above. Then, if there is time, the children can be asked to try out a short exercise themselves, say describing a flood in terms of lava running down the sides of a volcano, or a fire in terms of a hungry beast cating everything in its way.

PACIFIC 231—HONEGGER

The Train

The train lets out its steam
From the engine in a screaming blast
Slowly the great iron wheels begin to move
The pistons force out the energy
For the powerful train
Still slowly moving forward
Like a strong man gathering up his strength
For a famous task.
The iron giant moves forwards,
Faster and faster the wheels turn
Round and round again and again
Along the shining steel rails
Eating up the miles,
Faster and faster it tears into the country
Nothing can stop the powerful train now
So fast is it going through mountains
Through valleys, past farms and villages,
Eating up the miles
Faster and faster
Always faster

Nothing can stop
The train.

(Stuart, aged 10 UC)

En Saga — Sibelius

The low fog and mist was all around us the fog horn was blowing and the ships engine was quiet and only the ripple of the water and the fog horn could be heard. Then suddenly out of the fog came a ship then it hit us the ships were sinking fast all the men were jumping I clung on to the debry and I sink slowly under the sea.

(Ian, aged 10 UC)

Record of a Drum Beating Ominously, then Violently

In the jungle it is wild
The trees are big and gnarled,
Twisting creepers are all round the trees
It is very hot and makes your skin crawl
It is dangerous and fearsome and wild
You can hear strange noises of the animals
Groaning, roaring and trumpeting
And then you hear the drum which
Goes through your head, louder and louder
Frighteningly. Then you start to run and run
Fal down and everything is dark.
Then you wake up in bed,
You know you dreamed it all.

(John, aged 9 C)

Further Suggestions:

Almost any music could be used and teachers will probably have items of their own which will provide good stimulus. The following are fairly generally available in libraries and Education Departments:

Daphnis and Chloe *Ravel*
Pictures at an Exhibition *Mussorgsky*
Night on a Bare Mountain *Mussorgsky*
Grand Canyon Suite *Aaron Copeland*
Cranival of Animals *Saint-Saens*
The Leminkinan Legend *Sibelius*
La Mer *Debussy*
The Moldau *Smetana*
Pavane from Capriol Suite *Warlock*
Four Sea Pictures *Britten*
Sorm from 'The Tempest' *Sibelius*
Hary Janos *Zoltan Kodaly*
En Troika *Tschaikovsky*
Opening of 'The Creation' *Haydn*
Danse Macabre *Saint — Saens*
The Firebird Suite *Stravinsky*
Les Jeux d'Eaux a la Villa d'Este *Liszt*
L'Apres-midi d'un faune *Debussy*
Overture to 'The Mastersingers' *Wagner*
Peer Gynt Suite *Grieg*

1. Using recorders, piano, xylophones, cymbals, triangles and any other instruments, make up some music for the sea, or the sky, or the forest, or the city, and write some accompanying poems.
2. Listen to some music and paint a picture suggested by it. Then write some images, or stories or descriptions to go with the paintings.
3. Make up a story in sound effects only, without words. Each group devises a 'tape' story and tries it out on the rest of the class.
4. Using sound effects and words, do a tape-recorded documentary with the title 'A Day in School' or 'A School Outing.'

5. Retell a fairy story on tape, using made-up music, perhaps on a pentatonic scale. (See *An Introduction to Words and Music* Lawrence and Montgomery.)
6. Make up a story about instruments in a music shop.

Tape Recorders

Apart from using the recorder for children's voices reading their own work and so on, there are numerous other uses in connection with children's writing that are worth commenting on. One obvious use is the recording of relevant bits of music, which avoids the necessity of wasting time trying to find the right place on a record and perhaps scratching it in the process. But possibly the most interesting application is the use of the machine to create evocative sounds. A little experimentation will suggest all sorts of possibilities but for the benefit of those to whom this is new I shall list a few ideas below:

1. Crushing paper, cellophane, straw, cooking foil can sound like a fire, ice breaking up, an avalanche, buildings crumbling. If this is recorded fast and played back slow, the effect is more striking.
2. Blowing, whistling or humming softly across the microphone can produce the sound of wind, sea, rain, and, if the speed is varied, this can evoke the idea of wild desert or waste landscapes.
3. Tapping something near the microphone or the microphone itself, or moving it about on a wooden surface, can, if the speed is altered, produce uncanny and ominous noises which can sound like echoes in a cave or in the mountains.
4. Blowing across the top of a bottle or metal tube (e.g. that attached to a vacuum cleaner) sounds like wind in a tunnel or, when the speed is altered, like the distant fog horn of a ship.
5. Shaking a sheet of metal is the age-old way of making thunder of course, but a large sheet of cardboard can

produce the same effect when the volume is turned right up.

6. A large glass beaker or the lower notes of a piano can sound like bells ringing in the distance, or to take a suggestion from Debussy's 'La Cathedrale Engloutie,' bells under the sea.
7. And, of course, there is no end to the possibilities of distorting the human voice. If the reader is not averse to her family or colleagues thinking that she has gone completely out of her mind, she can, by playing around with the speed, produce sounds of trains ploughing over ravines, primeval monsters wallowing in fathomless swamps, or ghosts cavorting in wild mountain valleys at midnight. Whatever the sound required, there is some way of making it on a tape recorder and all it needs is a little ingenuity—and a thick skin.

Here are some pieces by children stimulated by sounds from a tape recorder:

> It sounds liek the ski is faling down on the erth and everythink is been distride and all the people was cild wen the stars fel doun on them. The was an orful thndering crash liek roks and mowntins braking open in shatrng peeces. Then the giunts came in with grate big boots crunshing the roks and howsis but all the peepole got away and the giunts chast them til they got out of breth and fel in the see. The story ends when they got drowndid.

(Nick, aged 7 UC)

I thought I heard the wind
It sounded pretty fierce
Slashing itself over the waves at sea.
I thought I heard the waves breaking themselves on the beaches.

In a gale like this I should think there are no people
on the beach
But as the gale went on nothing moved.
Under the sea it is so quiet.
Turtles, jelly fish, star fish are under the sea.
There are wrecks.
But nothing is moved by the gale
Only the little fish that swim about are on the move.

(Janette, aged 9 C)

The sound is of a thousand animals pounding across the plain burnt by the African sun. Something has frightened them. What can it be? The unheard of noise of aeroplane engines or the sharp crack of a hunter's rifle or the terrible noise of a forest fire which scares the noble animals to run for there very lives.

Some dreadful event has made that young zebra run to his mother's side and she knows that death is lurking not far away as she begins to make a run for it. Soon the other in the herd sense the common fear and they all move forward into deafening stampede which churns up the dusty earth from the sandy desert plain into huge clouds. Then the birds feel the fear and take wing into the burning blue sky. Little wings are fluttering anxiously and great wings of flamingoes and storks beat steadily lifting them into the dusty air. It is their only escape. Soon the birds give warning to the giraffe, the deer, the leopard and the hyena. The elephants will hear the warning too and charge in a mad fear without knowing what it is.

Everywhere is alive with animals on the move away from the terrible danger threatening them. There is only one animal who stays undisturbed by all the commotion. He lies there by the drinking pool sunning himself. He is the lion, king of beasts whom no noise can make afraid.

Apart from music there are now available records of sound

effect which are excellent for the stimulus of free writing. The BBC produce numerous LPs and also, in many cases, there are cassette versions. See particularly:

Radiophonic Workshop REC 196
Dr. Who REC 316 (Cassette ZCM 316)
Out of this World REC 225 (Cassette MRMC 040

and, for those disposed to the macabre:

Death and Horror REC 269 (Cassette ZCM 269)

See also Voices Records Argo PLP 1112-7.

PICTURES

As with sound, visual stimulus can be used as a development of the sense exploration dealt with earlier in this book or it can be used as an end in itself; that is, the class can be encouraged to notice shape,colour, pattern, texture, or they may be allowed to write freely as their imagination directs. Any pictures could be used but it seems that the less naturalistic the painting, the freer the writing is as a rule — short of completely abstract painting which often seems limiting. The paintings I have found most successful are those which have surrealist qualities or which tend to employ symbols or evoke a certain mood, such as the work of Max Ernst, Georges Braque, Umberto Boccioni, Picasso. The problem here is getting hold of prints large enough for everyone to see, since postcard reproductions have little impact. Occasionally, large prints may be borrowed from libraries separately mounted or in large art books. One way out of the dilemma is to use film strips or slides. These do offer a very striking impression of the painting and the moment of unveiling, so to speak, can be quite dramatic, especially if the room can be darkened. Magazines are a source of material of course and the children will sometimes bring alone useful pictures. Other sources are advertising and travel agencies who put out quite lavish material which is sometimes appropriate.

The simplest way to introduce a lesson with pictures is to tell the class they are going to see a picture and that they may then write anything they like about it: what it looks like, what it suggests to them, how they feel about it, any story it suggests. When they are all ready, the picture is displayed or projected on to the screen and they write as soon as they are ready. I think it is best to leave the picture on view while they are writing. Here are some examples. (The title of the picture was not given to the children until they had finished writing. The reason for this is that the title would sometimes be inhibiting and sometimes simply confusing).

Houses and Light — Luigi Russolo

I was in a dark tunnel
And I felt very lonely
because there were spooky colours
it was very cold and frozen.
And I felt very frightened and it was arch shapes
and it felt all soft and sogy.
I felt as if I was floating on water
and everywhere I looked
there was crustals and cobwebs.

(Julie, aged 7 UC)

The Force of the Street — Boccioni

The picture reminds me of a planet far out in space where everything is cold unless you have a space suit. When the bright stars shine down everything on the planet reflects the light so that there is intense heat in some of the rocks. It is unbearable when the light comes tearing out at you like lightening.It can be very calm or very violent on the planet called Isolar...

(Geoffrey, aged 10 C)

Nature at Daybreak — Max Ernst

There is a mysterious and hideous place
Entangled with twisted thorns and crawling vines.
No man can escape there for
It is a place of horror and death
Where long slimy and writhing slithery
Fantastic creatures move like prehistoric dinosaurs
From a dead world.
If you stand very still
You can hear the thick leaves growing
They grow so fast
There is no hope for a living creature who stands still.
You must move away into the light and air
Then you can breathe freely once more.

PICTURE OF THREE COWBOYS — (TAKEN FROM AN ADVERTISEMENT)

Tex

Tex looked out across the plain into the distance. His eyes strained through the hot sunshine shimmering the distance, but he could see a little cloud of dust. That is horses he said to himself, that dust. He couldn't hear any sound but he could see that little cloud moving slowly in his direction and he knew it would be the men after him. He wiped the sweat from his forehead and flicked it onto the rock he was learning on, then he pushed his hat back on his head and rested his hand on his gun, his trusty old forty-four. He felt the notches with his thumb and then the old leather of his holster tied up to his leg. I am ready if they come he said as he looked at the dust.

They felt the horses sweating under them as they galloped across the plain to the mountain. There was dust everywhere so they wore their neckerchieves up but it didn't stop the dust getting into their mouths. They spurred the horses on faster towards the rocks. One by one they took out their irons.

(Gary, aged 11 UC)

Suggestions for Pictures

Students will probably have their own preferences for certain pictures. The following happened to be available in slide form and were discovered to be useful:

Cabin in the Alps *Kirchner*

Spring in Flanders *Heckel*

Les Amis d'Alice *Ernst*

A Forest *Schmitt Rotluff*

Thorn Heads *Sutherland*

Catalan Landscape, The Hunter *Miro*

Elasticity, Dynamism of a Cyclist *Umberto Boccioni*

The Gare St. Lazare, Soleil Levant, Houses of Parliament, Water Lilies *Monet*

The White Edge, On White *Kandinsky*

Filmstrips and slides are often available from Education Committees. Otherwise they may be obtained from the following:

BBC (Radio Vision) Portland Place, London W.I.

Educational Productions Ltd. East Ardsley, Wakefield, Yorkshire.

Miniature Gallery, 2 Birds' Hill Rise, Oxshot, Surrey.

Visual Publication Ltd., 197 Kensington High Street, London W. 8.

UNESCO Slides for Art Teaching Aids.

Images (slide set) Oxford University Press (there is also a teachers' book).

Many of the more recent anthologies contain excellent visual stimulus — see, for instance, Junior Voices (Penguin), Passwords (Oliver and Boyd), Wordscapes, etc. (Oxford), English Project *Stage One* (Ward Lock).

Poems & Extracts

The Chinese Queen, *Julia, aged 10* WSP.

A blob of ink *Melvyn Broderick, aged 11* YI, I.

Tutankhamun *Jonathan Duncan Reynolds, aged 9* WSP.

11

Training of Senses

Allo human beings have five senses through which we gain our knowledge of the external world (setting aside questions of revealed and mystical knowledge, extrasensory perception, etc.). The more sharply these senses are developed, the more we are likely to take in and so the more we have to think, write and talk about. It seems reasonable therefore, to devise patterns of work which will encourage the children to become more aware of their separate senses and the experience they receive through them. Of course, some children have sense defects and the teachers has to make allowance for this and use natural and professional understanding and ingenuity to overcome it. Students will, one hopes, develop these faculties, and practising teachers will realise that this is a matter of experience and the 'tricks of the trade.' Also, without venturing into the complex question of intelligence, children do differ in general ability and this will affect their sensory awareness. Hence, as any teacher knows, one ought not to expect the same sort of response from every child, although teaching classes of 40 and over sometimes makes teachers wish that this were possible.

Sight

One might begin by discussing the five senses—what they are, which they use most, which they enjoy most, etc. The teacher then brings the discussion around to sight. The way in which this is done is clearly a matter for the individual teacher but the children might be asked to say what they can see in the classroom or through the window: then, if convenient, the class might go outside into the playground and 'see' as many things as possible, trying to ignore sounds etc. (though, of course, they won't do this entirely). When they return the teacher asks them to write down in any way they like what they have seen. With some this will simply result in a list, for example:

> I can see the railings
> I can see the trees
> I can see the walls
> I can see the white markings on the playground
> I can see some bicycles and a car
> I can see windows.

(7-year-old C)

Some teachers and students get depressed by writing such as this. The thing to remember is that this may be regarded as a point of departure, but also that a list of impressions is a viable 'from' in itself. This, with the discussion, might perhaps take half an hour (e.g. 10 minutes discussion, 10 minutes in the playground, 10 minutes writing) or longer. The teacher should not be over-concerned about time; it is more important to let the lesson develop naturally.

The next stage is to narrow the concentration down to one item in the list of things seen, e.g. the trees. The teacher perhaps says, 'How many things can you notice about the trees?' They then go out into the playground and look:

> I noticed the leaves resulting, jogging up and down and the twigs scraping against each other. The leaves were all wet and some were shining. The tree was very big and it had a thick bark and deep cuts in it, this was the bark. It looked like a giant with big feet, it had thick roots in the earth.

(8-year-old C)

One might go further with this concentrating on some aspect of the tree, say the branches or trunk. They are still concerned with what they can see but other senses are bound to come into play in their descriptions and should not be excluded, since we often have to describe one sensory impression in terms of another. Here is an example from a fairly bright child:

> Some branches reached up into the sky and some drooped down as if they were sad. They started thick and rough but when they went further out into the air they were petering and small. You could hear them moving through the air some were very heavy and groaning, some were wisking the leaves about lashing them at each other wildly. They were tormenting each other.
>
> *(10-year-old UC)*

The fact that the child has used a word like 'petering' in a way not normally acceptable to an adult seems to me of less importance than the fact that he has conveyed very clearly the idea of the branches appearing to diminish in size. Also the involvement and concentration which are prerequisites of good writing are clearly evident.

The teacher might ask the children to make lists (or offer suggestions for a board list) of words which describe how things look—their shape, colour, size, texture, etc. This may be done in the classroom in terms of the objects within the classroom, or outside if the teacher prefers it. The children read out their words and the teacher leads the class in a discussion of the particular qualities of those words, 'dramatising' them to bring out these qualities, while ensuring that some words from the most intellectually improverished child are 'performed.' Here is one 9-year-old's lists:

oblong	fawn	great	rough
cornered	pale yellow	small	smooth
round	like sea	huge	gentle
rounded	grey green	gigantic	soft
shaped	sunshiny	bigness	delicate
edge		like a tower	cutted

·folded	towering	craggy scratching thick

These words were offered under the categories suggested above but there is nothing special about such categories; any would do. In the list words like 'soft' and 'craggy' can be contrasted in sound as well as meaning (think of the way one can pronounce these words to emphasise this contrast). The teacher may then write interesting words on the board—an opportunity for enforcing the correct spelling and for lending words the prestige and dignity conferred by publication on the blackboard. After the lesson or at the end of it these highly-prized words may be copied into a book for class use or into individual word books ('Our Best Words,' etc.). The committed interest of the teacher in the words and expressions the children offer is absolutely vital if their enthusiasm in searching for words is to be stimulated and maintained. The creative writing lesson, as can be seen from this, is a lesson in which the teacher is actively participating. Students usually want to know how long all this takes: that is, how many lessons are to be devoted to this particular theme. So much depends upon the class and the teacher and the amount of time available. If the work is going very well, the children are interested and the time-table is flexible, one might go through all the stages at one time. Otherwise two or three lessons might be spent on Vision, perhaps in the same week.

A further extension of this particular theme might arise as a result of a visit, or perhaps an optional assignment. The teacher might suggest that the children who are able to go into the market on a Saturday morning take notice of the sights to be seen and then write about them. There is nothing like first-hand experience, of course, but the next best thing is imagination. If the interest is maintained the teacher might give the children 15 minutes in which to write on a theme of their own choice, e.g. Things to See at the Fair, In the Market, At the Railway Station, The Circus, Farm, By the River, according to the locality of the school and the environment of the children. All-important, we need hardly say, is the discussion which precedes this, and particularly that which centres on the most striking and evocative words.

Here are two examples of children's work which emerged from the situation described above:

The Station

This old railway station is usually very quiet when you go there in the week. It is very draughty if you stand on the pavement alone, waiting to get the numbers and you can feel solitary looking down the deserted lines which disappear together into the distance. But if you go there on a Saturday then things are very different. Everything seems to be going on at once. Trains are coming in spurting out steam, people are rushing about chattering, the porters are charging about with their trolleys, they are hauling the luggage and carrying the parcels dodging and weaving in and out fo the passengers and clumsy packages. Everything is bustle and jostle on a Saturday at the station, but go there on Sunday and all is stillness, silence and nothing. The station is taking its weekly rest.

(Neil, aged 10 VC)

In the wood everything is still
And I move silently along the ground
All covered with leaves
And with pine needles. It is dark,
But not too dark to see the shapes of huge giants,
The trees who stand as though they are dead
As if they have been dead for years.
Then comes the sunlight and lightens up all the wood.
There are great beams of gold
All shooting through the trees,
These are angry shapes, dark in the wood
Who hate the sunlight.

(Alan, aged 10 VC)

One peculiarly attractive feature of this poem is the imaginative way in which the child has seen the trees; not just as shapes, but as 'angry' shapes. In other words he has invested them with human attributes—a degree of anthropomorphism we find quite striking in a child of 10,and worth comment in a discussion.

We think it is always a good thing, if there is time available, to wind up a lesson of this sort by reading a poem or a bit of prose which exhibits the kind of technique or theme the children have been using. For example:

Stocking **and** Shirt *James Reeves* PQ
Grey *James Reeves* MGR; WS
The Term *W. Carlos Williams* H; WS
Silver *Walter de la Mare* OB, III; ILTP
What is White? *Mary O'Neil* WS
The Painting *Oscar Wilde* OB, II
After Rain *Helen Waddell* OB, II
Bessey the Kilkmaid *John Clare* OB, II
The Balloons *Oscar Wilde* OB, IV; YI, I
Shadows *Patricia Hubbell* JV, I
Full moon; Summer Night (Haiku) TC,I
The Paint Box *E.V. Rieu* ILTP
The Arrival *John Walsh* MW

Gerard Manley Hopkins is a poet whose use of the precise and evocative word makes him especially interesting in the context of sensory but, of course, most of his poetry is beyond the reach of children of Primary age. "Pied Beauty', however, with some discussion is generally accessible and after a lesson which has been concerned with looking hard at things it usually makes a clear impact.:

Glory be to Got for dappled things—
  For skies of couple-colour as a brinded cow;
    For rose-moles all in stipple upon trout that swim;
Fresh-firecoal chestnut-falls; finches' wings;

Landscape plotted and pierced—fold, fallow, and plough;
And all trades, their gear and tackle and trim.

All things, counter, original, spare, strange;
Whatever is fickle, frekled (who knows how?)
With swift, slow; sweet, sour; adazzle, dim;
He fathers-forth whose beauty is past change:
Praise him.

(TWD)

The curious thing about this is that it seems to present difficulties to adults which do not exist for children. A student sometimes finds it hard to accept, say, the colours in an evening sky as looking like the pattern of colours on a cow, whereas country children, at least, just take it naturally. This may be largely due to a kind of sophistication on the part of the adult. It is the sophistication of abandoning the 'passion' of life for its 'prose' (to use E.M. Foster's terms), which comes with the movement through adolescence into maturity, where poetry is a questionable indulgence. This is an attitude students ought to reassess when they begin to teach. Perhaps this is a good place to make the point that as teachers we are often rather conservative about the kind of poetry children can understand and enjoy. We tend to have an idea of poetry suitable for juniors which is perhaps formed from such an anthology as *The Book of a Thousand Poems.* Apart from the fact that there are now many excellent anthologies for the Primary School-listed at the end of this book and on which we have drawn very heavily—we can find plenty of usable poems in adult anthologies.

Sound

In some ways, sound is easier to deal with than vision because the teacher can produce it and thereby direct attention to it. But in the first instance the children should be made aware of the sound about them—in the classroom, corridor, playground. Concentration is, of course, essential and here one can ask them to close their eyes and listen to whatever sounds there are. It is most unlikely that there will be complete silence but if by some strange chance this should happen the teacher will have to provide what is necessary. Four or five entirely different sounds are enough to begin with, say, coughing, shuffling across the room, closing the door, scratching of pen on paper, etc.; in other words the ordinary everyday sounds which may or may not have impinged upon the childrens senses. After a brief discussion about what the sounds were and, how they differed, the children might go out into the playground, stand for a couple of minutes with eyes closed and then return to the classroom to record what they have heard. Again the lists of items will probably be common:

In the playground
I heard a bird singing,
The leaves rustling.
A man whistling,
And a dog barking.
It was cold out there,
and the people were shivering.
There were people talking
and people walking.
Out in the playground.

(Wendy, aged 10 UC)

But if one looks at even this simple piece objectively, one can't help but feel that this is something more than a list. The child has arranged the thing in lines like a poem, not a piece of prose, and the very arrangement gives emphasis to her ideas. Here is another piece which displays a rudimentry sense of form and more personal involvement:

The trees shivered as the wind went through them
the birds sang in happiness on top of them
At the bottom of the playground
The birds pecked
In happiness.

A dog barked
The birds flew
A man whistled
In happiness.

(Angela, aged 10 UC)

Another child concentrates more specifically on the variety of sound:

> The leaves are resulting themselves in the trees and the trees are moving, groaning heavy sound. The twigs are crackling snapping and spluttering. They crackle and pop when you crunch them with your foot. The children scuffle and shuffle across the playground. They kick stones with a scrubbing sound. You can hear an engine in the lane wining wizzing down the bank. We can hear the childrens voices talking. They sometimes make the birds twitter but the chattering birds have gone away to day. It is winter. There is silence.

(John, aged 9 UC)

At this point a tape recorder comes in handy. The children can make sounds themselves which are recorded on the tape, or the teacher can, of course, select and pre-record sounds. Anything can be used to produce sound, provided the result in sufficiently varied; in addition, unusual effects can be produced by recording at fast speeds and playing back at slow speeds (see section on Direct Stimulus, p. 90 off.). The purpose is to get the children to listen to the tape and then write down a list of words and expressions, including similes (one need not use this term; it is enough to say, 'Like a ...?) The children read out their lists and the teacher comments on the particular qualities of as many as possible or reasonable, writing the most interesting or evocative on the board. These are then copied into their book or books.

All of this may take one or two lessons, but after the vocabulary work it is a good time to introduce some poems which exemplify what they have been doing and which are simply enjoyable in themselves, for example Clare's Pleasant Sounds' (ws). It is also a good idea to read out the work of other children of the same age. This can work as a marvellous incentive provided, naturally, the teacher does not imply unfavourable comparison with their own efforts.

The next stage is to give the children an opportunity to put the skills they have been developing into practice. Subjects such as Sounds at the Fair, Sounds in the Kitchen, At the Railway Station, may be attempted. As always with this kind of work, first-hand experience is ideal, and if the writing can follow an actual visit so much the better. However, it is not always possible to have a visit just when you want it and writing from imagination and memory is better than no writing at all. Certainly the subjects we have suggested are all easily within the child's experience. The following examples will perhaps illustrate. Before writing the children were primed pretty thoroughly; that is to say, there was vigorous discussion about the sounds one might hear at the fair and in the kitchen. Care must be taken not to tell the children what they might hear. The ideas have to come from them. This is a trap many students fall into. We suggest they ask such questions as 'Well, what things *are* there in a kitchen that would be likely to make noise? What do you do in a kitchen? If your mother was in the kitchen at breakfast/dinner/tea time and you were standing outside with your eyes closed what would you hear?' And so forth. The idea is to place the children there in imagination and prod their imagination into doing the work. After the digression here are the pieces:

Sounds at the Fair

Millions of sounds at the fair, Engines and machines roar and wirr, clanging and hissing. The steam sizzles. The music roars and pour on the people talking, singing, shouting, laughing. Rifles crack and ping at little pipes. The men shout come and have a go at the coconuts, She at them, Clack they go bouncing off into the tent. On the dogem cars they have poles that run along the net and scrap and flicker and crackle off sparks. The cars bump and thud at each other, they look like big boots kicking each other. Noises, noises all round deafining our ears.

(Janet, aged 9 UC)

In Kitchen

In the kitchen the washing machine hums and drums, the spindrier wizzes, it wisles in our ears and our dad says it drives him mad its so loud it ort be mended. When our mom is getting the tea you can hear the cups and sorcers clater clatering. You can hear it anywhere all over the house. In the Kitchen we can hear the knives spoons forks in the draw dashing about and clanging as well. Sometimes you can hear water glugging down the drain in the sink as it sloshes down.

(Tony, aged 8 UC)

I would suggest that the degree of concentration exhibited in these pieces, the quality of observation and the precise yet flexible use of language are equal to if not in excess of, the same features as they might be found in much longer composition. Not that we would wish to discourage longer work from those children who can sustain it. With a class of lively children one sometimes find that having been allowed to exercise their skills over a wide range of ideas they enjoy being given a single simple idea to worry at, for instance the sound of a clock ticking, the wind blowing through the trees, a fly in a room. Anthony Thwaite has a very good poem about this last idea in *The Owl in the Tree* (O.U.P.) Here are the first two stanzas:

The Fly

The fly's sick whining buzz
Appals me as I sit
Alone and quietly,
Reading and hearing it
Banging against the pane,
Bruised, falling, then again
Starting its lariat tour

Round and round my head
Ceiling to wall to floor.

But I equip myself
To send him on his way,
Newspaper clutched in hand
Vigilant,since he may
Settle, shut off his shriek
And lie there mild and weak
Who thirty seconds ago
Drove air and ears mad
With shunting to and fro.

And here is an 11-year-old's effort on the same theme:

I sometimes lie reading my books in bed
Where it is very quiet,
There I can concentrate in the silence.
Then the idiot moth blunders in.
He thumps against the light fluttering his wings.
Round and round he goes, swinging, and thumping,
Banging and stuttering into the light bulb.
He must be stupid to keep bashing himself at the bulb.
It takes my mind of my books and I can not concentrate.
All I can think of is the noise of this moth
Fluttering, whirring, swizzing, flickering,
Until I get out of bed and throw something.
That stops him. It is a shame really.

(Maurice, aged 11 UÇ)

Although there is here clearly some imitation of Thwaite's poem (not that this matters—we learn by imitation anyway), the piece we think, vividly conjures up a very real experience. The child has made the idea his own and has recreated in his own words the sounds and the feeling of the moment.

Further Suggestions

1. Different kinds of noise or sound, perhaps recorded on tape: sharp, echoing, soft, loud, scuffling, scraping, muffled, etc. Special sounds might be included, e.g. drum, recorder, triangle. Children makes lists of words, with plenty of discussion, including the effect certain noises have on one, i.e. frightening, saddening, joyful, elevating, etc.
2. Noises at home: pots and pans banging, children calling, cat purring, dog barking, sausages frying, water being poured into a jug or kettle, doors squeaking.
3. Noises we can hear in the classroom or in the playground.
4. The Village Green; A Street in the Town; The Factory; The Swimming Baths; Noises at Night; Noises at the Seaside; Noises in the Park; Space Sounds; Sounds Under the Sea; Sounds We Don't like/Do Like.
5. At the railway station, fair, street, noises at night, etc. Use of tape recorder to evoke ideas about sounds in outer space, under the sea, in a jungle.

Poems and Extracts

Village Sounds *James Reeves* PQ

Bells *James Reeves* BP, IV

The Shell *James Stephens* RR, Yello; YI, I; SSV; TC, I

Sounds in the Night *Coventry Patmore* OB, II

Extract from 'The Pied Piper' (II.196-206) *Robert Browning* BP, III

Engineers *Jimmy Garthwaite* FBNV; BS

The Train *J. Redwood Anderson* PI, IV

At the Baths *girl, aged* 11 EW

Sounds of the Night *girl, aged* 9 EW

Tom Sawyer *Mark Twain* (Beginning of chapter 9)

The Washing Machine *Jeffrey Davies* MW

Gravel Paths *Patricia Hubbell* JV,II

Noise *J. Pope* POCO

Spring Morning *Dylan Thomas* WS

Touch

The other three senses are less easily treated than the first two but that is no reason for neglecting them. The impressions from these senses can be as powerful as the experience from the others and there is perhaps an even greater need to give practice in finding suitable modes of expression.

A simple way to begin is to allow the children to go out into the playground and find, say, a dozen different textures, emphasising that they must be as different as possible. They could do the same thing in the classroom. They make lists and then attempt to find suitable words with which the describe these textures. Here is an example:

The playground was rough and knobbly but it had little smooth stones in it. The dustbin is smooth and it has a dusty feeling to it. John's hair was sticky and oily and smooth. By the tree it is wet and slimy and a bit squelchy. The bricks were very hard and rough and sharp and a bit prickly. The grass was soft and a bit prickly. Shoes are smooth and leathery. Our blouse is soft and delicate like silk. It is not silk it is cotton.

Smooth as silk.
Rough as a brick.
Thick as iron.
Squelchy as mud.
Knobbly as a tree.

(Susan, aged 9 C)

The five similes which conclude this piece were volunteered by the child from her own experience in the playground and, therefore, have some real significance for her in a way in which the sort of substitution exercise one frequently encounters in text books does not.

After discussing the peculiar effectiveness of the worlds and similes offered, the teacher might then suggest a few, e.g. coarse, hairy, plush, sleek, gnarled, oleaginous (an oddity has curiosity value), sharp, cold, tepid, tingling, etc. It will be noticed that in an attempt to describe texture one tends to use words appropriate to the thing itself (coarse, etc.) and also words which describe the sensation (tingling, etc.). It is possible with some classes to emphasise this distinction and turn it to good effect, while it will only confuse other children. Nevertheless, it is useful for the teacher to remember it since it might open up other avenues for work and it certainly helps if you are trying to think up words of a precisely descriptive kind. Further, in this topic, and also in Taste and Smell, more time should be devoted to discussing words, since most children tend to find greater difficulty in describing experience related to them than the other two. One way to improve the situation is for the teacher and children to bring to school items of textural interest. We are thinking of materials such as velvet, silk, cotton-wool, sacking, fur, sandpaper, coke, metal, cork, foil, rubber, water, oil, sand. The object is to identify as many as possible and to find words and images appropriate to describing them. This can begin as a game with children blindfolded. Here are some descriptions taken from the work of several children following the above exercise:

The velvet is smooth as a flower.

Silk like tinsel.

Jagged, ragged, scrapey, scrunchy, spiky is the coke.

The oil is sloppy and slippery and greasely and smooth.

Cotton wool smooth and soft like a snowflake.

It (the velvet) prickles and tingles.

The metal is like the water.

The fur is slick (possibly for sleek but not necessarily)

Rubber is like cork.

In the discussion following this, it emerged that it was possible to describe one thing in terms of another, and once the idea caught on that this was effective and might improve the description it almost became an assimilated technique, although, as one might expect, with some children the technique tended to invalidate the comparison (e.g. sandpaperis not really like fur, though it might be like foil, as one child suggested) and the point had to be made clear. One very interesting thing that comes out constantly in these lessons is the extent to which children are at first frustrated by the fact that they get a distinct sensory impression (e.g. from brushed nylon) and are unable to find a mode of expression which satisfies them. In this case the simile 'like velvet water' (which eventually came up after a consideration of efforts such as 'metal like water') provided a satisfaction that most found agreeable for the description of brushed nylon.

Again we feel if necessary to stress that this is work in which the teacher has got to participate fully if it is really to become meaningful. Also she has to be prepared for disappointments. Sometimes the lesson seems to take a wrong turn or the mood changes and one feels that the purpose is becoming lost. This may happen with any kind of activity, of course, and an experienced teacher learns to cope intuitively so that as little as possible is lost, but students naturally find it disconcerting. All one can say by way of encouragement is that when the lesson goes well the children's participation is extremely gratifying since there is a feeling of getting to the heart of the matter and also that their capacity for expression, interesting and vital expression, has been considerably extended. The problem of finding a suitably appealing theme which necessitates the imagined use of the tactile sense is more acute than with some of the other topics. But one idea which usually works is Aladdin's Cave. You suggest that the children suddenly find themselves in the cave. It is completely dark and the cave is filled, not only with treasure but with fine fabrics, jars of oil and wine, casks, unusual objects, etc. Obviously they will have to feel their way about and identifying things by touch. What sensations do they experience? This is difficult because they have to work the opposite way round, as it were. They have to imagine the things visually in the first instance and work back to the sense in question, and one must expect some confusion of the senses:

> I could feel the floor all rough and sandy and then we felt the jewels all like glass, slippery. There was bits and pieces every-where like bars of gold all smooth and heavy and silk clothes and turbans, rubies, pearls and diamonds glittering.
>
> *(Madge, aged 10 C)*

The desire to describe in terms of other sense impressions is irresistible and we think it is false to insist upon their exclusion. On the contrary, they should be encouraged as a further techniques to be utilised. However, here is another piece, this time in verse form, which keeps strictly to the letter of the law:

> A blind man feels his way
> In the dark.
> He feels his crooked stick jigger on the pavement.
> He can feel the flowers in the park
> By touch he can tell if it is a rose
> or a tulip or a bush
> He can always know if it is day or night
> By the damp or warm on his skin
> For it is very thin.
>
> *(A boy, aged 10 UC)*

If is fairly certain that the child was striving for a rhyme in the last line and a teacher might be tempted to suggest some modification here, but it is worth considering that by 'thin' might be implied. 'extreme sensitivity.' This may be reading more into the line than is there, but one has to give the child the benefit of the doubt, even if he does not seem certain himself. Another word worth drawing attention to is 'jigger.' This does, of course, exist as a word but it is not normally used in the way the child has used it. What he seems to be using is the sound of the word, which to me suggests the intermittent, perhaps uncertain tapping of the stick on the pavement, and the vibrations of this transmitted through the man's hand.

Now we are fully aware that few teachers can find time for this kind of analysis of the words in one child's poem. We are simply trying to point out that a richer meaning is or might be there than seems likely at the first cursory glance, and one should try to encourage more often than ignore, Also, in the matter of the evaluation of children's work, it seems to me desperately important that such features are taken into account. So often we are only concerned with the outward and visible signs, e.g. hand-writing, spelling, punctuation, etc. Important though these, are, should they predominate?

Further Suggestions:

1. In a garden; in a draper's shop; on the beach.
2. Write some advertisements or a T.V. commercial for fabric, draperies, textiles, carpets, dress materials, etc.
3. Waking up on Christmas morning in the dark.
4. Imagine the 'feel' of one of these animals; cat, bird, fish, mouse, rabbit, snake. Try to describe him but don't say what he is until the end—in other words, make it into a kind of riddle.
5. The blind man.
6. Under the sea.
7. In a mine or undergrond cavern or pothole: the light goes out.
8. You are a T.V. hero and you have been left unconscious in a cell or place with no light at all. Feel your way around and find your way out.

Some of these items occur later in the book as separate topics and practice given here on one aspect of these topics can provide a basis on which to build the later work, since by exploring one dimension in detail the children can be encouraged to draw their ideas from others. For instance, 'Under the Sea' is treated separately but the tactile aspect of it, if it has been used, could be the starting point for their work. On the other hand, some children as well as the teacher, may wish to treat later ideas in a different way—see Intercurricular Strategies page 220.

Poems and Extracts

The Wendigo *Ogden Nash* FBNV; BW

Extract from 'Fish' *D.H. Lawrence* (see page 20)

Eve of St. Agnes (first or second stanza or simply one or two phrases)*John Keats* TW, IV

Alley Cat *Esther Valck Georges* PL, III.

Sink Song *J.A. Lindon* R.R. Green; WS; JV, III

Contentment *Diane Baines* MW

My Hands *Pamela Spratt* BW

Taste

Begin with a general discussion of the things children like to eat, or things they have had for breakfast or lunch, or things they have eaten in the last week. Depending on the circumstances, all or some of these items may be written on the board. By now it will be clear to the children that the lesson is on taste. 'Yes,' you say, 'it's taste.' We want you to concentrate on the thought of eating things, the flavour, the feel in your mouth [few children need encouragement to do this]. Food has a taste and a feel about it. Think of a potato crisp: it has a salty taste and it also has a crispy feel when you eat it. Write down some things you like eating and say what they taste like and how they feel.' This will be enough for some children, while for others it will be necessary to have further discussion in order to make the point clearer with more examples. Following this, the teacher and the children read out what they have written and the teacher draws attention to good descriptions. Here is an example:

> Jelley is sweet and squashy. Mints are spicey and crunchy. Rock is hard and sweet. Kali is prickly and sweet. Chewing-gum is rubbery and dull tasting. Rubob is funny its sort of stringy and makes your mouth water. Marang is fluffy

> and sweet. Lemons are sour and sloshy. Fish is a bit stinky and chewy.
>
> *(Sally, aged 8 UC)*

(Let's hope she was exaggerating about the fish.) This is a fairly middle-of-the-road example. Some children write only a couple of lines of common observation such as:

> Milk is wet and not taste. Suc [sweets] is sweet, Ice [icecream] is cold and slopy.
>
> *(UC)*

—while others run to a dissertation on the virtues of throughout mastication and the peculiar composition of cod roe. But the start has been made and it can be reinforced by a further lesson in which direct stimulus is provided. Here one might incur the displeasure of the health authorities, but provided the contingencies of hygiene are observed there should be no difficulty. (One of our students chopped up milk straws to about two inches long and the children dipped these into the samples). About four sets of small dishes or saucers are needed, depending on the size of the class, so that each group can have one of each sample. On the dishes the teacher may put all or any of the following: salt, lemon, rhubarb, vinegar, alum, licorice, garlic, honey, spice, etc. This can become a little game, e.g. how many flavours can you recognise? (the items being unlabelled). This may be extended by offering examples where texture is important, e.g. crisps, jelly, olive oil, etc. The children then write a short piece about any or all of these. Some teachers may prefer to begin with direct stimulus, or perhaps to avoid it altogether as something messy and difficult to control, but a teacher who has established a good relationship with the class should find no difficulty. Here are two examples:

> I like the rhubarb especially when it's dipped in the sugar. It makes your mouth water it's so squelchy and crunchy and nice. It tickles your tongue and makes your

tongue go funny. The lemon is sharp and makes your eyes crinkle up. It is sour. The biscuits are hard at first but they go sloppy and wet but they taste dry. The jelly is wobbly and floppy and tastes of orange. It feels a bit like the oil.

(Gillian, aged 9 C)

Taste

Salt is sandy
But sugar is sweet.
Flour is dry and thick
But jelley is good to eat
Crips are crumbly
And lemon is sour
The opposite of flour
Spices are sharp
Apples are nice
And so is rice.

(A boy, aged 10 UC)

This piece promoted some discussion about contrasts and opposites in taste and texture, and, of course, the appropriateness of certain descriptions. In what ways, for instance, could salt be said to suggest sand?

This practice can now be put into effect by tackling another theme, e.g. 'You are the Lord Mayor of London. Order a banquet.' If there has been some work in geography or history which coincides (such as food in Elizabethan times or food in other parts of the world) then this is worth pursuing. Some years ago the late Queen of Tonga provided a sumptuous banquet for our Queen, an account of which would be a splendid stimulus; or one might start by describing the limited diet of a poor man anywhere in the world. Alternatively, the teacher might read out and discuss a menu from which the children choose and describe a meal. Clearly the theme will have to be suited to some extent to the class and we can hear many teachers saying 'Our children wouldn't know what a manu is!' Well this might be a good opportunity for them to find out painlessly. Before we go any further, here is one child's banquet:

> Hear ye, hear ye. We are the Lord Mayor of London and this is our noble banquet. We shall have delicious lamb chops and thick slices of lamb, beef and thick pork chops with plenty of juicy gravy to dip our bread in. We shall have custard and jelly and sliced peaches and bananas and pears and oranges and dates. We shall have tons of cream is silver buckets and raspberry ripples. Then we shall have Mars bars to chew. We shall have gallons of lemonade with ice-cream in it and fizzy red pop.
>
> The lamb chops are sweet and taste of mint sauce and the pork chops are chewy. The gravy is great, it is oily and smooth. The jelly is sweet and sloppy in your mouth and the peaches are smashing and juicy, the juice runs down your chin. The ice-cream is cold and flaky but is soft and sweet. The lemonade is tickling our tongue. We can't drink any more.

(Geoffrey, aged 11 C)

For those children able to cope with the idea, concentration on a single experience, such as eating raw carrots, jelly, tripe, apples, strawberries, toffee, and so on, achieves good results. Some examples:

> A raw carrot you get form the garden is scrumptious, munchious and delicious. You can break it off with a snap and pop a bit in your mouth to crunch up and chew and when you chew it tastes sweet and juicy, cold and crisp in your mouth. Then you hold it tight and bite into to with a terrific crack! You can feel great chunks of it being ground up by your teeth and every chew is mouth watering and sweet. It is a rich and juicy thing a carrot is like free ice cream.

(Raymond, aged 10 UC)

Apples

Apples are sweet
Apples are crisp
Moust and juicy
Delicate colouring
Dark red and yellow green and all
Pale bright smooth skin
Soft and smooth to eat
Tast lushus lovely
Round and hart shaped
Thats what apples are like.

(Philip, aged 10 UC)

The Taste of Things

Jam is sweet and sloppy
Bread has a taste of moisture
Meat is tasteless soft and sleek
Watercress is clean and fresh
Sugar is chewy and cool
Custard is horrible at our school
Custard at home is nearly always nice.

(Valerie, aged 9 UC)

Further Suggestions

1. Find out about and describe a meal in Roman times, mediaeval times, etc.
2. You are Robinson Crusoe, You imagine a meal you would like to eat if you were at home.
3. You are a visitor from space. You find yourself in a grocer's shop. You have never tasted these foods before. Write about the experience.
4. Imagine you can go into a sweet shop and have whatever

your like. Have as many things which are different as you like and describe them to a pen friend who doesn't know about such sweets.

5. Write about one thing you would like to eat that you have never tasted.

6. Write the words for a T.V. advertisement for a particular food or sweet, e.g. jelly, jam, crisps, peanuts, butter, cream.

Useful Books

A History of Everyday Things in England (four volumes) *M. and C.H.B. Quennell* (Batsford)

Food Penguin Primary Project, also the unit handbook Charlie and the Chocolate Factory *Roald Dahl* (Penguin)

Poems

Salt, Mustard, Vinegar, Pepper *trad.* JV. 1

This is Just to Say *Wm. Carlos Williams* TWD; Ws

The Biggest Cream Bun in the World *Mary Calvert* YSH

Feast *James Joyce* WS

Pete's Sweets *Eve Merriam* JV, 1

Crumboblius Cutlets *Edward Lear* BW

Making Pancakes when my mother was out *Paddy Kinsale* BW

A Cure *Anon* THW

Smell

This and the sense of taste are so closely allied that some people might feel inclined to combine both. However, the topic can be treated separately although it is to some extent dependent on the season, e.g. in the winter we are deprived of the scent of flowers, fruits, etc. Most people find it impossible to imagine the particular quality of a scent (although it seems to work the other way around-scents easily evoke memories) so that direct stimulus is very important if the eventual writing that is to accrue is to have real verve. Yet it is difficult to provide a variety of stimuli in the classroom. We shall, therefore, make suggestions on the assumption that direct stimulus is limited. One might begin by a consideration of the kinds of smells there are.

As many teachers will realise, a lesson on such a subject will provide most children with some indelicate amusement, and on this account some teachers might prefer to avoid the subject. This is really a matter which depends upon the nature of the class/teacher relationship and, generally, teachers develop their own technique for dealing with the kind of reaction to which we refer. It is usually a matter of diverting their attention and keeping on top of the situation with a joke.

One may begin by attempting some sort of classification. For example, *Garden smells:* flowers, wet grass, bark of trees, pine trees, vegetables, etc. *Kitchen smells:* vinegar, onions, cabbage, spices, lemon, etc. *Burning smells:* leaves, cigarette, tobacco, paper, coke, cloth, etc. *Special smells:* Petrol, wet wool, a new book, oranges, gas, brandy, etc. Of course, these categories are only suggestions to get the lesson going Almost any sort of arrangement would do and children will suggest groups of their own.

The next stage is to find suitably descriptive words, the children supplying as many as they can and the teacher making a few suggestions, perhaps beginning with alternatives for the word suggestions, perhaps beginning with alternatives for the world 'smell' itself, e.g. odour, fume aroma, fragrance, perfume, scent. Then might come the adjectives, e.g. musty, sharp, pungent, yeasty, rancid, fragrant, spicy. The words they favour then go into their word books. Alternatively the teacher and the class might provide materials which offer a direct stimulus, such as, nutmeg, orange, flowers, incense, paraffin, meths, metal polish, mint, camphor, moth-balls, floor polish, perfume, coffee, etc. The children record their reactions and after further discussion they are given a theme to explore for themselves, e.g. Bonfire Night (burning wood, fireworks, roasted potatoes, sausages. onions, chestnuts), or the Grocer's Shop, the Market, the Fairground, the Seaside, a Shop we Know, a Country Lane, Streets, the Kitchen Here are some examples:

The Town on Saturday

The town is full of odours
Drifting down the streets on a Saturday.
Saturday is the day of smells,
The cabbages, the onions and then comes to you
The smell of the mouth-wearing hot-dog stand
Onions and sausage!
The beer smells from the public houses
Mix with fish and chips and sticky sweets
From the stall for boiled sweets.
But last of all there is the fragrant smell of daffodils
From the woman who stands with a basket in the gutter.

(Clarice, aged 11 UC)

The Seaside

The seaside is full of pungent smells
The seaweed stinks
The sea smells salty
The crabs smell tasty and there is a stall
That sells whelks and cockles and jellied eels
All around the people smell it.
On the beach we have our dinner
And what do you think it is?
You can smell its fish and chips
Lovely fish and chips.

(Lillian, aged 9 UC)

In the initial stages, the children show a marked reluctance to abandon the search for rhyme, however it inhibits the sense, and this is natural since rhythm and rhyme are developed in a child very early on the they expect a poem to rhyme. But as they begin to realise that they do not necessarily have to make rhymes, some children find the freedom of *vers libre* an opportunity to express themselves in a way not offered by rhymed verse or prose. We say some children because there are always those who are dissatisfied and perhaps a little frustrated by this freedom. We think it should always be left to the child to decide on the form, although the teacher can encourage the child to branch out a little and try a poem for a change.

It might be argued that the last piece printed above could without any loss have been written out as prose and as such it would have been less appealing. We think the word 'appeal' the right one here. This is, of course, the point. The arrangement of the words on a line might be capricious, but the caprice itself is expressive of individuality, a personal view; it is part and parcel of what is being expressed. Normally in poetry a new line tends to provide emphasis and sometimes to isolate a meaning only partly accounted for by the syntax. Without wishing to claim much skill for the writer of the above piece one can reasonably argue that the second and third lines suggest something about the nature of the (in this case imagined or recollected) experience; that there was a feeling of the individual smells activating the senses, also that these two lines offer a rhythmic balance against the foregoing.

Here is another piece:

The Grocer's Shop

If you stand still and close your eyes in the grocer's shop you can feel hundreds of smells. You can smell the coffee a clear and spicy smell. You can smell the cheese, a fresh smell, and the bacon all ready for the pan. Tea and sugar have a scent of mint. Spice has aroma like snuff, it makes you want to sneeze. There are hundreds of smells in our nose.

(Robert, aged 8 UC)

Considering the form of this in comparison with the preceding piece one might feel that it could have been written out as free verse and that this would have improved it, in that some of the child's similes would have stood out, e.g. the scent of mint. (Tea and sugar don't evoke the scent of mint for me, but we suppose they might to a child since tea, sugar and mint all have a sharply individual smell.) Nevertheless, we would be inclined to leave the piece as it stands and suggest to the boy that in future he might like to arrange his writing as a poem, and leave it at that, since he is young—possibly too young to understand a more detailed explanation without thinking that the teacher is dissatisfied with his work; we want to encourage him rather than arouse a feeling of that kind. Ultimately, of course, it is a question of the teacher's knowledge of the child. The child might understand.

Further Suggestions

1. In a chemist's shop, bakery, garage, corn-merchant's, gasworks, herbalist's, fish-and-chip shop, decorator's, factory, farm, carpenter's, etc.
2. Make up an advertisement or T.V. commercial for coffee, tobacco, perfume, soap, soup, a plant nursery, pickles, etc.
3. Write down all the things you can think of that have distinctive smells. Then write against them words which would describe them. Then cut the list in two so you have two strips. Which words fit and which don't?

There seem to be few poems which are about smells or which employ specifically olfactory imagery. Possibly this sense is not particularly well-developed in poet either, as Christopher Morley comments in his poem (PL, IV).

Smells

Why is it that poet tell
So little of the sense of smell?
These are the odours I love well:

The smell of coffee, freshly ground;
Or rich plum pudding, holy-crowned;
Or onions fried and deeply browned.

The fragrance of a fumy pipe;
The smell of apples, newly ripe;
And printers' ink on leaden type.

Woods by moonlight in September
Breathe most sweet; and I remember
Many a smoky camp-fire ember.

Camphor, turpentine, and tea,
The balsam of a Christmas tree,
These are whiffs of gramarye—
A ship smells best of all to me!

Other poems to look at are:
Seaside Smells *Dylam Thomas* WS
House Smells *James Kirkup* WS

All Senses

Now that the children have had plenty of practice in using their senses separately and a good stock of words has been built up, together with the idea of describing one sense in terms of another, the next logical step is to put it all together in one exercise. This is bound to be rather mechanical at first, especially with some children who are less able:

> In our school there are all sorts of sounds. There is banging and talking. You can smell the dinner when its time and you can smell your clos when they are wet and your coat is rough but the desk isn't its smooth.

(Girl, aged 8 UC)

It is important to get across to the class eventually if not straight-away that you do not insist that they rigorously write down something about each sense. The idea must be dispelled that to use five senses is excellent, four good, three satisfactory etc. Experienced teachers would not make this mistake, they would perhaps casually point out as the occasion arose that there might be an overwhelming impression of sound, or sights, and it might be artificial to write about anything else. Generally speaking one can explain this quite clearly to older children, but it can confuse the younger ones. The best way, probably, is to comment on it individually where necessary.

The usefulness of the exercise is really that it can become a point of reference in future work or during visits or in more ambitious work such as long stories or novels (see section on Stories, page 196 ff.)

It is a good idea at this stage to arrange a visit somewhere to exploit as many sense impressions as possible, e.g. a farm or factory, or the swimming baths. If this is not convenient one or two of the subjects previously treated might be used ()fairground, town, village, etc.). A useful thing to remember is that it is helpful if the children are allowed to concentrate for a short period of time, preferably with their eyes closed, immediately before writing, and then write in silence. This seems to create the best atmosphere for intense concentration.

On page 17 is an example of writing using all senses on the theme of the market. Here is another piece, this time following a visit to a factory:

> At first it was deafening. You couldn't hear a thing if anybody spoke to you. There were black oily machines everywhere spinning their drills like silver needles churning out the blue metal in long winding coils all over the floor which was like thick black mud. You had to mind you didn't slip. A bit further down there were some men welding with masks on like men from outer space. They had torches shooting blue flames which you could not look at because they might blind you. There was a terribly chocking smell coming from these welding torches and we could taste it in our mouth a long time after we got back to school. Every time a man finished a job he threw a piece of metal into an iron box and this made a deafening clang! We only stayed in there a few minutes

and we were not allowed to go close but it was enough for us. We never want to go there again.

(Gail, Aged 10 UC)

This piece clearly reveals the powerful impact of first-hand experience. The teacher could never have conveyed this sense of reality however much she attempted to recreate it verbally. It is perhaps worth mentioning for the benefit of students that the factory had novelty appeal in a way that a walk just outside the school would not have, although this would probably be better than nothing. There is nothing quite like taking children to a place they would not ordinarily see if you want some really fresh and lively writing from them. However, there is another way to look at this question of first-hand experience, which concerns the training of the imagination. We think it is legitimate to encourage children to recreate in words the memory of an experience. In a sense, of course, they would be doing this if they were writing after a visit, but in that case it would certainly be vividly imprinted on their minds. If they are asked to imagine, say, a place they know well, to close their eyes and concentrate on what they might see, hear and feel, etc., if they were at that place, what we normally term imagination is being more actively exercised, provided, of course, the teacher has generated enough enthusiasm for the children to want to do this. If the enthusiasm is not there, then naturally it becomes something of an imposition, proportionally difficult, and is of little or no value compared with the exercise of writing that would result from a visit. But how does one generate this enthusiasm? One way is to present the class with examples of other childrens' work (work of which they are personally capable, naturally), and/or extracts of prose and poetry which the teacher can use as the basis of a discussion. Exactly what the teacher says here depends on so many factors that it is impossible to lay down any general rules—factors such as the age and ability range, the work the children have been doing previously, where they live, books they have been reading and of course the actual passages chosen as most suitable, the teacher's personality, relationship with the class and how the teacher's personality, relationship with the class and how the teacher has interpreted what we have said so far. In case the student feels that we are wriggling out of an answer, we will describe a lesson we took with a class of 11-and 10-year-olds in a small country town. We had never seen the children before and there was no doubt a certain novelty in the presence of somebody new in the classroom. We began by talking about the five senses, asking them to tell me what sort of things they would notice if they went to a sweet shop, a market, etc. They suggested other places where there would be a variety of experience. We asked them to close their eyes and imagine they were in a fairground, and after a few minutes to open them and tell me whatever they had thought of. We then briefly went through each of the five senses in the way we have described the approach in the earlier sections of the book. Then we presented the children with the following piece, the market (see page 17),and some of the items in the list on pages 62-63.

In the Playground

Today is a wonderful day with the sun shining all morning. Everyone was ready to go out into the playground waiting and eager. When the bell went everybody finished their milk, gulping it down, and dashed outside. The children were shouting, wooping and calling to each other to play at ball, hopscotch, skipping, hide-and-seek and leapfrog. You could hear the girls calling skipping games and boys calling each other names. Some children charged into each other or ran about in different directions and some just stood in groups, but everybody was happy because it was such a nice day. The sun was warm and it was nice just to stand in the sun to be warm and taste the fresh air and smell the grass being cut by the lawn mower, and smell the onions from the kitchen, on such a lovely day.

(A boy, aged 10 C)

I read each piece in a way we hoped would bring out certain qualities which we thought might appeal and after each we asked the children to point out any bits they liked or noticed, asking why they thought they liked them; if they were not able to tell us, we suggested a reason. All of this took about half an hour, perhaps less. We let the discussion follow its natural course and we only concern about time was to leave some 20 minutes for writing. We asked them to write about any place they knew very well and made one or two suggestions, such as local places they might be familiar with. Our only injunction was silence while they were writing. Before giving one or two examples of the work produced in this lesson (none of which we are claiming as remarkable) we would like to stress that we don't offer this as a model lesson; in fact we have like to stress that we don't offer this as a model lesson; in fact we have purposely chosen a pretty run-of-the-mill affair. The way we presented things was dictated by the situation. The following pieces are, we think, representative and are printed without correction:

It's a hot day and dowels brook babbles and rushes on its way to the river. The dry mud crumbles underfoot as you walk along, a squirrel runs up one of the many pines in the forest and a trout lies like a huge airship tethered to its mooring tower Suddenly a kingfisher darts like a streak of blue lightening into the stream and a faun shyly creaps away. The faint rattle of a woodpecker floats through the forest and a sparrow hops along the path. Then all is silent as you tramps over a bridge and the forest you have passed settles down to live peacefully again.

At the Fair

It was noisy and the people were shouting at each other, Music was drowning the screams came from the people of the big wheel. It was night and we could seethe lights a long way off. The boats on the river were also lit up. Steamers were blowing their hooters and were slowly going up and down the river. Speedboats were gliding. On the Waltzers people swang round and held on tightly. There were bingo stalls and men shouting out the numbers. The moon was full and it shone down on the river. Each roundabout was stopping and starting and going round fast like a spinning top. It soon became midnight as we looked the our bedroom window we could see no more, the lights of the fair, hear no more, music of the roundabouts. The fair had finished and now the night was quiet.

(A boy, aged 11 C)

On the Beach

The bells on the fishermen's rods tinkled as the fish bit at the bait. When a fish was caught the people left their games and came to look at the fish.

You could hear the chugging of motor boats as they went bobbing up and down on the calm smooth sea. On the horizon there were big gliding, sailing yachts. On the promanards children were shouting excitedly to each other as they rode, ungainly on the loveable, grey donkeys.

Farther along the beach were some people playing games and running races. After each race the crowd got even more excited and more noise came from them.

(A girl, aged 10 UC)

Further Suggestions:

A big shipping store, school bus, a garden, going home, town at night, the park, a football match, Bank Holiday, carnival, feast day, the parade, cricket match, fete. Pick one of these and makeup some images to suggest all you might see, hear, touch, etc. Or write a free description. First close your eyes and imagine the scene as vividly as you can. (Pictures, slides or sound effects might be used as a starting point).

Poems and Extracts

Transformation *Jeane Richards* RR, Yellow

Morning After a Storm *William Wordsworth* RR, Yellow

To Autumn *John Keats* RR, Yellow

Little Trotty Wagtail *John Clare* OB, 1

School's Out *W.H. Davies* TW, II

Morning *Clare, aged 9* BW

Caligari Market *D.H. Lawrence* YI, I

12

Teacher Assessment

Here in this chapter we are particularly concerned with the scope and impact of the assessment initiatives that have been brought about by the 1988 Education Reform Act. Highly visible to all sectors of society — be they teachers or consumers — the requirements of the national assessment programme must be rated as one of the most controversial of the Government initiatives. The high-profile debates about technique and manageability that characterized the introduction of standardized assessment captured, as far as education was concerned,an unprecedented degree of media attention. Rather less generally visible, but arguably just as important, were the significant numbers of new obligations that were placed on teachers in relation to making, recording and reporting assessments more generally. In what follow we shall briefly review the evidence on how the teachers in our study saw assessment before the impact of National Curriculum assessment. We will then explore the nature and significance of the changes the have impacted on them in this respect.

As in the other chapters of this book that deal with the impact of various different aspects of the legislation, our attempt to explain the changes in teachers' assessment practice that this chapter documents will be informents by the key themes of power, values and understanding. More specifically, these themes translate into issue concerning what assessment is (understanding), how it may most profitably be used to promote learning (values) and who should decide on the purpose, nature and use of assessment (power).

As indicated in previous chapters, we shall argue that the principal dimension of change in relation to assessment which brings together many of the tensions concerning understanding, values and power, is the shift from provisional to categoric assessment, from assessments that are essentially intuitive and idiosyncratic to assessments that are explicit and based on a common language of achievement.

Teachers Approach Assessment Before the Education Reform Act

Until the advent of the 1988 Education Reform Act relatively little research had been conducted on assessment in primary schools and little had been written for teachers to support their professional practice. Why was there such an apparent lack of interest in primary school assessment? Certainly, part of the explanation lies in the fact that with the demise of the 11 plus in most areas in the 1960s, most primary schools no longer had to grapple with formal assessment requirements. Not only did they no longer have to prepare children for formal tests, they were not required to provide formal written reports for parents. Indeed, one of the effects of post-Plowden, child-centred, ideologies was to provide a rationale for a very different approach to pupil assessment. Thus, to motivate children and as a basis for communicating with parents, assessment was seen as a much more intuitive, holistic and informed procedure. Previously, the teacher would have been likely to communicate with pupils through a statement of marks awarded for work in different subjects and would have used the same explicit form of communication to report to parents. However, with the advent of more child-centred ideologies such evaluative insights were increasing communicated to pupils and their parents in the form of descriptive comments referenced to the teacher's overall assessment of the child's intellectual capability, behaviour and application.

As Sharp and Green (1975) argued in their classic study, such holistic evaluative judgements were further related to the known personal circumstances of the child, especially ethnicity and home background, to provide the basic information for an individualized pedagogy. The PACE study has confirmed he findings of previous studies (e.g. Ashton et al., 1975; Broadfoot and Osborn, 1993), which showed that English Primary teachers' professional ideologies are centred typically on providing learning experiences that meet the emotional, as well as the intellectual, needs and interests of the individual child. This ability to interpret pupil behaviour in relation to existing assessments of a pupil's strengths and weaknesses, needs and interests, and to make pedagogic decisions accordingly, has arguably become a central element of professional competence in the contemporary English Primary classroom.

This broad background tc the current programme of change highlights a number of points that are helpful in interpreting the progress and significance of assessment developments in primary schools. First, we can note that primary teachers' existing views of and practices concerning assessment are explicitly *ideological,* reflecting the broader professional ideology held by the teacher. This of course, as we saw in Chapter 6, embraces their approach to curriculum and pedagogy as well. Second, it is apparent that the teaching of primary age children is not *inevitably* associated with a particular ideological approach. This is made clear by the experience of countries in which both teaching and assessment are much more formal in content than has been the case in England. For instance, it is significant that the French Government's current concern to make teachers more responsive to the differing learning needs of children is manifest in a nationally imposed comprehensive programme of diagnostic assessment.

In this chapter we explore further some of the issues raised above. We report findings concerning how the teachers in our study saw the role of assessment, how they used it and what they perceived to be its effects on children. Many of these findings are drawn from conversations and observations with the teachers involved in our detailed classroom studies. Others are drawn from interviews with teachers in our larger sample of 48 schools.

How did Teachers See Assessment at the Time of Our Study?

When asked what role they felt assessment ought to play in

infant classrooms, teachers' responses were structured around three main dimensions: frequency, purpose and mode (see Table 1).

In terms of *frequency,* all the teachers who took part in our detailed classroom studies stressed the need for assessment (and associated feedback) to be continuous and immediate —- part of the on-going dialogue of teaching. Many of the teachers adopted a constructivist view of learning and talked of the continuous, intuitive, diagnostically orientated mental process they 'had always used.'

It's an integral part of the process of teaching.

I think that it should be diagnostic, I think it should be the teacher's way of carrying the child from A to B, noting whether you have to go from A to A1, A2, A3 before you get to B. Note whether you can skip over C because the child is good and go on to D and to record that somewhere, whether it be an internal school record informally with other colleagues that can help you and then later on to pass that informational on to the next teacher, to discuss with parents how they can help if you feel that something external might be influencing what's happening in school, but purely diagnostically because the children are assessed externally. They have their reading tests, their maths test and I think that's sufficient.

TABLE 1

Mode, Purpose and Frequency of Assessment

	Assessment to support the construction of knowledge	**Assessment to monitor the acquisition of established knowledge**
Mode	Covert/intuitive	Over/explicit
Purpose	Encouragement/guidance	Accountablilty
Frequency	Constant	Intermittent

In terms of *purpose,* the emphasis was on needing to assess in order to make pedagogic decisions. 'We've always been assessing. As teachers we need to assess in order to know where to go next.... now it's written down on paper you feel more constrained.' This clear emphasis on assessment to inform teaching decisions was associated with the antipathy felt by many teachers towards National Curriculum assessment. Their essentially informal, holistic approach was contrasted with what was perceived to be the reductionist requirements of 'ticking boxes' associated with National Curriculum assessment. The latter was seen as making assumptions about the 'established' nature of knowledge, with which may teachers could not agree.

The *mode* of assessment most often mentioned was a mental record. Perhaps the most extreme representation of this approach was those teachers who were unable to describe their approach to assessment.

> *I think we just take that for granted — I don't know that I've ever questioned that aspect of it.*

> *I'd have said [assessment shouldn't have] a very big role, mainly because you've got so many other things to cope with; assessment needs to be something that should come later.*

Implicit in these responses concerning the three headings of frequency, purpose and mode is a continuum of practice. At one end are those teachers for whom assessment is almost entirely an explicited, almost unconscious, integral part of the process of decision-making on which their teaching is based. It is implicit in their work. At the other end of the continuum are those teachers who are increasingly-explicitly making a conscious and active distinction between this constant intuitive evaluation and feed-back relationship and the quite separate activity of recording evidence for later use in reporting and accountability.

Interviews with Year 2 teachers in 1991 produced a very similar picture to those conducted in 1990, when our cohort of target pupils was in Year 1. However, the same strong stress on holistic, intuitive, informal monitoring was increasingly contrasted with the formal, explicit, externally imposed, detached assessment which for them was associated with the National Curriculum. One other noticeable difference of emphasis was the addition of an *affective* element in the identification of assessment purposes. Several teachers mentioned the role of assessment as a source of encouragement for pupils as well as of guidance for themselves. For instance:

> Every time a child brings a piece of work up I do make sure that I read it, read it with them, or they read it to me and then if there's anything there that is to do with language, to do with spelling, to do with organization, I'll draw it out of them hen and there. I mean, spellings hit me immediately, I notice them, straight away and if I can use something that's a howling mistake with all of the children, for instance the spelling of 'ou' sounds we were doing this week. So many were putting the spelling of 'ow' or whatever, then I'll draw that out for the whole class. But I suppose in time — I'm not sure — I don't often accept the piece of work as it is, I'll always try and make some constructive comment about that piece of work. Either 'Yes, that's lovely handwriting, that's very neat, you've really worked hard on that' or 'Can you see what mistake you've made with this?' So there is an assessment going on with every piece of work.

In teacher's minds there would appear to be a clear distinction between assessment that is quite explicitly carried out to promote the learner's confidence and motivation, by providing *reinforcement* and *enjoyment* for the child, and assessment for *diagnostic* purposes. Such diagnosis of progress made may be further divided into *general* curriculum evaluation, for example collecting up a list of words that the class *as a whole* is spelling wrongly and setting them as the spellings to be learnt for the week, and *individual* curriculum evaluation, which might lead to teaching of the specific words that a particular child was finding difficult.

Another difference noticeable in the 1991 responses was the growing feeling of assessment pressure reported by teachers as the combined effects of the children growing older and the increasing implementation of national assessment made themselves felt. This was well described by one teacher, who used a 'trick box.' This was a box into which the children put their work when they had finished it and/or at the end of the session. The teacher then checked the work later.

> *I have a cursory glance at it, and if I've noted 'Oh dear that is wrong' then I will deal with that child. If it's right, then I give them a little praise and then it's on to the next task. If it is really good, I'll try and spend a minute (well it's not a minute, I would reckon it's about fifteen seconds if you actually timed it) of praise, but then it goes in the tick box. At one time I would read through every essay with the child, every story and make the discussions. I'd try and do that with each child once a week, you know, read through their story with them—correct punctuation, discuss punctuation, etc. — and now the work goes in the box and I have to look at it at home. Each night I take the box home and I assess what I see. Now I would have done that anyway with children, but with them, and discuss it with them.... But I can't now because the tasks that I've set myself to do have taken time away from that. So the child hasn't got that reflective feedback on their work; I'm going to somehow try and do a reflective period where I gather all the files together and I actually look through them with them I'm going to try and fit that in, I don't know when, but I'd like to try, so that we can get, perhaps once a week if I did three files, and we look through them and we could reflect that way on, you know, the past half-term's work.*

Like many other respondents, this teacher was being forced to move from her preferred professional approach in which assessment involved constant monitoring coupled with immediate feedback to the child, to a situation in which she felt she had 'lost that sitting back and looking time.' She felt that assessment was now more time-consuming but less valuable because its emphasis — on the greater externalization of information — was different.

It was thus possible to identify a number of contrasting features in the assessment practices operated in the primary schools we studied — features that articulated with the constructed and established dimensions of knowledge and learning, which we first discuss in Chapter 3.

Of course, in one sense assessment is an integral part of the second-by-second process of teacher decision-making in classroom. These decisions are informed by concerns such as the management of the classroom, discipline, keeping children's attention, intellectual extension and the need to encourage effort and motivation, and then filtered through each teachers' specific set of judgements about the current state of achievement for each child. There was some evidence that this detailed, intuitive assessment process, was which largely occurred in the past without the and of an explicit language of objectives, being facilitated by the provision of the detailed learning targets embodied in the National Curriculum because of the provision of a language for thinking about and communicating such decisions. As one teacher put it,

> *If they're doing specific activities as part of the National Curriculum work, if I've perhaps asked them, for example, to write a story about something to do some sequencing work in story form, then I'd obviously be trying to assess whether they're achieving writing simple words on their own or whether they are beginning to write in sentences, or sequencing their story in a logical way, so I'm making those sorts of assessments as we go along, so that I know the kind of work to give them next and the kind of help they're going to need to move on to the next stage.*

This comment is much more structured in terms of specific curriculum targets than most teachers' comments about their assessment. In fact, assessment was typically described in a rather general way;

for example, correcting mistakes, completing the work set following instruction or demonstrating certain work-related social skills. However, it is worth emphasizing that the issue of *what* is assessed came across as much less important than the 'how' and 'why' of assessment in teacher's responses.

Teachers Respond to the New Classroom Assessment Requirements

The PACE study of the impact of national assessment began in mid-1090, when the first SATs for Key Stage 1 were about to be piloted and teachers were just beginning to implement assessment in relation to National Curriculum attainment targets. Interview data generated at this stage showed that many of the teachers' reactions were based on both their experience of the National Curriculum to date and their anticipation of the changes to come. When they were asked, 'How do you feel the needs of your pupils relate to the requirements of the National Curriculum?' teachers' spontaneous comments in 1990 included 24 percent who felt the teacher assessment procedures were useful and relevant, against 76 percent who felt that it was the assessment procedures in particular that were unrealistic and time-consuming.

In view of the contrast between the assessment requirements of the National Curriculum and the preferred approach to assessment that characterised our teachers, it is not surprising that changes in assessment and record keeping combined to produce a large source of changes in classroom practices. In 1992 these changes were mentioned by 44 percent of teachers — as against the content of the curriculum, which was mentioned by 58 percent. Although the physical constraints of the environment, the size of the class and pupil characteristics were identified as the major constraints on teaching approaches, in 1990 in the early stages in national assessment implementation, 22, percent of teachers identified assessment as a source of constraint on their teaching approach, and this rose to 25 percent in 1992.

Of the changes teachers had experienced, more record keeping had far and away the most significant impact, with 60 percent of teachers remarking on the way it had changed their work. Meanwhile an increase in assessment (33 percent) and changes in curriculum content (34 percent) were perceived as broadly equal sources of change. However, by 1992, these feelings had changed to emphasize changes in teaching methods (45 percent) and curriculum content (40 percent) rather than assessment (18 per cent). The emphasis appeared to change with the implementation phases of the legislation and with the ebb and flow of public debate. More generally, although nearly 47 percent of teachers were broadly positive about the changes they were making in their own classrooms in relation to the National Curriculum, 30 percent disliked those associated with assessment.

TABLE 2

Emphasis and Recent Changes Felt by Teachers Concerning Different Types of Assessment (Row Percentages)

Type of assessment	Year	Do you use these forms of assessment?			Has your use of these forms of assessment changed recently?		
		Yes	A little	No	More	No	Less change
Standardized	1990	15	11	73	3	93	3
tests	1992	24	22	52	12	82	3
Marking	1990	61	30	8	8	92	0
written work	1992	91	7*	0	9	88	3
Pupil	1990	32	28	39	14	86	0
self-assessment	1992	44	28	27	15	77	8
Listening to	1990	80	14	6	22	64	14
children	1992	87	4	9	11	80	8
Discussion/	1990	82	11	7	27	71	3
review	1992	74	13	12	11	85	4

Source: PACE 1 teacher interviews.

Sample: 88 teacher in each year.

Date Summer 1990 summer 1992.

In an attempt to identify the precise nature of these changes, we asked teachers in our larger sample to describe the approaches to assessment that they typically use and any changes in this respect of which they were conscious. From Table 2 it appeared that in 1990, not surprisingly considering the age group, very few schools were using standardised tests. Marking of written work, by contrast, was frequently practised, particularly by 1992, with the emphasis on doing it *with* the child, often with some tick, 'smiley face' or message to provide personal reinforcement and encouragement. This collaborative approach was also in evidence in the use by 32 percent of teachers in 1990 and 44 percent in 1992 of some form of pupil self-assessment, which typically involved the children with the teacher or with each other discussing their work and assessing its quality. In a few cases the use of self-assessment was more formalized. One school, for example, had a school policy of children self-assessing their topic work and undertaking an annual self-assessment.

Listening to children was, not surprisingly, frequently practised, through the impact of the National Curriculum on this seems to have been variable. Some teachers in 1990 felt they had less time for this very important area than before, others that the obligation to formalize the assessment of children's listening and speaking had transformed listening and speaking from being simply an assessment vehicle into an assessment focus. In some cases this was felt to be good because it justified and systematized something that had always been done; in other cases teachers found such assessment very difficult and resented it.

Discussion and review were widely practised, both with individuals and with the class as a whole. One example involved children being invited to talk about their work to the class at the end of a topic. Another was for the children to plan daily activities with the teacher, set targets and review whether these had been achieved at the end of the day. Some respondents mentioned explicitly that standards had improved as a result of this approach.

In 1990 many teachers planned to implement more changes in the future, with 22 percent mentioning in this respect such assessment procedures as developing the skills of listening to children more conscientiously. Changes in methods of recording achievement were anticipated by 17 percent of teachers. Reference was also made to assessing more curriculum areas separately from each other than hitherto, to assessing personal and social dimensions and to cross-curricular assessment.

Some respondents felt that their teaching had changed in response to assessment requirements. Becoming clearer about teaching objectives was mentioned, as was the need to pose problems for children at different levels of achievement. There was some evidence of the impact of new assessment practices on relationships, with teachers giving more attention to talking with children and their parents. This was partly to help gather more information but was also associated with teachers using the assessment process to clarify learning goals with children, to provide reinforcement and encouragement and to set individual learning targets. A very formalized example of this was in relation to one LEA's primary language record, which required teachers to interview every child and their parents regularly so that a contract between teacher and parents could be drawn up and used as the basis for on-going comment by both. However, some teachers were unhappy with this kind of formalization, feeling that, as one teacher put it,

> Teachers get the feel of children and just know things. It's not always necessary to assess formally.... it should be on-going without tests.... just general... Teachers should be assessing and have always continually assessed to know what to do next and when to move into new work. It's the breaking down of subjects that makes a huge workload.

The tension between what can be seen both as encouragement to greater structure, discipline and accountability in assessment under the legislation and as its manifestation as undesirable, time-consuming, bureaucratic paper-pushing was quite marked. It was a tension that characterised many other aspects of the Education Reform Act's provision, since it reflected the changing balance of power between teachers and the Government. By far the most commonly perceived pressure, predictably, was that of time. For one respondent, assessment that used to take place at the end of a term or year had been replaced by regular assessments of different things for different groups throughout the year. Another found she had to set aside one week at the end of each half-term for assessment. Others mentioned the need to cut corners; for example, their attempts to formalize observation of particular tasks.

There was thus some evidence at the beginning of the project in 1990 of teachers beginning to use assessment creatively to support learning according to the diagnostic and formative purposes of the Government's Task Group on Assessment and Testing (TGAT) Report (Des, 1988). Teachers were stimulated to experiment with creative new approaches to assessment as it moved increasingly centre stage in professional development and as in-service training programmes were mounted by local education authorities. Such approaches were often characterised by collaborative approaches to assessment involving pupils and parents, and by the use of a wide range of techniques for gathering and storing evidence of attainment. At the same time, such developments did not appear to reflect widespread enthusiasm for change, set as they were against a background of essentially reluctant acquescence and generally low morale.

How Did Teachers REspond to Record Keeping Requirements?

Many of the changes in record keeping practice echoed those identified in relation to assessment techniques. The virtually ananimous view among teachers that record keeping had increased was variously explained by the need to develop and try out different methods and forms, the need for careful curriculum planning and evaluation to ensure full coverage of the appropriate attainment targets, and the extension of records to cover subjects, such as science, not hitherto the subject of records.

In 1990 the picture that emerged was a teachers spending a considerable amount of time devising and completing their own records or completing records imposed on them from outside, such as from their LEA. Much of this work was carried out in teachers' own time and against a background of anxiety or even panic about how to do it, guilt about not doing it well enough, cynicism about its potential value for pupils' learning and resentment about being made to feel inadequate. The words of one respondent ably summarized this feeling: 'All these changes make you feel that unless you're good at documentation in the National Curriculum, you can't be a very good teacher.'

Equally striking was the enormous variety of records being used. Subject records were mainly centred on science, maths and English, with more than one record being used for some subjects, such as an 'at a glance' record and a more detailed 'broken down' record in maths or an oracy, reading and general record in English. A number of respondents mentioned their use, or anticipated use, of 'profiles' and records of achievement, particularly in terms of keeping children's work for later review and discussion with them and their parents.

The theme of time recurred consistently in the responses:

> *I could be doing it all the time.*
>
> *It stops you spending time teaching.*
>
> *'You have to spend your own time dealing with it.*
>
> *We're making a big effort to keep it up.*
>
> *I feel guilty.... I should do more but I've no more time.*

The concern was undoubtedly exacerbated by a general lack of *confidence* among teachers that they were doing what would be required centrally in terms of recording or what would be demanded of them by parents, and by the lack of value they perceived the records to have.

> *But staff are still not recording in enough detail to meet the requirements. We have a reading record book and individual records to take home, brief evaluation of individuals in the weekly planning book and each child has a pupil profile book.*

Well, if children learn the National Curriculum in terms of following improved attainment targets and the levels... If I'd been doing it I'd know exactly what they'd been doing but they don't. And no amount of writing it down like that will actually tell me.

We always have assessed — now we're filling in tick sheets.

While the conduct of such assessment may have become easier with the passage of time and growing familiarity, this seems to have done nothing to reduce teacher's resentment and frustration at the amount of time they were having to spend on procedures for which they did not see a value. As Table 3 sets out, in both 1990 and 1992 virtually all teachers reported a huge increase in the time spent on record keeping and a growing number reported negative feelings about assessment and record keeping. A further question elicited the nature of these changes (Table 4).

TABLE 3

Changes in the Amount of Time Spent on Record Keeping (Percentages)

Change	1990	1992
A lot	81.0	90.0
A little	8.0	7.0
No change	1.0	2.0
Expected to change	10.0	0.0

Source: PACE 1 teacher interviews.

Sample: 88 teachers in each year.

Date: Summer 1990 and summer 1992

The key to understanding these feelings does not entirely appear to be concern about parental pressure or even worry about the direct effects of assessment on pupils. Although more that half the teachers interviewed in 1992 thought that the National Curriculum was exerting a negative influence on teacher-pupil relations — a figure almost double that of two years earlier — very few teachers (9 percent) identified assessment directly as a factor in this respect. Equally, almost as many teachers identified an increased emphasis on partnership with parents as reported an increase in the requirement for assessment information.

TABLE 4

Nature of Changes in Record Keeping (Percentages)

	1990	1992
More written recording	99.0	98.0
Less written recording	0.0	0.0
More direct work with pupils	11.0	9.0
Less direct work with pupils	2.0	1.0
More work with colleagues	30.0	9.0
Positive feelings about assessment/record keeping	8.0	3.0
Negative feelings about assessment/record keeping	56.0	66.0
Mentions records of achievement	27.0	24.0
Other	20.0	0.0

Source : PACE 1 teacher interviews.
Sample: 88 teachers in each year.
Date: Summer 1990 and summer 1992.

Rather, the major source of teachers' resentment is hinted at by the response to a question that required teachers to identify their own strengths as a teacher. Whereas 61 percent mentioned curriculum-related skills in this respect in 1992, only 2 percent mentioned assessment. While many curriculum-related skills may in practice include many of the intuitive and individualized assessment decisions referred to above, it is clear that very few teachers regarded the overt and deliberate assessment that was required by the introduction of the National Curriculum as something that was part of their own professional competence.

Equally revealing in this respect were teacher's 1990 replies to an open-ended question ('What does professional responsibility mean for you as a teacher or head teacher?') that had been included in an initial postal questionnaire to all teachers in the sample. Although responsibility in relation to assessment and evaluation was mentioned spontaneously by a relatively small proportion of the sample (16 percent) as compared to, for example, relationships with colleagues (47 percent) and teaching approach (39 percent), this represents a significant increase on the answers to a similar question, which was asked as part of the Bristaix project in 1985. In that study only 7 percent of English primary school teachers included assessment as an explicit element in their conception of their professional responsibility.

So far, this chapter has addressed questions concerning teachers' responses to the new assessment and recording obligations that the Education Reform Act imposed. In summary, the picture that emerged over the three years of the project showed much greater emphasis on formal assessment and record keeping; some considerable resentment at the time demands and the perceived unnecessary formalization of much assessment work; fears about the potential impact of intrusive assessment and recording procedures on teaching-learning processes; and concerns about relationships with parents and the pupils themselves. At the same time there was some evidence of the beginning of a more positive phase of development in the use of assessment, as teachers' growing confidence and knowledge allowed them to mediate external requirements towards more professionally acceptable ends.

What did Pupils Understand About Assessment?

To explore only from the teacher's point of view the significance of the momentous changes that have been taking place in infant classrooms would be to miss the opportunity to explore the even more important question of the impact of such developments on pupils. How infant teachers' preferred intuitive approach to assessment affected pupils' learning, and the significance of increasingly explicit assessment and reporting procedures in his respect, are questions that are of central importance in any attempt to research the significance of the 1988 Education Reform Act.

Unfortunately, however, whereas a considerable body of research exists concerning the apparent impact of different pedagogic and curriculum strategies in primary classrooms, there is a lack of equivalent base-line research in relation to assessment. We simply do not know how different assessment practices impact on children's learning in primary classrooms. Moreover, we lack a conceptual framework that would help to identify the key variables with which to address this issue. Thus, before we turn to an examination of the possible effects of National Curriculum assessment it is appropriate to examine in a little more detail what our data had to say about pupils' awareness of, and reaction to, assessment.

Given that, as we have seen classroom assessment in primary schools has rarely been explicit, it was not possible to enquire directly of such young pupils in a meaningful way. Rather we asked a series of more indirect questions of the 54 pupils whom we observed as part of our detailed classroom studies in 1990 and again in 1991. These questions were designed to address the more tangible sources of pleasure or anxiety of which a pupil might be aware in relation to assessment interactions such as 'Do you like it when your teacher asks to look at your book?' The result of this question is shown in Table 5.

TABLE 5

Responses of Pupils to the Question Do You Like it When Your Teacher Asks to Look at Your Book?' (Percentage)

	Positive	Negative	Mixed	Normal
Year 1	57.4	22.2	14.8	5.6
Year 2	51.9	20.4	20.4	7.4

Source: PACE 1 child interviews.

Sample : 9 Year 1 and Year 2 classes.

Date: autumn 1990 and autumn 1991.

In both 1990 and 1992, over half the children gave positive answers to the question. Among the main reasons children gave for feeling 'good' were so that they could go on to something else, because they got a reward — a smiley face or a sticker — or because they felt pride and satisfaction. As some of them put it,

> *I feel good because I can get it over with and go on to something else.*

It's good because I've done good work and she's pleased with me and I get a sticker like this.

I feel OK — proud of myself.

Because I can find out if I've done it right.

Yes, 'cos she might mark all of them right. When she ticks them, I feel like doing three more pages.

The main negative reasons given were not waiting to do the task again or fears of being told off or not being praised:

Because I'll never be super.

I doesn't want the teacher to look at it.

In case I have to do it again.

I worry in case it's wrong.

The mixed responses expressed sentiments such as 'I like the teacher to look at my work if it's good but not if it's bad.' Significantly, these pupils appeared unable to predict what the outcome was likely to be on any given occasion. Thus their responses combined both pleasure at having the teacher's attention and anxiety because the work might be wrong. Most children clearly liked, and actively sought, teacher praise. Indeed, they seemed to depend on it to regulate their own pace of learning and appeared to have little capacity to judge this for themselves. There thus appeared to be a tension for many pupils between wanting attention in order to receive praise and to get the necessary curriculum guidance, and wanting to avoid possible censure for not following instructions or having to repeat tasks:

Sometimes, because sometimes I rush a bit and sometimes I take my time. I like it when I've done it really neat and tidy and keep within the lines.

Quite happy because sometimes she sends us to other teachers and they give us smiley faces and stars.

Sometimes I do and sometimes I don't ..... Because it's not very good sometimes, but sometimes it's quite good....

When it's good, I feel quite nice and when it's not good I feel sad. I don't want to get shouted at.

Yes, when I done it wrong, I feel upset and when I done it right, I feel happy.

There was no apparent difference between the schools studied in this respect or between boys and girls.

When asked, 'Does it matter if you don't do things the way your teacher wants them,?' the children responded in two different ways. Some cited educational reasons why it mattered, such as 'Otherwise you won't learn anything.' Others cited extrinsic reasons, such as the need to avoid getting told off! However, in both years, 70 percent of children recognized the need to follow the teacher's requirements and instructions. The majority cited educational reasons for this: 'Yes, it matters — she tells instructions. If you don't follow you don't learn.' A significant number referred to potential teacher disapproval: 'Yes, otherwise you get told off.' The reaction of this group to the question thus depended somewhat on whether they thought the teacher would be cross — perhaps because they had been messing about — or would understand and be tolerant of mistakes:

Yes. If you do it wrong, you have to start all over again and it wastes time and we get told off.

No, she rubs it out and she says, 'I know you listened quite well, but you got it wrong.' Once the whole class got it wrong.

From the previous discussion of teachers' attitudes to assessment, we may deduce that the ways in which teachers react to individual pupils in these circumstances would have been governed by their assessment of what was likely to be most constructive and appropriate in leading to better work from each individual pupil.

A few children responded to the question in a way that reflected very clear views of themselves as learners, and their relationship with the teacher as one in which they accepted their teacher's power unconditionally. For example:

> *I haven't tried it [not doing things the way the teacher wants them] so don't know what it's like.*
>
> *I always do it right.*

In summary, it appeared that children perceived the assessment interaction of the classroom in terms of three issues:

(i) task management — knowing what to do and/or not being fund out if the task was incorrectly done;
(ii) affect — pleasure at receiving praise and pain at being told off;
(iii) intellectual — being told what educational tasks to engage in next.

This analysis of children's understanding of assessment purposes is in line with the analysis of Mavrommatis (1993) concerning assessment in Greek primary classrooms, in which he identifies *teachers'* use of assessment as spanning three main dimensions: the psychological (affect), the intellectual (cognitive guidance) and the managerial (behaviour).

Interestingly, children's understanding of these various facets of assessment were also reflected in their interpretation of why some children do better than others. The children were asked: 'Why do some children do better at school work than others? Their answers were coded and analysed and, at Table 6 shows, there was a considerable imbalance in the reasons given for some children doing better than others at school work!

Examples of the kind of response given for each category are:

Age: Because they're younger.
They have been there longer.

Effort: They don't mess about.
Because they get on with their work and don't mess about or nothing.

They don't 'Miss, Miss,' they just get on.
They just try harder.

Ability: Because they think in their minds.
Because they've got more clever brains.

Skill: 'Cos they do gooder pictures than the others.
Some just do round circles for eyes and nose and half a square of body.
Tidiness 'cos they can do it neater.
Some do big writing and some do nice writing.

TABLE 6

Responses of Pupils to the Question 'Why do Some Children do Better at School Work than Others? (Percentages)

Reasons given	
Age	12.7
Effort	45.1
Ability	18.6
Skill	13.7
Don't know	9.8

Source: PACE 1 Child interviews.

Sample: 54 children in Year 1 and Year 2.

Date: autumn 1990 and autumn 1991.

It seemed from their responses that many children had begun to develop a perception of teachers' assessment criteria. Pupils were particularly aware of the importance of 'effort,' with no fewer than 45 percent mentioning its importance.

These responses echoed the teachers' evaluative criteria that Pollard (1985)identified in terms of three broad domains of 'productivity,' 'behaviour' and 'individual responsibility.' Relating to productivity and efficiency at school work the evaluative criteria he identified were:

Effort: Let's make a really big effort today.

Perseverance: Try a bit longer.

Neatness: That's a nice page.

Regularity: Is that your best work?

speed: Has anyone finished yet?

Relating to behaviour and social relationships were:

Self-control: Stop being silly.

Obedience: Did you hear what I said?

Politeness: That's not a very nice thing to do.

quietness: Silence now.

Truth: Let's have it straight now.

Respect for authority: Hands up if you want something.

Relating to individualism and competitiveness were:

Achievement: Have you got that right?

Individualism: Do it yourself.

Hierarchy: Why got ten out of ten?

Self-reliance: Go and find out.

It may be significant that, in talking about reasons for achievement, some children mentioned actual learning *behaviour* while others referred to circumstantial characteristics over which pupils have no control, such as age, language and gender. While it is not possible to make a great deal of this distinction at the present time, it is possible that these explanations were linked to individual pupil's learning attributions and thus could by significant in influencing their future learning. In future stages of the PACE study we shall be able to pursue this further.

A third aspect of assessment activity that we explored with the children concerned their attitude to rewards. When they were asked, 'What happens if someone does their work really well?', pupils' responses were coded to produce the analysis shown in Table 7. Not surprisingly, the most explicit rewards for good work, such as praise and symbolic rewards, were the ones most likely to be remarked upon by the children. However it was interesting that boys were more likely to stress symbolic rewards, such as ticks, stars and smiley faces, than girls and that girls were more aware of praise.

TABLE 7

Responses of Pupils to the Question 'What Happens when Someone does Their Work Really Well? (Percentages)

	1990		1991		Overall
	Boys	**Girls**	**Boys**	**Girls**	
Praise	28.6	25.0	21.4	50.0	31.2
Symbolic Reward	50.0	32.2	60.8	35.8	44.7
Material reward	7.2	10.8	7.2	10.8	9.0
Choice	10.8	10.8	3.6	7.2	8.1
Nothing	0.0	3.6	0.0	0.0	0.9
Don't know	8.6	8.6	3.6	3.6	6.1

Source: PACE 1 Child interviews.

Sample: 54 children in Year 1 and Year 2.

Date: autumn 1990 and autumn 1991.

Certainly relevant to this question is the bitter envy expressed by some of the children in discussing teachers' rewards. It provides clear testimony to the potentially negative, as well as the positive, affective impact of assessment, even when it is not directly addressed to a particular child:

> *I feel I like I want to do it — I feel like taking their work away from them.*
>
> *I get angry 'cos I want a star too.*
>
> *You feel jealous.*
>
> *You show it to the class. I get jealous; they stand up and get clapped sometimes.*

She shows us it and she goes 'look at this work — it's wonderful.'

While our evidence is to scanty at present to support any firm conclusions in this respect, it does suggest that the more explicit the assessment procedures used, the more differentiation between pupils will be made explicit. This is likely to affect pupils' motivation and self-esteem.

How did the Classroom Assessment REquirements of the Education Reform Act Impact on Pupils?

Our data suggest that the advent of National Curriculum assessment, with its emphasis on explicit learning targets and overt assessment criteria, is transforming the assessment culture and its associated language. Although the children themselves are too young for it to be possible yet to make any such comparison from their point of view, some testimony to this is provided by interviews with teachers in our classroom study schools. Asked if they thought the National Curriculum and its assessment were raising children's awareness of differences in achievement, most teachers thought that children, even at the infant school, had always been aware of differences in their levels of achievement. However, teachers felt that young children were unconcerned about such differences because they were not aware of their meaning and significance in the way that older children would be. Although there was some feeling among teachers that SATs, in particular, would make even infants more aware in this respect, teachers largely felt they could protect children from such pressure through praise for efforts made and by recognizing alternative achievements. The majority of the teachers questioned did not feel that National Curriculum assessment had yet significantly changed the classroom climate. However, most teachers felt that the constraints of reporting children's achievement in the controlled format of the new requirements would prevent them from showing a genuinely individual and hence diagnostic picture of a child's different achievements. Only one teacher described the benefits of having a clear structure on which to base curriculum coverage, diagnosis and progression.

Asked about their strategies for minimizing such effects, teachers mentioned the use of praise for alternative achievements, planning the curriculum to embrace children's particular perceived talents, adjusting tasks to facilitate pupil success and explaining differences in attainment by giving non-threatening reasons, such as age. The use of these strategies was reflected in the pupils' explanations discussed earlier. One teacher mentioned grouping by 'ability' so that the differences were not obvious — at least with the groups. However, it is significant that teachers did not always find it easy to articulate their strategies in this respect. For some, their responses to individual pupils appeared to be part of more intuitive behaviour in which assessment activity was implicit.

Although it is too early in our longitudinal study to characterize the impact of new assessment procedures on pupils, the above data do enable us to be a little clearer about the key dimensions of assessment activity in primary classrooms. Assessment activity may usefully be regarded as a form of language that allows for the communication of evaluative messages between teacher and pupil. It thus contributes to a given classroom's culture, in which particular symbolic forms are imbued with evaluative meaning for those interacting within it. We may hypothesize that pupil's capacity first to *understand* the way in which such cultures operate and subsequently to learn to *operate* successfully within it is likely to influence their future success as pupils (Filer, 1994).

Conclusion

In this chapter we have suggested that, in the infant classroom prior to the 1988.Education Reform Act, the particular value system informing teachers' evaluations of pupils and their work was likely to have been unclear both to the teacher herself and to her pupils. For many teachers this value system was typically bound up with their more general professional ideology about the task of teaching and about how children learn.

As far as assessment is concerned, we have seen that this ideology was structured in terms of teachers' understanding of the *mode, purpose* and *frequency* of assessment. For teachers who could be described as having constructivist views of knowledge and learning, such understanding has been characterized as an approach to assessment that was intuitive and continuous with the central purpose of providing instructional feeding, which the Education Reform Act has brought, involved teachers developing their assessment repertoire considerably. As well as the diagnostic and formative assessment activity in which they had always engaged, teachers were now required to undertake summative and evaluative assessment, which emphasized the explicit categorization of pupils' achievement.

The dislike of many teachers for this requirement was not simply because it meant an increase in their workload or required skills that they did not feel they had. Rather their resistance was rooted in an objection to the use of the coercive power of the law to impose on teachers the obligation to operationalise a different set to understandings concerning the role of assessment in primary schooling. This conflict of understanding in turn reflected a fundamental challenge to the values typically held by primary school teachers concerning how children can best be helped to learn, and the particular role of assessment in this respect (see the discussion of dimensions in Section 3.5).

We have suggested in this chapter that before the advent of national assessment requirements, assessment was typically not a separate domain of activity but part of a broad web of professional strategies. We have described how these strategies are constantly being manipulated by teachers in the light of their on-going judgements about appropriate interventions to meet the intellectual, emotional or behavioural needs either of individual pupils or of the class as a whole. As teachers have begun to respond, in various ways, to the challenge of formalizing the assessment process. it is becoming clear that a more refined model of the relationship between educational ideology and teachers' assessment practice is needed.

Of particular. interest here is the model of Mac-Callum et al. (1993), which identifies three distinct types of teacher approach to assessment within the National Curriculum. MacCallum et al. contrast 'critical intuitives' whose child-centred approach leads them to concentrate on the 'whole child' in their assessment; the 'evidence gatherers' for whom assessment is largely a periodic, summative activity to provide an evidential record of judgements made; and the 'systematic planners,' more or less overt in their approach to assessment, who deconstruct the issue of achievement I tom any interpretive context.

The spectrum of increasingly deliberate and explicit data gathering and interpretation on the part of teachers as identified by MacCallum *et al.*,accords with the finding reported in this chapter concerning the salience of timing, purpose and mode as defining variables in assessment practice (See table 1). Perhaps more difficult ot represent are the differences in understanding concerning how children learn and the nature of knowledge. Such conceptions incorporte a complex mixture of more or less clearly thought-through view concerning how pedagogy, classroom organization, curriculum materials and, not least, assessment should be arranged to facilitate learning. At one extreme is what we introduced in Chapter 2 as the 'elementary ideological tradition in primary education, with its conception of education as the initiation of children into a corpus of established knowledge. This ideology is readily associated with both didactic pedagogy and the carrot and stick approach to assessment, with its emphasis on competition and sanctions. At the other extreme is the developmental ideological tradition, with its conception of education as the provision of a curriculum ladder individual to each child. Teacher intervention is designed to support learners in constructing pogressively higher levels of knowledge and understanding.

Most teachers' ideology is likely to be a mixture of these different elements, and their practice will be informed by a mixture of pragmatism and habit as well as educational philosophy. By the same token, assessment practice is likely to reflect a similar mixture of influences. The value of such models is thus not to provide for the 'mapping' of individual practice but rather to reinforce the importance of the relationship between teachers' views and practice of assessment and their more general professional understanding. It is only with such an appreciation that the true significance of the conflict between the Government and teachers, to which the imposition of national assessment has led, can fully be understood. In terms of each of our analytic themes of power, values and understanding, the challenge of national assessment could hardly be more fundamental. We have described the ways in which teachers are adjusting to these requirements and incorporating them into both their practices. In reporting these changes the most significant question in terms of the overall purpose of the PACE study must be the extent to which teachers were finding it possible to integrate national assessment requirements within their professional practice. Did this reflect a change in their educational values and understandings? Or did it reflect a change in the values and understandings implicit in national assessment itself, as these were originally conceived, in the process of its realization in the classroom? On the answer to this question will rest not only the outcomes we may predict from the imposition of national assessment *per se*. Given that the assessment requirements of the Education Reform Act arguably represent the most explicit expression of the ideology on which it is based and the most powerful mechanism for imposing this ideology on schools and teachers, the fate of the whole reform initiative is likely to depend on the way in which national assessment comes to be realised in practice.

It is at the apex of the power struggle between the Government and the teaching profession. At present there is little to suggest that there has been any significant change in the values informing the classroom assessment culture since the Education Reform Act. We must anticipate, however, that the pressures of the educational market, in which assessment information is the currency, may well bring about changes such as an increased emphasis on achievements that can be formally demonstrated and recorded and an associated increase in the emphasis given to competition.

13

English through Weather and Animal

The weather is always with us, so we might as well put it to good use. It often dominates the mood of the class and one valuable side-effect of writing about it is that the exercise of writing can help to dispel this mood. If, for instance, it has been snowing as the children arrive at school, the chances of them concentrating on maths singlemindedly are remote, but if they can work out their fantasies about the snow in writing first, as they would in the infant school, they are much more amenable to what might seem to them alien disciplines. Any kind of weather can provide the theme for writing but obviously it is only sensible to capitalise on prevailing conditions.

Wind

Let us take, as an example of lesson, 'The Wind,' or 'A Windy Day.' The class may be taken outside for a while with the question in their minds 'What is the wind doing?.' Back in the classroom they discuss this with the teacher. The discussion may be confined to what can actually be observed in the playground or it may extend to what the children know does happen what it is windy, i.e. washing on the line, dustbin lids clattering, leaves blowing about, kites flying, a man's hat being blown off, smoke being blown about, tiles torn off the roof, ships tossed about at sea, in fact as many different things as they can think of. The teacher might wish to emphasise certain aspects of the wind, such as its force,or the sound of it, according to whether she considers it desirable to give the work a particular direction. If this is the case the discussion might be extended by playing taped wind effects or some music such as

Vaughan Williams' 'Sinfonia Antarctica.' If however the children have got into the habit of writing freely then it is as well to let them get on with it. If necessary they might precede their writing by a rough sketch, pictorial or verbal, of the effects the wind has, together with lists of appropriate words and images. Here are some examples of writing from lessons begun in these various ways:

The wind is blowing the trees about
The wind is blowing the paper
A terrible sound in the entry
Comes wooshing out at us when we pass.
At night you can hear the moaning wind
In the chimneys, getting everywhere.
Wind terrible and strong.

(Georgina, aged 10 UC)

The wind comes in a fearful hurry, stirring and twisting and bellowing into the town. It scatters the paper in the gutter like snowflakes blowing about in the sky. It wriggles howling down our chimneys. It swishes through the trees which bend and groan as if they are very old with aches and pains in their old limbs. Everything shakes at the merciless wind, which always goes its own way. it goes down entries and gardens and round the backs of houses never ceasing to raise up the dust in people's eyes. And when the wind is tired of playing in the town it leaves to wind its fearless way in the country across the hills and wood and at least it hurtles across the sea.

(Jennifer, aged 9 C)

It makes our think of the wind blowing across the ice and snow in the Antarctic. Everywhere is deserted, there are no people to be seen and only a few seagulls. It is getting dark and it is beginning to snow again, the snow comes wirling down and it is beginning to blow into a blizzard. You have got to fight against the snow and the screeming wind. The wind is howling and tearing at our clothes and we can feel it on our cheeks biting. There is nothing to see for miles across the wasted snow and ice but wizzing flakes hurling past like bullets. It is very lonely here and we have to stay for months yet until the relief ship comes from the Filkland Islands. Then we shall have fresh food and we shall be able to light our fires again instead of using it only for cooking. The wind is still howling but we must go out and look after the huskies.

(Martin, aged, 9 UC)

This was written a short while after the film 'Scott of the Antarctic' had been shown on television and we suspect that the boy was writing with the lingering memory of that experience triggered off by a recording of Vaughan Williams' music played in the classroom.

The following piece was written by a boy who had become a reluctant writer but was fascinated by an account of a hurricane in the West Indies:

Hurricane

A hurricane is a hotfoot in great haste, giving an uproar of violence a nomad roaming from place, leaving distress and sorrow, leaving people perplexed and bewildered, leaving damage indescribable. It looks like a storm on the sea, all pucker, leaving wrinkles and folds,a revolution getting revenge for some unsettled score, causing riot everywhere. It looks like a scrawny piece of cloth ragged and ripped, until now kept remote and undisturbing, secluded.

(David, aged 11 C)

Snow

Few things are more likely to disrupt school work than the appearance of snow. If it starts during a lesson you might just as well abandon the lesson and talk about the snow. Let us suppose that this did happen and that the classroom had large windows through which the children could see the playground, houses, trees, etc. They will already be looking through the window so that the concentration so necessary to good writing is ready to hand. The children might be asked how the snow flakes fall, what they look like, how they could be described to someone from a hot country who had never seen snow, how they feel to the touch, how they settle to the ground, what snow sounds like when you walk on it, what it does to your hands when you have been snowballing, what snowflakes look like under a microscope, what it would be like to be in a blizzard, what it would be like to be an Eskimo, and so on. Then the class might be asked to make suggestions for good words, the teacher offering one or two to get the ideas across, e.g. words describing movement—fluttering, whirling, twirling, flying, skipping; words describing sensations of touching, tasting, and so on — crisp, tingling, sharp, biter, sweet; words describing appearance — delicate, feathery, scintillating. Alternatively, the teacher might simply approach it as a verbalising exercise and ask the children to write down as many words as they can think of the describe the snow, after which they read their words out. One might begin with one of the least able children in order that others can add what may be the more unusual words. This avoids the situation in which the least able child is being asked to read his list mainly composed of words already mentioned by the quicker pupils. After this exercise they are encouraged to write a poem or descriptive piece. Here are two short examples:

All the lacy lines,
Pattering drifts of snow
Show me all the secret paths
Where the thrush and robins go

Where the ducks left the frozen pond
I see their footprints clearly
When I follow then I would know
For they would see the tracks of me.

(Girl, aged 8 C)

I am white
And I fall from a hedge

I cover the ground
And don't make a sound

(Boy, aged 8 C)

Incidentally, this last piece has the quality of some of the old riddles, which children enjoy imitating for their own sake (see Techniques, page 165-6):

White bird featherless
Flew from Paradise,
Pitched on the castle wall;
Along came Lord Landless
Took it up handless,
And rode away horseless to the King's white hall.

Heat

Equally distracting is a particularly hot day which may furnish the subject 'Heat.' The teacher might ask such questions as: What effect does the heat have on us? What effect does it have on animals? What effect does it have on anything? Pools dry up, fish die, the earth cracks, things become dusty, grass may be scorched, plants wither, etc. The children might then be asked to suggest appropriately evocative words or similes.

Here are some examples of children's work:

Heat

The heat is lying on us heavily
Every where is still with the heat,
The cats lie in the shade as if they are dead
Even the birds do not seem to move.
You can hear people's voices but they seem to be
Chocked with heat.
Nothing can move in this blistering day
And even the air shimmers so hot
Like above a brozier in the winter.

The heat has stifled everything and we can only think
Of cool places in the world,
Or the water, cool, blue and refreshing.
By a lake you could dive in deep out of the hot air.
Nothing is so cold here now. The butter melts,
The milk goes sour, the bread is dried up.
Even the water is warm.
And it will et hotter.

(A boy, aged 11 UC)

I am lying in a garden on a very hot day. The sun is beating down on our like hot rain. Everything is too tried and weary to move. It is too hot to move out of the sun. The dog is sleepy. He crawls into the shade to stretch out. He does not jump and joggle today. Nobody can hardly breathe it is so hot. Your blouse sticks to you and you are so weary. All the trees and leaves are dead still without air to move them. We want a cool wind coming slowly.

(A girl, aged 9 C)

There is great heat in the valley of the Nile.
The red hot sands flow against the temple walls
Where no man can put his hand down
And it is not be scorched with fierce heat.
The heat is everywhere
Dragging us down
Weary
And sad.
It is scorching the dry cracked earth
And nothing will grow except the cactus plant.
All people and animals are slow in the suffocating air.

(A boy, aged 11 C)

I think it is worth drawing attention in the last poem to the way in which the boy has used the word arrangement in the sixth, seventh and eighth lines to reinforce the sense. It is not necessary to make a great thing of this, only to point out that it is a good idea which somebody else might like to try sometime.

Fog

Fog is not easy to describe, yet on a foggy day children are very much aware of it, perhaps because it tends to turn them in on themselves (other things such as people, buildings, vehicles are obscured and therefore excluded by the fog), and also perhaps because it might get worse and there is then a chance of leaving school early; one need not of course draw their attention to that! Here are two pieces by children, the first of which we have found a useful introduction to writing on this theme:

A Foggy Day

> The fog creeps and crawls along the road, swirling and puffing around the lampposts, and dancing in and out of hedges. All along the bushes there are cobwebs with little drops of silver all over like diamonds. The cars crawl along the road with dim lights staring into the thick, dark grey smoky fog. People hurry home all wrapped up with scarves to keep out the wet air and they cough and splutter as they go, anxious to get home by the warm fireside. You can see the lights in houses and street lamps shining tinily like stars as if they were struggling to get out. Nobody has a good word to say for the fog and everyone is miserable, waiting for it to go.

(Michael, aged 10 C)

The Fog

The fog is boiling up this morning.
It sticks in the trees like cob webs
Silvery flickering little pearl drops.
And everything is very quiet and still,
Sometimes a motor car is heard as it

drawls its way along the road.
Everything seems very quiet and lonely
but a few muffled shapes come loming up at you and then
They disappear in the choking fog.
The fog stops everything.

(John, aged 10 UC)

Rain and Storms

I suppose the fascination of watching raindrops running and converging on a window pane is something we all indulge in sometimes, and in the following poem the child has speculated on the power which seems to activate these raindrops:

The rain comes pattering down
the rain comes pattering on my window-pane
Where does it come from
Where does it go. Many people tell me
And many do not know.

I love to see the raindrops on my window pane
I love to see them racing from the topmost frame
Where is the engine where is the fuel
People say they have none
But still I am not sure.

(Wendy, aged 9 C)

This child was in a class where creative writing was a normal thing and children wrote freely on almost any subject, so that very little preparatory discussion was necessary. In the following piece from a boy in a different class the marks of the student's introduction are clearly evident. Here it was necessary to make suggestions, to encourage the children to make suggestions about what the rain does, what it is like to be out in it, and so on.

Rain rushes down gutters, gurgles down the drains, spits

on the footpaths like sparklers crackling. It bites at your face, blinding your eyes. The wheels are wet on the cars and bikes and they screech and squirt water on the children's legs, but it's all right for us because I've got our wellingtons. Everything is dull and dreary except the rain running down rivers on the window panes. You can see the joining up together in big drops like river meeting until they all go together in one big woosh, right down to the bottom.

(Peter, aged 9 C)

Some teachers feel that by discussing ideas before the children write, their creative energies are being channelled and their natural or individual awareness is somehow being stultified. Certainly this is possible with an insensitive teacher who dominates the class in such a way that they feel obliged to write to satisfy rigorously applied conventions, but surely this would happen whatever techniques such a teacher was employing. Where the teacher approaches this work in a sensible and sympathetic way,the children will have every freedom to use any suggestions in any way they like, as did the boy who wrote the above passage which, for all that it has a framework, still possesses and individual quality. Furthermore, most classes in primary schools contain only a very small proportion of children gifted with the sort of creative imagination which is likely to be inhibited by the approach we have been discussing, and any reasonable teacher would give such children every opportunity to develop their talents in a variety of different ways. And in the case of the less able child there is greater opportunity for expression when he has something to express that he can make his own in his own individual way. There are times, of course, when a discussion preceding a lesson will help a child like this to recall his own experience.

So far we have been considering the sort of stimulus that might arise on a fairly dull day when the class might go into the playground for a few minutes or simply look out of the classroom windows. A day which is stormy clearly provides much more dramatic opportunity especially if there is thunder and lightning, since most children respond to the violence of a storm and indeed have very deep fears of it. Here are some pieces written during a storm:

Bang! Crash! Shattering noises!
Thundering and hurling across the sky
Goes the terrible thunder train
A wild blundering prehistoric beast,
Moaning, groaning, howling about
In the sky. Terrifying all the people.
All will flee for their lives.

(John, aged 11 C)

Everywhere is very dark as if there was an eclipse of the sun. In the school and houses there are small lights dimly shining but outside all it dark and threatening. People are hurrying away to their own homes in case the dreadful thunder should crash or if the lightning might charge out of the sky. The lightning is a great spear of light that comes shooting jaggedly out of the black sky. You can only see it for a second then it is gone to strike into the earth or a tree or a tall building. That is why they have lightning conductors on churches if the lightning should strike. Every time there is a flash it lights up the sky and you can see the rain coming down in great sheets and torrents. Flooding everywhere.

(Leslie, aged 11 C)

Further Suggestions

1. Write about a walk home or across some fields on a windy day.
2. If you have ever been in a boat on a rough sea write about what it was like, or write an imagined account.
3. Find out what you can about tornadoes, then give an account of one. First think of the effects it would have.
4. Describe a frosty day, perhaps by making a list of images.

5. Imagine you had to bale out of an aircraft over the desert.

   Write about your trek to the nearest town (a whole day's journey).

6. Imagine you have to visit a relative across the other side of town when a snow storm blows up.

7. Read *Everest Climbed* by Ian Serraillier and write about climbing a mountain or coming down a mountain in a blizzard.

8. Describe a walk home through fog, or a walk through the town on a foggy day. Or write a story called 'Lost in the Fog.'

9. Look out through your window on a rainy day.

10. Imagine you are in the mountains in a thunder-storm.

11. You go with a party of children up a mountain. You get separated from the others when it begins to snow. Write about your journey back.

12. You live in a crowded city in a heat wave. Describe the heat. You borrow a bike and cycle out to a pool in the country.

About Animals

Everyone knows that children are fascinated by animals and will write about them without much prompting. There is no difficulty in arousing the interest; the difficulty arises in prompting the verbal use of all the minute observation, all the sensory awareness children naturally have of animals. It is for this reason that we think it is a good idea to begin with creatures for which most children seem to have a revulsion, or at least a curiously ambivalent interest, e.g. insects, spiders, reptiles.

Animals Exciting Revulsion or Fascination

Naturally the best stimulus is that which is immediate; the living animal in the classroom or in its natural surroundings is better than a picture, but a picture is better than nothing. Grass snakes, newts, spiders are not difficult to come by but, failing this, pictures are usually available from libraries or, if the teacher has some artistic ability, a much enlarged picture of something like a common fly drawn in black ink is extremely effective. The next important step is the discussion which emerges from this initial stimulus. The children might consider how the creature moves, the texture of its covering (furry, rough, slimy, scaly), what is lives on, where it lives, how it lives, the sounds it makes, etc. Then the teacher can encourage suggestions for precise words with which to describe these attributes and the way the children feel about them. The point at which the writing begins is obviously a matter of the class reaction, if this is being done as a class lesson; if the children are in groups it is probably as well to let them begin as they wish, and this applies particularly to young children. Sometimes a poem or an extract from a poem by a child of their own age will help to sharpen their incentive to write, while at other times this might tend to be inhibiting if they feel that they have to produce something of the same kind when they have specific ideas of their own. It is clearly impossible to make rules about this; the student must to a certain extent react as the situation demands. But here are some examples which may illustrate different approaches. The following piece was written after five minutes looking at a newt, with no other stimulus:

He is a sad dragon waiting his chance;
He waits for the world to change again.
His ancestors were the kings of the earth
And he watches with his beady eye
For something to fall out of the sky
So that he can roam about free
Like the dinosaurs from out of the sea.

(John, aged 11 C)

The following piece was written when the class had been shown a model of a large spider made from a ball of brown wool and pipe-cleaners, which was stuck to a large sheet of white paper on which was drawn a web. A real spider suspended from the ceiling would have been much better but you can't expect them to appear to order and at least the model had the advantage of size. There was no discussion here—the children were simply asked to write whatever they liked about it:

> An awful great brown spider crawling slowly over his web. His body is brown and furry and it makes your skin tingle to think about it, the scrawling creeping spider waits for a prey, the lonely buzzing fly who doesn't know that the web is a black silky trap and that once he touches it he will never be able to escape to freedom again. He will never fly in the air when the furry brown monster grasps him with his bony claws and eats into his heart. But he will not know because the spider will inject him with a sleeping poison to sap away his strength so that he cannot struggle for his life. He will be eaten alive by brown twisted manacles [*sic,* for mandibles?] of the demon in the web.

(Ronald, aged 10 UC)

Naturally, in the same class there were different degrees of imaginative involvement and the above was probably the best. Here is an example of the less involved:

> We had a model of a spider on a white paper. It was made out of brown wool we think and it had little yellow spots on it. It looks like a spider crawling on his web. This is painted on the card in black ink. The spider looks creepy.

(A Girl, aged 9 C)

This child's writing apparently normally lacked gusto, but then one does not expect that from every child. What is to be commended in her work is accuracy of description, and this in itself should be encouraged. Naturally one hopes that presenting her with a variety of incentives will arouse a more active interest in writing, but if this is not so the child should not be made to feel that her work is inferior: one must accept that there are differences in temperament, as there are different interests.

With another class the stimulus was Robet Horan's poem 'Little City' *(Faber Book of Modern American Verse).* After a good deal of discussion about the way in which spiders lie in wait for insects the children wrote their poems.

Little City

Spider, from his flaming sleep,
staggers out into the window frame:
swings out from the red den where he slept
to nest in the gnarled glass.
Fat hero, burnished cannibal
lets down a frail ladder and ties a knot,
sways down to a landing with furry grace.

By noon this corner is a bullet-coloured city and the exhausted architect
sleeps in his pale wheel,
waits without pity for a gold visitor
or coppery captive, his aerial enemies
spinning headlong down the window to the trap.

The street of string shakes now and announces
a surprised angel in the tunnel of thread.
Spider dances down his wiry heaven to taste the moth.
A little battle begins and the prison trembles.
The round spider hunches like a judge.
The wheel glistens.
But this transparent town that caves in at a breath
is paved with perfect steel.
The victim hangs by his feet, and the spider
circles invisible avenues, weaving a grave.

By evening the web is heavy with monsters,
bright constellation of wasps and bees,
breathless, surrendered.
Bronze skeletons dangle on the wires
and a thin wing flutters.
The medieval city hangs in its stars.

Spider lumbers down the web
and the city stretches with the weight of his walking
By night we cannot see the flies' faces
and the spider, rocking.

And the children's work:

The big black spider in his web
Is waiting for a nice juicy fly.
He prances about in his silver city
Hoping a wasp or bee will be his prey
Today his little danger holds in every corner.

(David, aged 10 UC)

The spider makes his web so big
To catch his dinner.
The trap is waiting for a moth or fly
To come into the web's eye.
The fly sees the web's eye,
Bang, Too late.
The fly will die.

(John, aged 9 UC)

The spider
with its eight legs
climbs
up the web.

Further on
up the web
is a small grasshopper
which
has been caught
in a tangle
of sticky
cob-
web.

(Robert, aged 10 UC)

The simplicity of expression here is, we think, quite powerful; it achieves the kind of directness much praised in the poetry of e.e. cummings and William Carlos Williams. It is poetry of this kind that some students and teachers find difficult to appreciate. They expect their poetry to be passionate or full of high sentence — what Hopkins called 'Parnassian'—and consequently, having their own taste settled long ago, perhaps by unfortunate encounters with poetry at school, they tend unconsciously to reject children's work which lacks some evidence of their *idea* of a poem. This is a pity since it blunts their sensitivity to what is good in children's work. In a way this book is a plea for greater understanding on the part of the teacher, for greater awareness of the positive values in children's writing. The teacher's reaction to the above poem by David ought to recognise two important values: clarity of conception and clarity of diction. A teacher thus disposed will see the interest in a good deal of children's writing.

Predators

The predatory nature of animals seems to fascinate most children, possibly because there is something of this in themselves. At any rate to introduce the word 'predator' is usually enough to start a discussion. This quickly gets under way with cats stalking birds, spiders and flies, snakes, vultures, foxes, wolves, tigers, etc. Robert Horan's poem, quoted above, makes a good introduction and can be supplemented by Tennyson's famous poem 'The Eagle.' Here are some examples of children's work written following discussions about predators:

> The chameleon is like a demon with a long tongue. He is a menacing creature with crooked claws like steel nails. He uses them to grip the branch so then he is fixed to it and he can stay without moving so that his prey doesn't notice him at all. He will not move a muscle while the unknowing insect comes into his reach, fluttering around him until his tongue flicks out a flame of hot deadly fire into the air and the innocent insect disappears never to be seen again. He does not move and nobody even knows he is there waiting for the next time, the silent demon who changes colour to suit himself.

(Romy, aged 10 C)

The Vulture

The vulture is a hideous creature.
He sits perched on a bit of broken branch in the desert,
Waiting for some animal
Or for a lost man.
His beak is like a great hook which tears flesh.
While he holds it with his crooked claws.
His hook is tearing flesh, and blood drops from his jaws.
He keeps still a moment listening for something near.
Is it another animal he wonders.
It is only the sound of his dirty work.

(Michael, aged 10 C)

A Kill

Down by the water hole where the antelope are drinking,
A lion is ready to pounce on his prey
His tail flickers

His head is high.
Then he runs, he pounces and just misses an antelope.
The zebra run and cry as a vulture is heard.
The chase is on.
Suddenly the lion seizes a zebra
Blood is coming from his throat as the lion
Tears him limb from limb.
And when the meal is finished the vultures eat the remains.

(Romy, aged 10 UC)

Pets and Familiar Animals

Our dog Sam is a mongrel, a one-eyed terror is he. They call him a mischievous beggar because he will fight anybody. He fights other dogs who are too big for him, he fights cats and chases them up trees and people throw buckets over him but he does not care because he has a thick skin. He just goes off somewhere and finds a bone he has buried and lies about in a hedge. He has lots of fun because he likes adventure. He is supposed to be white with black markings on him but he's usually not very clean when he comes home, he plays too much to keep clean. When we wash him he comes up lovely and his coat is white and wiry and tough. He lost his eye in a motor car accident once when he was run over. we thought he was dead and had to be put to sleep but it just knocked him about a bit and glazed his eye and the vet said he wouldn't be able to see out of it very well again. We were very unhappy at the time but he doesn't seem to care very much so we got over it. The one-eyed wonder we call him now. He doesn't mind, he knows we're only joking and he has a lot of fun in him. He can take a joke. He's a tough dog, and we have some good times.

Pets and familiar animals can provide an absorbing theme for writing which genuinely involves the child, as we think this piece shows. It is a good idea to give children some warning that you want them to write about their own animals, perhaps suggesting that they might like to make some notes about the behaviour of the animal in question.

Town children are perhaps at a disadvantage in that their range of acquaintance with animals is limited, but cats, probably the commonest of pets, seem to offer unlimited scope, as the number of poems about them in any anthology appears to testify. Children know they can be fierce, vicious, gentle, docile, inscrutable, agile, lethargic, comic. A reading of Eliot's *Old Possum's Book of Practical Cats* will provide stimulus for a considerable assortment of cat-like activities.

Our cat sits by the fire
Quietly licking his paws.
He doesn't seem to care for anything,
He looks as if he wouldn't hurt a fly
But when the night time comes and everywhere gets dark
His eyes begin to gleam
And round he starts to prowl
Glaring with a scowl.
He knows his friends are waiting
Getting ready to go hunting in the dark.
Their claws are ready for some violent deed,
Perhaps they will go on a visit to the park.
They all begin to screech and howl
And then go quietly into the dark.
Next time we see him he will be lying asleep
As innocent as you please
And no one will ever know
What he did in the lonely night.

(Angela, aged 11 C)

Cat

Just one ball of soft fur,
Curled up round and small,

Purring when its happy
Me-owing when it's sad
Tail wagging when it's angry
The so timid little cat!

(Romy, aged 10 UC)

And here are some representative examples of work written following a brief exploration into the environs of country school:

The Butterfly

The butterfly, flutterby,
A delicate and dancing creature
Goes zig-zagging in the air.
He has wings like daffodil petals,
All creamy-yellow and light,
A glorious flower in flight.

(Charlie, aged 9 C)

When we went out we found an ants' nest in a small mound of earth. We disturbed a bit of it to see what would happen and then there was some activity! They began to rush out in a fluster all over the place, to left and right, in circles and straight lines. They all looked as if they were going somewhere special but when you watched them carefully you saw that they did not really go anywhere. It looked as if they were pretending to move about to draw away the scent. We know they don't really have scent but if they had been peewits they would move like that to attract your attention. If you stood looking at them for some time you got the idea of a great battle or an army moving about, each one carrying out instructions. It is easy to see why they could conquer the world if they had the chance.

(Gordon, aged 11 C)

The Flies

I noticed the flies buzzing everywhere
They were nearly getting in my hair.
They made an awful sound
As they were going round and round.

(Mary, aged 9 C)

Fantastic and Comic

Few things please children so much in literature as the comic and the fantastic and this interest can be readily given expression in writing about animals. Apart from the fun that children derive from such writing there is also opportunity to exercise the imagination in making up unusual images and in playing with words (see Techniques, page 147). Here are two examples:

The Kingcuas

The kingcuas is my imaginary bird,
It has five red heads and blue black fur,
It walks like an elephant, it runs like a dog,
It flies like a dragon, and has tusks like a hog.
It is ten miles long, three miles wide.
It has hundreds of spikes on every side.
Its eyes are like a radar screen,
It's cruel and horrible and extremely mean.

Its appetite is three thousand men.
It won't eat pigs or any hens,
For it only eat human flesh,
Nothing different, nothing fresh.

The horriblest parts are his heads,
Nobody is safe from him till he is dead.

(R.D. Griffiths, aged 10 C)

Rattle and battle
And chuckle and clang
Goes the elephant bird
Called the Chinese Wang.

Round and about
In the air he goes
He's got no nose
And he's got no toes.

He digs in the earth
With the nose of a mole
And a spike on his back
Like a telegraph pole.

(George, aged 11 UC)

Before ending this section on animals we should like to make some comments on the emotional content of the children's work. What one begins to notice about it, and particularly the pieces dealing with animals, is the absence of sentimentality; feeling is there, but not the spurious feeling one finds in so many of the poems written by adults for children, such as may be found in large numbers in many of the older anthologies. When adults write 'little poems' about 'sweet woolly rabbits,' etc., not only do they side-step all direct awareness of the creatures in question, they grossly distort the emotional response of the child reader by indulging their own fancies about the child's feeling for animals. Junior children by and large are not sentimental, although, because they are vulnerable their natural feeling can be played upon by people who *are* sentimental. And of course if they are brought up on a diet of poems and stories designed to play upon their feelings to the exclusion of all else, it will not be surprising if what they write exhibits similar tendencies. It realise that the dividing line between genuine feeling and sentimentality is sometimes obscure and certainly there are many poems about which enlightened critics disagree as their tastes differ; also fashions change and one generation will accept literature which another generation will reject. Allowing for all of this we think it is still possible, working from the extremes of the emotional scale, to develop a standard of judgment about what can legitimately be used to evoke certain feelings in children and what is emotional bribery. We hope that the poems we have listed give some indication of the kind of writing about animals which is commendable because it evokes images undistorted by sentimentality.

Further Suggestions

1. Observe some animal (cat, bird, insect, snail, hamster, etc.) and write as much as you can about its movements, how it looks, what it does.
2. Write a comic poem about some unusual animal in the zoo.
3. Mythical animals: phoenix, dragon, sphinx, roc, unicorn, behemoth, minotaur.
4. Extinct animals: dodo, mammoth, tyrannosaurus rex, pterodactyl, peliosaurus.

   Find as much information as you can about one or more of (3) and (4) and write poems or short but vividly descriptive passages about them. Or write a story about one that comes to life.
5. Write a poem about a snake moving through the grass or through the water. Then rearrange the lines so the pattern moves down or across the page (see Techniques, page 160).
6. Write a short passage or poem about gnats over a pool, a flock of pigeons circling around, moths around a light, daddy-long-legs in a room, crows in a field, swallows in flight.
7. Write a story about some creature that is trapped or caged or tied up and finally achieves its freedom.
8. Create a completely fabulous creature and describe it and its habits in a poem or story. See James Reeves' *Prefabulous Animiles* if you want some ideas.

9. Suppose you have a very special pet, like a lion or an eagle or an elephant or a dolphin. Describe an adventure with it. Suppose you were able to help such a creature—how might it show its gratitude? [See 'Ranjit and the Tiger' (BW) and 'Androcles and the Lion' (THW)].

10. Write an 'adventure' for some wild creature such as a badger, fox, falcon rabbit, etc., perhaps introducing hunters or a chase or a rescue.

Poems and Extracts

Animals Exciting Revulsion or Fascination

Spiders see *Margaret Langdon,* 'Let the Children Write,' pp. 8-17

The Bat *Theodore Roethke* POCO; JV, III

Man and Bat *D.H. Lawrence* H; CDS

Snake (extract) *D.H. Lawrence* Selected Poems, Penguin Flies *David Daniels* BW

The Fly (first two stanzas) *Anthony Thwaite* (see page 39, above)

The Tom Cat *Don Marquis* PL, IV; JV, IV

The Water Snakes, from 'The Ancient Mariner' *Coleridge* PL, IV Rats *Nannette Colleen Burt, aged, 13* PC

Tiffin and Son, Bug destroyers to Her Majesty *Henry Mayhew* GSH

Snakes *A.K. Ramnujan* TH

Predators and Preys

The Eagle *Tennyson* RR, Yellow; WS; TC, I

The Wild Boar *Shakespeare* TW, IV

From 'Reynard the Fox' *John Masefield* RR, Yellow; TC, I

Circus *Margaret Stanley-Wrench* RR, Yellow

Badger *John Clare* WS

The Tigress *Clifford Dyment* HJ; TC, I

The Red Cockatoo *Arthur Waley* H; WSP

Ranjit and the Tiger *Paddy Kinsale* BW

Garden Scene *Anthony Evans* PC

The Battle *Kevin Campbell* PC

Escape *S. Cardy* PC
The Stoat *boy, aged 11* EW
Now from the Woods *Robert Bloomfield* WS

Pets and Familiar Animals

The Runaway *Robert Frost* BP, II
Mick *James Reeves* TW,II
Hedgehog *Anthony Thwaite* H
The Colt *Raymond Knister* OB, IV
Lone Dog *Irene McLeod* BP, IV; ILTP; POCO
The Stallion *Walt Whitman* OB, IV
Man and Beast *Clifford Dyment* OB, III
A Cat *Edward Thomas* H
Blue-Tits *Phoebe Hesketh* HJ
The Flies *Alan King* LCW
The Swan *Jill, aged 8* YWYR
The Puppy *Allexander Solzhenitsyn* WSP
Tortoise *David Speechley* WS
A Squirrel *girl, aged 10* EW
A hamster at large *Phillipa Pearce* RSH
My Dog Sam *Barbara, aged 10* WS

Fantastic and Comic

The Kraken *Tennyson* PL, IV; CDS
The Unicorn *E.V., Rieu* PQ
The Hippocrump *James Reeves* H
The Wendigo *Ogden Nash* FBNV
The Prince *Walter de la Mare* PdM
The Jumblies *Edward Lear* MGR
Macavity *T.S, Eliot* BP, IV; TC, I
The Platypus *Oliver Hereford* RR, Yellow
The Adaptable Mountain Dugong *Ted Hughes* CDS
The Yellow Door *Barry Maybury* Images

The Dodo *Hilaire Belloc* FBNV
Polar Bear *Christopher Richards, aged 10* PC
The Fish *June Crabtree, aged 11* PC
The Magical Mouse *Kenneth Patchen* JV, II
The Snitterjipe *James Reeves* ILTP
The Doze *James Reeves* BW
The Traintiwontigongolope *C.J. Dennis* BW
Riddles in the Dark *J.R.R. Tolkien* GSH

Exotic and Powerful
Lion at School *Phillipa Pearce* YSH
Androcles and the Lion THW
The Tyger *Wm. Blake* OBP
India *W.J. Turner* H; WS; POCO
The Whale *John Donne* DT
The Lion *Jane Horlock, aged 12* PC
The Flamingo *Jeanne Pook, aged 14* PC
Kangaroo *D.H. Lawrence* MW
Fish in Pacific Waters (from 'The Ballad of Kon Tiki')
Ian Serraillier PL, IV
The Wangsun *Arthur Waley* H
Wild Horse *Hillary Allen, aged 9* WS
Dolphins in Blue Water *Amy Lowell* WS
The New Horse *Jack Schaefer* WSP

Others
Feel like a bird *Mat Swenson* JV, IV
Summer Insects *Leonard Clarke* POCO
His First Flight *Liam O'Flaherty* WS
The Rockfish *Liam O'Flacherty* TH
The Conger Eel *Liam O'Flaherty* WSP
Horses *Paddy Kinsale* TH
Adolf *D.H. Lawrence* TH
Men have been in our woods and killed our badgers YI, I

Poems and Extracts

Wind

Wind *Ted Hughes* JV, III

When the wind is strong *Tanikawa Shuntaro* BW

Mid-Country blow *Theodore Roethke* TC, I

Hurricane Flora *13-year-old Tobagan bōy* WSP

The Wind *James Reeves* BP, III

Storm Wind *Christina Rossetti* OB, II

The Wind; And it was Windy Weather *James Stephens* OB, III; WS

Stocking and Shirt *James Reeves* PQ

The Wind *Emily Dickinson* TW, IV

The Wind *N. Carey, aged 11* PC

A Windy Day *Andrew Young* WS; POCO

Snow and Ice

The Snowflake; Snow *Walter de la mare* PdM

Stopping by Woods on a Snowy Evening *Robert Frost* H; ILTP; TC, I

Hard Frost *Andrew Young* ILTP; WS

Snow Towards Evening *Melville Cane* OB, III

Sheep in Winter *John Clare* RR, Green; POCO

White Fields *James Stephens* PL, II

White Snow *Susan Young, aged 7* PC

Icicles *boy, aged 11* WS

Heat and Sun

A Hot Day *Dylan Thomsa* WS

Lying under a Tree *James Nimmo* OB, III

A Hot Day *A.S.J. Tessimond* HJ

A Summer Noon *Carlos Wilcox* OB, IV

Morning After a Storm *Wordsworth* RR, Yellow

Extract from 'A Prospect of the Sea' *Dylan Thomas* TH

Noon *John Clare* WS

In a Cornfield *Christina Rossetti* PL, IV

Fog

Fog *Carl Sandburg* WS

The Fog *W.H. Davies* PL, IV; JV, III

November *John Clare* WS

The Way Home *Rowena Farre* OBS, III

Cobwebs on a Foggy Day *girl, aged* 10 EW

A Foggy Day *girl aged 11* EW

Bibliography

Camp, Louise E., Lycan, Eva H., and Bair, Frederick H., *Creative Composition,* J. B. Lippincott Co., Philadelphia, 1932.

Canby, Henry Seidel, Opdycke, John Baker, Gillum, Margaret, and Carter, Olive I., *High School English,* The Macmillan Co., New York, 1936.

Chapman, Lucy H., *Using English,* Harcourt, Brace and Co., New York, 1929.

Craig, Virginia J., *The Teaching of High School English,* Longmans, Green and Co., New York, 1930.

Cross, E.A., *English Test,* World Book Co., Yonkers-on-Hudson, New York, 1934.

Dakin, Dorothy, *Talks to Beginning Teachers of English,* D. C. Heath and Co., Boston, 1937.

Eastman, Max, *The Enjoyment of Poetry,* Charles Scribner's Sons, New York, 1921.

Emerson, O.F., *History of the English Language,* The Macmillan Co., New York, 1922.

Featherstone, W.B., "The Place of Subjects in the Integrated Curriculum," *California Quarterly of Secondary Education,* Vol. 9, p. 242, 1933-4.

Fries, C.C., *The Teaching of the English Language,* Thomas Nelson and Sons, New York, 1927.

Ginsberg, A., and Inglis, R.B., *English Essentials Tests,* University Printing Co., Minneapolis, Minn., I925.

Glaser, Emma, *On the Teaching of Junior High School English,* D. Appleton-Century Co., New York, 1935.

Gosling, Thomas W., Chairman, "Junior High School English," pp. 99-123, "Tentative Conclusions and Recommendations," N.E.A., Department of Superintendence, *Fifth Yearbook,* 1927, Washington, D. C.

Greenough, J. B., and Kittredge, G.L., *Words and Their Ways in English Speech,* The Macmillan Co., New York, 1920.

Hackett, W. A., "This Thing Called Debate," *English Journal*, Vol. 21 (I932), pp. 810-816.

Hatfield, W. Wilbur, *An Experience Curriculum in English*, A Report of the Curriculum Commission of the National Council of 'Teachers of English, D. Appleton-Century Co., New York, 1935.

Hitchcock, Alfred, *Bread Loaf Talks on Teaching Composition,* pp. 60-90, Henry Holt and Co., New York, I927.

Inglis Tests of English Vocabulary, Ginn and Co., Boston, 1938.

Jespersen, Otto, *Growth and Structure of the English Language,* D. Appleton-Century Co., New York, 1930.

Jespersen, Otto, *Language, Its Nature, Development, and Origin,* Henry Holt and Co., New York, 1922.

Jones, W.F., *One Hundred Spelling Demons,* Hall and McCreary, Chicago, 1913.

Kennedy, A.G., *Current English,* Ginn and Co., Boston, 1935.

Lounsbury, T.R., *History of the English Language,* Henry Holt and Co., New York, 1907.

Mawson, C.O.S., (Ed.), *Roget's International Thesaurus of English Words and Phrases,* Thomas Y. Crowell Co., New York, 1935.

McGee, John A., *Persuasive Speaking,* Charles Scribner's Sons, New York, 1929.

McKee, Paul, *Language in the Elementary School*, Houghton Mifflin Co., Boston, 1934.

Minnesota, *The Secondary School Curriculum and Syllabi of Subjects,* Bulletin No. B-I, English for Junior High School Period, Department of Education, St. Paul, Minnesota, 1933.

Mirrielees, Lucia B., *Teaching Composition and Literature,* Harcourt, Brace and Co., New York, 1937.

Neville, Mark A., "English as a Positive Factor in Correlation," *The English Journal,* pp. 44-49, January 1938.

New York State Education Dept., *Syllabus in English for Secondary Schools,* Albany, New York, 1934.

Parker, Roscoe Edward, *The Principles and Practice of Teaching English,* Prentice-Hall, New York, 1937.

Raubicheck, Letitia, *Teaching Speech in Secondary Schools,* Public Speaking, Chap. VII, Group Discussion and Debate, Prentice Hall, New York, 1935.

Scott, H.F., and Carr, W.L., *Development of Language,* Scott, Foresman and Co., Chicago, 1921.

Seely, Howard Francis, *On Teaching English,* American Book Co., New York, 1933.

Smith, Dora V., "American Youth and English," *The English Journal,* pp. 99-113, February, 1937.

Swift, G.A., "Creative Expression," *The English Journal.* pp. 27-32, January, 1938.

Thomas, Charles Swain, *The Teaching of English in the Secondary School,* Houghton Mifflin Co., Boston, 1927.

Wade, Harold H., Blossom, John E., and Eaton, Mary P., *Expressing Yourself,* Books One and Two, Houghton Mifflin Co., Boston, 1935.